CBD OF ARMIDALE NSW

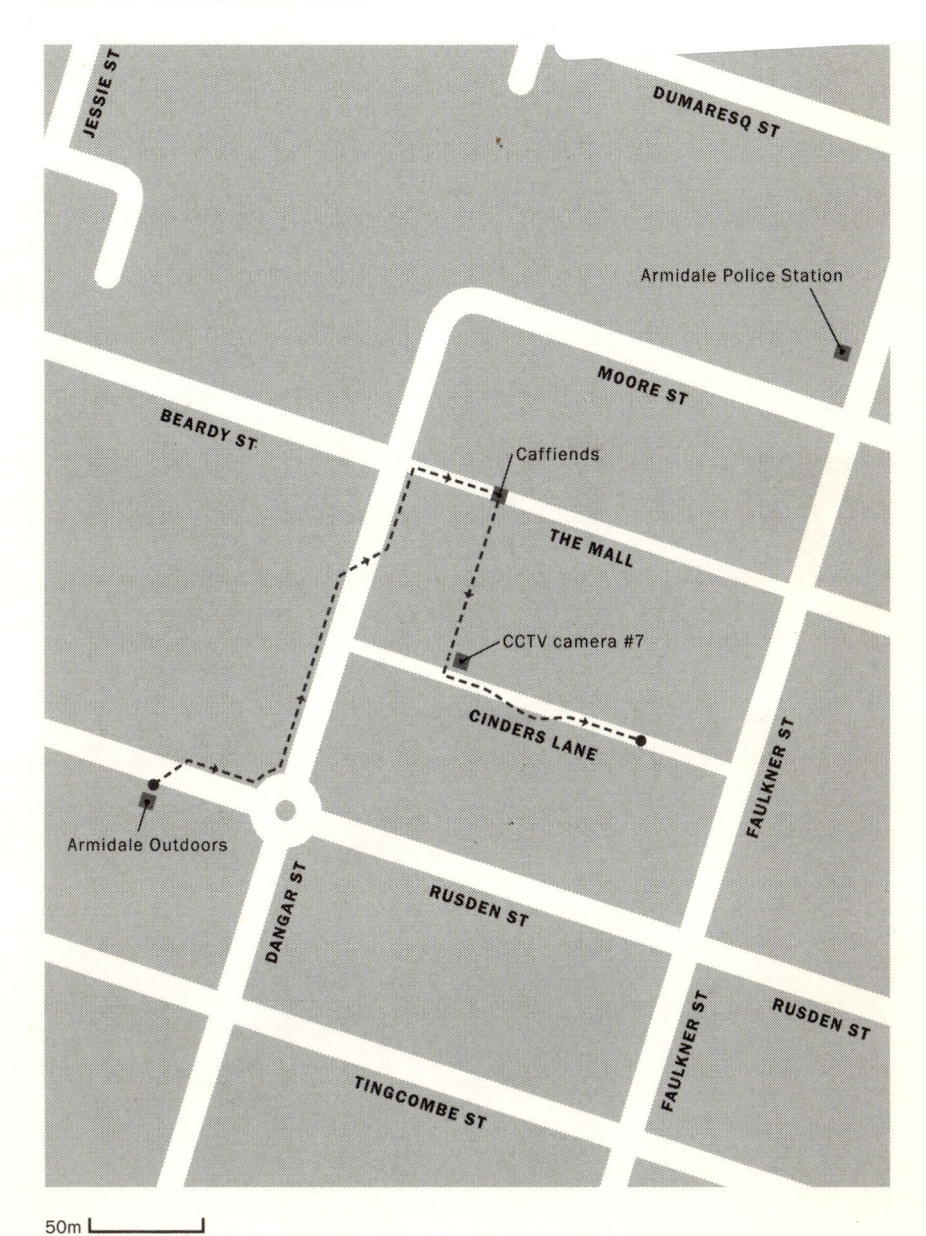

The path of Senior Constable Andrew Rich's pursuit of Elijah Holcombe, a distance of approximately 430 metres.

WAITING FOR ELIJAH

Kate Wild is an investigative journalist whose work with distinguished teams at the ABC has been recognised with three Walkley Awards and a Logie. Her reports from Darwin, where she lived from 2010 to 2016, laid the groundwork for a *Four Corners* story on juvenile detention that prompted the calling of a Royal Commission. Like Elijah Holcombe, Kate grew up in country New South Wales; she now lives and works in Sydney. *Waiting for Elijah* is her first book.

KATE WILD

WAITING FOR ELIJAH

SCRIBE
Melbourne • London

Scribe Publications
18–20 Edward St, Brunswick, Victoria 3056, Australia
2 John St, Clerkenwell, London, WC1N 2ES, United Kingdom

First published by Scribe 2018

Copyright © Kate Wild 2018

All rights reserved. Without limiting the rights under copyright reserved above, no part of this publication may be reproduced, stored in or introduced into a retrieval system, or transmitted, in any form or by any means (electronic, mechanical, photocopying, recording or otherwise) without the prior written permission of the publishers of this book.

Quoted material on p. 268 from 'The Old Fools' by Philip Larkin reprinted here with the kind permission of Faber & Faber; on p. 273, the line from Part IV of 'The Spirit of Place'. Copyright © 2016 by the Adrienne Rich Literary Trust. Copyright © 1981 by Adrienne Rich; also on p. 273, the line from Poem IX of 'Twenty-One Love Poems'. Copyright © 2016 by the Adrienne Rich Literary Trust. Copyright © 1978 by W.W. Norton & Company, Inc., from COLLECTED POEMS: 1950–2012 by Adrienne Rich. Used by permission of W. W. Norton & Company, Inc.

Typeset in Adobe Garamond Pro by the publishers

Printed and bound in Australia by Griffin Press

The paper this book is printed on is certified against the Forest Stewardship Council® Standards. Griffin Press holds FSC chain of custody certification SGS-COC-005088. FSC promotes environmentally responsible, socially beneficial and economically viable management of the world's forests.

9781925322736 (paperback edition)
9781925548914 (e-book)

A CiP record for this title is available from the National Library of Australia

scribepublications.com.au
scribepublications.co.uk

To Kay Masman

There is no wholeness outside of our reciprocal humanity.
    Bryan Stevenson

PART ONE

PART ONE

PROLOGUE

The image I keep returning to is of a car parked on a quiet street in a country town. The windows are blank with condensation. A young man lies curled up on the back seat, slowly waking. The air outside is as cold as stone.

In another street in the same quiet town, a second man wakes. Senior Constable Andrew Rich gets dressed and joins the day. This is when things could have turned out differently. When everything could have been all right. It's 6.30am. Tuesday, 2 June 2009.

2009

1.

Elijah walks swiftly, pulling his jumper over his head. The right sleeve snags, and he tugs it free. The jumper lands with its arms outspread, misshapen, like a puddle on the asphalt. It is close to 2pm, 2 June 2009, and the people around him are heading back to work. Cinders Lane is a thoroughfare linking Armidale's mall to municipal buildings and a car park. Elijah crosses the lane and passes a woman in a bright red coat. She raises a thin arm and calls out, pointing to the ground. Elijah does not respond. A different voice is at his back — male, commanding, and closing in.

'Drop the knife, Elijah! Drop the knife!'

Elijah slips between cars in the open car park.

'Elijah, stop! Put down the knife.'

Elijah hesitates, slows, looks back and sees the gun. He stops and turns around.

Joan Whitburn watches from an office window. Voices had drawn her to the glass doors of her building, which fronts onto Cinders Lane. When she saw two men pass outside and up the lane, she followed them from window to window. Now she drags a phone along the desk towards her. She is metres from them, watching behind the glass.

The younger of the two men is standing still. His hands are in the air, his arms outstretched. The expression on his face is odd. The second man's back is turned to her, but Whitburn sees his wide-legged stance. He is training a gun at the young man's chest. Her mind works like a camera taking shots. Arms, face, torso, black gun. The young man's face, his messy hair.

'Don't shoot,' she whispers to the empty room.

Watching from his office above the street, Ambrose Hallman sees a man in a white baseball cap in the middle of Cinders Lane. He's pointing what looks like a handgun at another man.

'Lay down on the ground,' Hallman hears the gunman say. The second man is holding something dark and straight at shoulder height. Hallman stares, transfixed.

Joan Whitburn clenches the phone to still her hands. She dials emergency. Wrong number. There is shouting outside, but she can't discern the words; she dials a second time.

From his eyrie, Hallman hears the command again.

'Get on the ground,' the gunman yells.

Whitburn watches; the young man doesn't move. Hallman sees him sprint towards the gun. They hear a shot, and the young man falls face forward on the road.

A woman outside screams, 'You didn't have to do that!'

Hallman and Whitburn watch a circle grow like a shadow on the young man's chest.

Whitburn whimpers in the silent room as the gunman kneels to touch the prone man's neck.

'This is triple zero. Police, fire, or ambulance?'

'P-p-p-police,' Joan Whitburn stutters.

When Senior Constable Greg Dufty reaches the corner, he sees his partner at the far end of the lane. *So this is where they got to.* He spots a strange shape on the ground at Rich's feet. *Richie's pulled his jumper off or the guy has had a seizure. Maybe Richie's knocked him out?* Dufty sprints, arriving as Senior Constable Andrew Rich leans the shape against the gutter. Rich is shaking.

'Oh Duff, can you help him?' Dufty hears him say.

Rich is pale. As pale as the face of the body propped against the kerb. Dufty straightens, confused. His nostrils fill with gun smoke. A growing bloody circle comes into focus. Reality settles on his senses, and Rich's voice begins to float in Dufty's ears.

'You're going to have to put pressure on that wound.'

Dufty sees blood on Rich's hands and trousers, bright and sharp.

'Are you alright, are you cut?' Dufty asks his partner.

Rich leans forward, gasping in great breaths. He shakes his head, and Dufty hears the scream of the first siren.

'I had no choice, mate, I had no choice.'

Jordan is sitting on the kitchen counter beside a pile of cut-up pumpkin when the phone rings in Wee Waa, two hours later. She locks eyes with her sister — Laura is closer. Jordan's heels clap on the cupboard door. She holds her perch and wins.

'Hi, Dad. What's up?' she hears Laura say.

'What?' Laura shouts into the phone, and the air around the two girls changes.

Their mother races from the living room and wrenches the phone from Laura's hand.

'Jeremy, have they found him?' Their mother begins to shake.

'Why? Why would they shoot him?' Tracey Holcombe screams.

Jordan falls to the kitchen floor. Laura walks outside. The clothesline in the backyard is a skeleton holding hankies. Tracey's wail streams through the door and across the lawn. It winds and tightens like a noose.

'They've shot my boy, they've shot my boy …'

2.

The day after Elijah was shot in Cinders Lane, an image of three people giving CPR to a young man in the gutter filled the front page of the *Armidale Express*.

'A man carrying a knife was shot dead by undercover police in the centre of Armidale early yesterday afternoon. The shooting, which occurred around 1.50pm in Cinders Lane, came after a chase through the CBD streets …' the *Express* reported.

The dead man was thought to be in his early twenties. He was possibly from Narrabri, but the paper did not name him.

'The bloke had something in his hand and the two coppers asked him twice to drop it. But he charged them, one cop shot him and down he went,' a witness told the paper.

'The guy had a knife in his hand and then he just went for them,' a second witness said.

The following day, New South Wales police held a press conference in Armidale. Acting Assistant Commissioner Geoff McKechnie addressed the media. The officer involved in the incident was a 'relatively experienced' senior constable, McKechnie said. He was in plainclothes, he had acted alone; there had been 'no other choice but to use his pistol'.

'Obviously he is shaken and concerned by what has occurred. We're doing everything possible in terms of providing him and his family with assistance, as we are to the other officers who were working yesterday. That will be an ongoing process and hopefully he will come through it OK,' the Acting Assistant Commissioner said.

Someone asked when the senior constable would return to work. He remained on duty, McKechnie replied.

Details of the press conference ran on page two of the *Armidale Express* on 4 June. On that day, the front page was filled with the face of a handsome young man with brown eyes and perfect teeth. Elijah Holcombe smiled from beneath the headline 'Tragic waste of life'. The story had shifted.

The *Express* told its readers, 'Family and friends of Elijah Jay Holcombe are today mourning "a beautiful and intelligent young man". Elijah was shot dead after allegedly threatening a police officer with a knife. Three days after the tragedy a picture is beginning to emerge of the young man.'

The Holcombe family had sent Elijah's photo and a statement to the paper to set the record straight. The *Armidale Express* printed it verbatim.

'Given the spate of speculative reporting suggesting our Elijah was something other than the beautiful man we knew him to be we feel compelled to make public the following facts,' the statement said. Elijah was studying philosophy and psychology at a Sydney university. He was a talented musician. He worked part time. Over the previous twelve months, he had received treatment for a mental illness.

'Sadly, it manifested as episodes of intense paranoia where he lived in grave fear for his own safety,' the statement continued. 'His mental health practitioners based at a leading Sydney mental health unit did not consider his condition to represent a danger to any person. He was absolutely non-violent by nature and prior to the day of his death Elijah was completely unknown to the police and had no police record of any sort. The circumstances of Elijah's death are now under investigation by police. In order not to compromise that process this family will make no further comment to the media until the results of the investigation are known. Whatever the results, this family holds no ill feeling towards any person involved in this tragedy. That includes the police officer who felt he had no choice but to pull the trigger …'

A week after the family's statement was published, a Sydney newspaper challenged the claim that the officer had no choice but to shoot.

'Two women have independently sworn they did not see Elijah Holcombe armed with a knife and said he was at least fifteen metres away from officers when he was shot in the chest,' *The Daily Telegraph* reported.

'The women claim Mr Holcombe, who suffered from mental illness, was "calm" when ordered to stop by police in Cinders Lane, Armidale ... The second witness said Mr Holcombe's "demeanour seemed casual" and he was "in no hurry, just strolling along".

'"The young man turned around casually and I would say he had a look of bewilderment on his face — but he was fairly calm and casual," the woman said. "He just turned around and stood still. I can't remember anything about his hands — I was looking at his face. He didn't say anything."'

Journalists scrambled to take the story further, but, true to their statement, the Holcombes refused to comment. Without the family's rage or grief for fuel, the story disappeared until a reporter I worked with at *Four Corners*, the ABC's top investigative program, followed up a hunch. Quentin McDermott recognised Elijah's shooting as one in a series of fatalities where the person police had killed had a mental illness. Were mentally ill people demonstrably more dangerous or were police making that assumption, and using fatal force without good reason? Quentin asked. *Four Corners'* executive producer, Sue Spencer, agreed he should find out.

The Holcombes' silence meant Elijah's case was still a mystery, three months after his death.

'See if you can contact them,' Quentin said to me. 'Find out if they'd like to talk.'

We both knew what he really meant was, 'See if you can change their minds.' As a researcher at *Four Corners*, my job was to build relationships and persuade people to tell their stories. I was also the office country girl. Elijah's family were country people — I was perfect for the job.

It was six weeks before Jeremy Holcombe returned any of my calls.

I was expecting the chewed-over words of a farmer, but he spoke like a self-taught intellectual. Yes, the family's statement was genuine: they really didn't blame the officer who had shot Elijah. Police accepted a responsibility that no one else wanted. Jeremy's voice was rigid. The police officer was acting on the community's behalf; Elijah's death was society's fault, not the officer's.

'We ask a lot of people in his position. We basically ask people like him to do what he did, for us, and then we scapegoat him. There were so many things that let Elijah down, not just that one thing,' Jeremy Holcombe told me.

The intensity in his voice pushed me back in my chair.

Jeremy had separated from Elijah's mother, Tracey, but both had contacted police repeatedly in the months since their son's death. The message they got was always the same — Elijah's shooting was under investigation; all information was off limits. They had been respectful to begin with, Jeremy said, but they didn't understand why police couldn't tell them something by now. He hinted at a cover-up.

The only person close to the family who had publicly criticised the police was Elijah's wife, Allison. Two days after Elijah's shooting, she blasted them in a letter to a Sydney tabloid. Police had killed 'the gentlest, kindest person in the world', she wrote. I asked Jeremy if he thought Allison would speak to me. Possibly, he said, but probably not.

Four Corners wanted to tell Elijah's story, I ventured. Did Jeremy see any value in that? He said he would think it over.

We spoke and emailed sporadically for a month. Jeremy referred to Elijah's death in one conversation as an 'execution' by the State. The next time we spoke, he said he didn't want to be vengeful.

'You hear so many people on TV outside court say, "We came here to see justice", and I think, *bullshit*. You came here to get revenge. There's a big difference between justice and revenge.'

Jeremy knew nothing about the officer who'd shot Elijah — not his name, his age, nor how long he had served with the police. All the Holcombes' information came from media coverage or from witnesses who contacted them. Rumours were rife: the officer had been transferred to Armidale after a knife attack in Sydney. He wore a protective vest under his uniform all the time. He was a cowboy. He was a good guy. Jeremy relayed each story bitterly. He had no way of knowing what was true, but he refused to hate the man who had shot his son.

I waited for the show of saintliness to fall away. *Perhaps in the next call*, I thought each time, *Jeremy will drop his guard and give in to his anger.* Or we would dig a bit deeper somewhere else and find a justification for Elijah's shooting: a drug habit or a history of random violence.

'I think you may have made the assumption, as many have, that this is yet another case of "crazed mentally ill man tragically shot dead by police",' Jeremy wrote in an email at the end of August 2009. 'I can assure you the truth is way more complicated.'

Attached to the email was a sixty-page summary of Elijah's childhood, the history of his mental illness, and the days leading up to his death. It was a map of Jeremy Holcombe's grief, written in the months since Elijah's death. The Holcombes had decided to tell Elijah's story.

Elijah grew up in Wee Waa, a dot on the northwest plains of NSW, where cotton crops blot the horizon white in summer. His parents had been raised on the same flat land. Jeremy was a farm boy, Tracey was from Narrabri, the next town on the map. They met around a campfire at a woolshed party. Jeremy proposed to Tracey the night they met. He wanted to marry her at the local lookout. She was sixteen; he was a year older.

My parents, too, had grown up in a small town on the northwest plains of NSW. My mother was a townie, my father was a farm boy. They met at a dance in an old woolshed.

My best friend in high school lived in Narrabri. Her father owned the car dealership there and one in Wee Waa. In the holidays when

I visited her, we would go to the Blue Dove café for cappuccinos. We got drunk for the first time at a woolshed party and dreamed of meeting boys who would whisk us away and marry us.

Jeremy and Tracey left Wee Waa for Sydney in their twenties, but returned to raise a family in a district rich with relatives. Farmers on the Holcombe side, sports heroes on Tracey's. Jeremy built a house from scratch in the middle of the tiny town. 'The vanity project of my thirties.' He supported his family by applying the skills he'd learned restoring antique cars in Sydney to fixing farm machinery and family Falcons. Tracey settled in to having more kids. Elijah was already a toddler. Next came a brother, Tarney, then two girls, Laura and Jordan. They were all smart and musical, but everyone agreed Elijah had an extra dose of charm. His siblings nicknamed him 'Too Good' when he went to high school: too good to be true. But when he turned sixteen, something changed. One night, Elijah punched a hole in his bedroom wall.

'It's all dark, Mum. I don't feel anything,' he told Tracey.

Elijah was diagnosed with depression. Anti-depressants and sessions with a psychologist put him back on keel within a year, but his diagnosis had unexpected repercussions. Jeremy Holcombe listened to descriptions of Elijah's internal world — violent mood swings, suicidal thoughts, extreme anxiety — and found an explanation for feelings he himself had carried his entire life. The realisation was overwhelming. Jeremy was hospitalised with chronic depression and suicidal thoughts three or four times in the next two years.

I include this, Jeremy wrote in his account of Elijah's life, *because my illness was a feature of Elijah's formative years. I also believe, because of my own experience of mental illness I am qualified to some extent to offer an opinion as to the nature of Elijah's illness in the final year of his life.*

By the time he finished high school in 2004, Elijah's depression was a thing of the past, wrote Jeremy. He set his sights on university and enrolled in an arts-psychology degree at Macquarie University. The country boy with the big brown eyes was a hit on campus, especially with the ladies.

Elijah liked the American girls who came to Australia on exchange. He'd date them and wave each one goodbye at the airport when their semester was up. But one refused to say goodbye — a marketing student from Minnesota. Elijah put her on the plane, but Allison kept calling. He made trips back and forth between Australia and the States; there were break-ups, reunions, and phone calls day and night. It was a relationship that any adult who survived their twenties would recognise. In early 2007, the couple agreed that Allison would return to Australia and they would set up house together. When getting a permanent visa for Allison proved tricky, they solved the problem by deciding they would marry. Elijah took Allison home to Wee Waa in the middle of 2007 to break their news to his parents in person.

It was a trip full of surprises. Before the young couple could share their plans, Elijah's parents announced that they were separating. Tracey and Jeremy had been together for almost thirty years, but Jeremy was in love with someone else. Elijah's parents had agreed to tell their children face to face. They had waited for Elijah to be there, not knowing the news he'd come home to share.

Elijah and Allison stayed the weekend and left without revealing their plans. They wed in December in a Sydney registry office, with two friends as their witnesses. Allison returned to the States to pack up her life and return to Australia permanently.

Eight months after the wedding, in August 2008, Tracey received a phone call from Elijah.

It was the first time we became aware of Elijah's compromised mental state, Jeremy wrote, and described what Tracey had told him about the phone call.

'Hello?'

Silence at the other end. The sky outside was pitch-dark.

'Is that you 'Lije? Are you OK?'

'Have you heard anything, Mum?'

'What are you talking about — where are you?'

'I'm at the train station.'

'Where?'

'Epping.'

'Why? Is something wrong?'

'She wants to kill me, Mum.'

Tracey sat up and switched the light on. It was almost midnight.

Allison was plotting to have him killed, Elijah told her. Their flatmate was in on the plan — he was a member of the Turkish mafia. Elijah had fled the apartment with his passport and a thousand dollars.

Tracey spoke calmly.

''Lije, this doesn't make sense. Allison loves you. She doesn't want to hurt you, none of this is true. You have to go home.'

After fifteen minutes of Tracey's pleading, Elijah's phone went dead. She called Jeremy straight away.

'I think our boy might be a bit schizophrenic,' Tracey blurted out.

Jeremy was sceptical.

'Are you sure?'

She relayed her conversation with Elijah. He'd sounded terrified, she said.

'I think I should drive to Sydney in the morning. What if he sleeps out in the street or the park? We don't know what he could do.'

Jeremy relented. There was just one problem. Elijah and Allison had moved into a new apartment the previous weekend. Tracey and Jeremy didn't have Allison's new number or the couple's address. Jeremy offered to make calls to find the flat, so Tracey could sleep before she left for Sydney.

He called Elijah's brother first. Tarney lived in Sydney, too. He didn't know where the apartment was, but Elijah had shown him some places they liked online. Tarney began trawling real estate websites for anything familiar. Jeremy called around friends and family to check if Elijah had made contact.

Tracey watched the stars fade into morning. She was in the car at 5am, heading out of Wee Waa. She called Elijah's mobile every twenty minutes. At 10am, he answered.

'Hi, Mum.'

Tracey pulled off the road.

''Lije, do you remember last night? What you said to me when you were hiding at the train station?'

'Yeah, but it's alright, Mum, that was just silly stuff. Don't worry about it.'

'Well, I'm coming to see you, OK?'

'Hey Allison, Mum's on her way to see us.' He was back at the apartment.

Tracey sighed.

'What's your new address?'

'It's not normal, you know he's not well,' Tracey said to her daughter-in-law over lunch. Elijah seemed perfectly fine again now.

'I know.'

Allison had been in Minnesota with her family for six weeks. Elijah was fine when she left, she said, but when she got back, he was checking for wiretaps and reading coded messages on Facebook. Allison thought it was an elaborate joke at first, but the strangeness went on for hours at a time.

'I don't know what's wrong,' Allison said softly.

Tracey could see they were all out of their depth.

''Lije, we need to go to the hospital to sort this out.'

To her surprise, Elijah agreed.

'I'm fine now, Mum, this is stupid,' he said after an hour in Emergency, but Tracey refused to budge. The triage nurse at Concord Hospital sent them to the mental health unit, where doctors diagnosed 'a textbook case' of delusional paranoia. They recommended Elijah begin treatment in the mental health unit immediately.

When Jeremy heard the news, he was relieved. Elijah was in good hands. But Allison's reality broke. Her husband had an illness she had heard about in psych lectures. He was going into hospital and he might not be home for months. Elijah was the reason she had moved to Australia. Tracey repeated as gently as she could to her daughter-in-law what her son had told the doctors.

A few weeks earlier, Elijah had gone to a party alone while Allison was in the States, Jeremy explained in his timeline of Elijah's illness.

Elijah told us that he got extremely drunk at this party. He believed he had kissed another girl, but he could not remember if that was the extent of his indiscretion. He told Allison about it. Apparently, she did not consider it to be 'a big deal' and told Elijah to forget about it. Elijah invariably referred to this party as 'the start of it all', wrote Jeremy.

Doctors at Concord Hospital were confident Elijah's heavy drinking session had triggered a chemical shift in his brain, changing the way he experienced his own thoughts. They couldn't say for certain what had made his brain switch tracks — there was usually a genetic predisposition. A personal crisis or period of great stress could create conditions for the illness to develop, and all sorts of things could act as a trigger. Elijah's intense guilt was a classic feature of paranoid delusion, the doctors said. Allison's observation that he was seeing coded messages in Facebook postings was another. Elijah was re-interpreting situations to try and impose control on his internal chaos. The more opaque a situation was, the more intricate his stories became, in order to make sense of his changed reality.

Jeremy and Tracey's response to Elijah's diagnosis was so exemplary and rational I had trouble believing Jeremy's account was completely truthful. Allison's reaction aligned more closely with my expectations; except for her response to the party. Had she really been so relaxed about her husband's possible unfaithfulness?

Jeremy's descriptions of Allison were protective. She was young, 'insecure in a new country' and a 'long way from her family,' he wrote.

Could I speak with her? I asked again.

Elijah had ended his relationship with Allison days before he died, Jeremy explained over the phone. The Holcombes weren't sure what Allison knew about her place in his delusions or if she believed the marriage was at an end. She was a victim, Jeremy warned; he didn't want her hurt.

My days were taken up with phone calls tracking down witnesses to Elijah's shooting. The list of people I needed to find grew longer with every person I spoke to. When the phone in my office rang one morning, I assumed it would be an eyewitness from Cinders Lane calling me back.

'Hello, ABC, this is Kate.'

'Hello, I'm Allison,' said a quiet voice.

I rifled through a notebook, looking for a clean page.

'Hello.' I spun my internal Rolodex trying to place the caller. 'I'm sorry, Allison, I'm not sure why you're calling,' I admitted.

'I'm Elijah's wife. His mother said you wanted to talk to me.' She sounded like a shadow breathing. Her voice was so soft I could barely detect an accent, but the note of offence was clear. I scrambled for ground already lost. Was there anything important she could tell me about her husband that would help me understand him? I asked. She knew him better than anyone — what did she want other people to know?

Allison paused. Her voice grew a fraction stronger. She had photographs of Elijah and her together if I wanted them. *Four Corners* could use them in the program, but we weren't to publish her last name. She didn't want people at work to know.

'Would you like to say something about Elijah on camera?' I asked.

His parents knew more about what had happened. It was better they told the story, she said. I apologised for my clumsiness and tried to draw her out with questions about her own experience of Elijah's illness, but the call lasted less than a minute. Allison didn't want to talk about it.

She had criticised police in the newspaper, but she wouldn't speak to me. I had blown it.

True to her word, Allison emailed me photos of her and Elijah together.

So this was the woman he had chosen for his wife. Deeply tanned, with long chestnut hair, and brown eyes just like his. A narrow face and nose. Straight teeth. Allison nestled into the space under Elijah's arm. The grin on his face was broad. He was happy and proud. She wore an ivory top in silky satin; was it their wedding day? Allison looked like she'd stepped off a beach in California. A pretty American girl with her handsome Aussie. Elijah was the anchor in the picture, solid and stable; no sign of illness in his eyes or face. Allison clung to him. Something in the angle of her head strained towards the camera. She couldn't believe her luck that this man loved her.

How would it feel to lose that love? To watch it disappear into the waves of an illness that convinced your husband you were plotting to have him killed?

3.

Elijah was admitted as a voluntary patient into Concord Hospital's specialist mental health unit, but a month into his treatment he announced he was checking out, Jeremy wrote. His doctors tried to persuade him to stay, but, as a voluntary patient, they couldn't hold Elijah against his will. He returned to the apartment he shared with Allison; he deferred university, and kept appointments with a psychologist. Mental illness was part of Elijah's life, but it wasn't the whole story — he was still functioning in the world. He worked packing shelves at a supermarket, and socialised; most of his friends didn't know he was sick or that he'd been in hospital, his father wrote, but the delusions and paranoia persisted. Reality could falter for an hour or a day and then right itself just as swiftly. Everything was internal. What didn't change was the guilt that overwhelmed Elijah, even on the good days.

He was obsessed with discovering what had happened at the party. He saw that as the key to everything. On many occasions, he acknowledged that he was ill. He was trying to determine why, Jeremy wrote.

The stories Elijah concocted became more detailed as time went on. But Elijah did not hear voices or hallucinate, Jeremy insisted.

That is, he was not psychotic in the clinical meaning of the word. As far as I can determine, every event, every word and every conversation alluded to in his fantasies actually took place. It was his interpretation … and his predictions of where they may lead, that was so dangerously flawed.

In the week before Christmas 2008, Elijah called his father. An intruder had come into the flat to kill him, and he didn't know what to do except run, he said. He was hiding in parkland near the apartment. Jeremy told him to stay put. It was past 8pm, the drive to Sydney was seven hours. Tarney was home for the holidays and offered to share the driving.

They arrived at Elijah's Homebush flat at dawn. Elijah was back inside, but he didn't want to let them in. When he finally opened the door, 'He looked like shit,' Jeremy remembered.

'Where's Allison?' Jeremy asked.

'She's in America for Christmas.'

Jeremy pleaded with Elijah to return to Wee Waa with them. 'I felt like I was kidnapping him,' he recalled. On the long drive home, and then over Christmas, Jeremy gave his son some blunt advice. 'Forget about work and relationships for a while and stay home with us until you've recovered.'

Allison called from Minnesota multiple times a day. She wanted Elijah to meet her in Sydney to celebrate New Year's Eve.

By this time, Jeremy recounted, Elijah understood that his relationship was flawed. *What he didn't know was whether he was ill because his relationship was flawed, or his relationship was flawed because he was ill.*

I had so little information about Allison it was hard to know what Jeremy meant when he alluded to flaws in Elijah and Allison's relationship. She was a mystery figure but a familiar girlfriend — emotionally needy, beautifully packaged, and often a long way away from the man she loved.

Elijah took the bus back to Sydney to see in New Year's Eve with his wife, and a five-month silence opened up in Jeremy Holcombe's account of his son's life.

His records resumed with a phone call from Elijah at the end of May 2009, the week before Elijah was shot.

Elijah had ended his relationship with Allison. Would Jeremy come and help him move out of the flat?

'Sure 'Lije, if that's what you want,' Jeremy said. 'When do you want to do it?'

They settled on two days' time. Jeremy would drive to Sydney and meet Elijah at the flat, late-morning.

Jeremy stubbed his cigarette out against the wall and pressed the intercom.

Elijah was slow to answer and slow to the door when Jeremy reached the fifth floor. The apartment was dark. Elijah's face was streaked with tears.

'What's happening, mate?'

Jeremy put his arm around Elijah's shoulders and his son began to sob.

'I'm waiting for the police to come and arrest me. They're coming to arrest me and deport me to the US. They're going to put me on death row in LA for statutory rape,' he said.

'They can't do that, mate, I won't let them. Come on, we'll get your gear and I'll take you home. We'll get you some help.'

'No Dad, they can do that. There's an arrangement between Australia and the US. I took Allison out of the US when she wasn't mentally well. She wasn't a responsible adult. She set me up Dad — this is how she is going to get me. The last time we were in the US, Allison bought me an LA Dodgers shirt, and once I said something about dying alone and she said, "I won't let you die alone, EJ", and that's what it means. I'm going to be publicly executed in LA. A couple of days ago, she wrote something on Facebook about me being her little lamby ...'

Jeremy interrupted.

'No, mate, none of that's true. You're not well, 'Lije. It's a delusion. Come on, I'll help you get a few clothes together and we'll take you home and get you some help.'

But Elijah wasn't listening.

'I was walking to the bus stop the other day to go to work. A cop car came up beside me. The cop drove the car slowly along the gutter beside me as I was walking, just watching me. I looked at him, and then he sped up and took off.'

'That doesn't mean anything 'Lije. You know cops, they're suspicious of everyone.'

'No. They're watching me, Dad. Did you see any police downstairs?'

'No, I haven't seen a cop since I left Narrabri.'

'Why are you here, Dad?'

'You asked me to come and get you, 'Lije. Remember we spoke on the phone yesterday? You told me you were breaking up with Allison and asked me to come and help you move out.'

If Elijah's calm on the phone two days ago had been a window of lucidity, it had now passed. Jeremy's mind worked rapidly through his options. The police had replaced the Turkish mafia as the aggressors in Elijah's story. He could take his son to Concord Hospital for readmission, but with Allison so nearby in Homebush, she might attempt a reunion with Elijah. Since she was the focus of his delusions, that didn't seem like a good idea. Jeremy wanted to remove his son from any triggers until he was well again. The family's GP in Narrabri could manage his care, at least to begin with.

He put his hand on Elijah's arm and coaxed his son towards the door.

'Come on, mate, we'll go home. We can get your other stuff later.'

'OK, if that's where we're really going …' Elijah looked at his father intently. His phone buzzed.

'Why don't you turn your phone off, mate?' Jeremy prompted. 'Who is it?'

It was Allison, Elijah said. She wanted to know if it was really over. He walked onto the balcony, leaned his back against the wall, and slid to the floor with his knees pulled to his chest. He lowered his head and cried. Jeremy squatted down to lift Elijah's face and looked directly into his eyes.

'I love you, 'Lije. You have to trust me. It's all a delusion, mate. Nothing bad is going to happen to you.'

Elijah looked at him with a flicker of recognition.

'It's a delusion,' Elijah repeated, and the recognition fell away. But Jeremy had touched something. Elijah collected clothes and a philosophy book from his room. On the bed was a guitar Jeremy had given him when he left for university. Jeremy swept it up, and the two men walked down to the car together.

They drove north over the Hawkesbury River, past Gosford, into the hinterland at Maitland. Elijah became more settled the further they travelled, and Jeremy's fear he would leap from the car faded.

'Thanks for coming to pick me up, Dad.'

'That's OK, mate.'

They stopped in Muswellbrook for fuel, and a highway patrol car pulled in at the bowser behind them. Jeremy pointed it out deliberately.

'That's not freaking you out is it, mate?'

'No. I didn't even notice him.'

The morning's episode had waned. Jeremy refuelled and went inside to pay. When he came back out, the highway patrol officer followed him, deliberately walking through the narrow gap between Jeremy's car and the petrol bowser. Jeremy was back in the driver's seat. The officer peered through the window and shot a long, hard look at Elijah, who shifted in his seat uncomfortably. Jeremy saw the problem.

'Mate, you're sitting in a car next to a petrol bowser smoking a cigarette! No wonder he gave you a look. We're lucky we didn't get booked!'

'You reckon that's all it was?'

'Yes, mate. I'm sure. That's all it was.'

Jeremy shook his head and pulled the car onto the highway. Elijah sighed.

'Well, at least I'll get to spend my last few days with my family.'

Fragile and fed up, Jeremy snapped.

'Is that your plan, Elijah? Are you just going home to top yourself?'

'No! I just meant that I'll be home for a couple of days before the police find me and arrest me.'

'Jesus Christ, 'Lije ... That's not going to happen.'

They tracked northwest, stopping on the broad Breeza Plains as the sun dropped. Standing next to his father, pissing into the long, dry grass, Elijah commented on the beauty of the sky.

Elijah's wasn't the only case study Quentin McDermott was interested in for *Four Corners*. There was Tyler Cassidy, a 15-year-old who was shot in a Melbourne skate-park, six months before Elijah was shot. Tyler was waving two large knives and advancing on police when they fired. In the same month that Elijah died, Tony Galeano was tasered twenty-eight times in seven minutes by Queensland police, and died.

The most historical case we covered was the death of Roni Levi in 1997. Mental illness entered Australia's collective consciousness the day Roni Levi was shot on Bondi Beach by two uniformed police officers.

A decade before the ubiquity of mobile phones, it was a miracle a photographer happened to be on the beach that morning. Jean-Pierre Bratanoff-Firgoff's half-dozen images of Roni standing at the edge of the surf, wet overcoat flapping and a carving knife in his hand, were burned on Australia's retina and housed in the National Archive. Between reading Jeremy's summary of Elijah's life, I researched Tony, Tyler, and Roni's deaths. Their stories were shocking, but it was Elijah's that held me. I returned to Jeremy's document repeatedly, looking for the moment fate had turned.

Back home in Narrabri, Jeremy was roused by a knock on the bedroom door.

It was 7am; Elijah was dressed in his clothes from the previous night.

'Can I talk to you?' he asked his father.

Jeremy looked behind him to the bed. Fiona, his partner, was still asleep.

'Yes, mate. I'll be right out.'

Elijah sat at the table in the courtyard, smoking.

'What's up?'

Elijah raised both arms in the air as if to surrender.

'This is what I was supposed to do, isn't it?'

'What do you mean?'

Elijah lowered his arms and pulled his sleeves back, exposing jagged lacerations caked with dry blood at his wrists.

'Jesus Christ,' Jeremy exploded. 'What did you do that for?'

'That's what I was supposed to do, wasn't it?' Elijah asked again.

'What? Commit suicide? Well, you did a piss-poor job, didn't you?'

Jeremy guessed the cuts were not a genuine suicide attempt, but rather a staged performance to 'fulfill' some part of a delusion.

I was actually reassuring him that if he really believed he was to commit suicide he had made a feeble effort, Jeremy wrote in his account of their first morning back in Narrabri.

He phoned Tracey, who took the news of Elijah's self-harm calmly and offered to meet them at Narrabri hospital. Once there, Elijah admitted he had weaned himself off his medication three months earlier. He didn't believe it had helped his paranoia, and it interfered with his ability to think, he said. The doctor gave Elijah enough medication to get through the weekend and told him to make an appointment on Monday for an ongoing prescription.

Sunday passed quietly. Elijah was watchful. He asked Fiona to close the curtains by the table when they were eating breakfast.

'They've got the house bugged, Dad,' he whispered to his father later.

Jeremy slept in a single bed pulled up against Elijah's that night.

On Monday, Jeremy had chores to do before they went to see the GP. He explained to Elijah that they would drive into town, and he would go to the post office and then the ATM. After that, they'd go home for lunch, and then come back for the doctor at 3pm.

Jeremy parked the car just off the main street, leaving the keys in the ignition so Elijah could listen to the radio.

'I won't be long, mate. I'm just going to the post office and bank, OK?'

Elijah nodded.

The line in the post office was long and slow. Jeremy bought a stamp, pushed his letter into the dark slot of the mailbox, and hurried across the road. The screen on the ATM was blank. The bank's glass doors slid back on another queue. Jeremy checked his watch and swore. He'd been gone almost twenty minutes. Longer than he'd planned; if Elijah got scared, he might leave the car. Jeremy turned to leave and saw his Fairmont moving past the window. It stopped at the intersection with its indicator flashing, then slowly swung left onto the highway.

Jeremy sprinted, but Elijah was gone. He thought of calling the police but batted the idea away. It would only antagonise Elijah's delusions. He hurried to Fiona's workplace in the main street and marched into her office.

'Elijah's taken off in my car.'

Fiona grabbed her bag and they sped home. Jeremy searched upstairs. Elijah's phone was on his bed, switched off. Jeremy took Fiona's car and headed for the highway. She went with friends to search the back roads.

An hour later, Jeremy called Tracey. Again, they discounted calling the police. Jeremy started phoning Elijah's friends while Tracey called Allison, but no one had seen or heard from him. An hour after that, Jeremy sent a text to Tracey. It was time to contact the police.

Senior Constable Brett Allison ushered Jeremy into a quiet room and offered him a seat.

Elijah was mentally ill; he suffered delusional paranoia, Jeremy explained. The illness didn't make him dangerous, but he had taken off in Jeremy's car and he didn't have a driver's license. Jeremy needed help to find him, but there was a complicating factor: because of his illness, Elijah was terrified of police.

'Just help us find the car,' Jeremy said. 'Don't approach him — find the car and we'll come and get him.'

Senior Constable Brett Allison assured Jeremy the police could handle it. He asked for the registration, colour, and model of the car. Did Jeremy know where his son might be headed? Was there a photo of Elijah the police could have, and what was his condition called again?

'Delusional paranoia,' Jeremy repeated.

The senior constable was calm and reassuring. Before Jeremy left the station, Brett Allison put a note out on the police internal system to alert officers across the region to the details of the car and to Elijah's illness. Someone would call as soon as the car was spotted, he said.

Jeremy went home to check if there was any activity on Elijah's bank account — it was connected to his own. There had been two withdrawals that afternoon. One at a truck stop on the outskirts of Narrabri for about $100 and a second one for $1000, one hundred and fifteen kilometres southwest, in the town of Coonabarabran. Elijah had once told his father that if his paranoia ever got too much, he would hide at an uncle's house in Canberra. Coonabarabran was on the way. Jeremy called Senior Constable Brett Allison to tell him he was leaving to follow Elijah south. Mobile reception was patchy on the road to Canberra, so the police should contact Tracey if they found Elijah or the car, Jeremy said.

'If you call me, I'll probably be out of range,' he warned.

'I know Jeremy has said this already, but please don't let anyone approach my son in public. He won't hurt anyone, but if someone goes up to him he'll run,' Tracey said as soon as she sat down. 'I know how these things go sometimes, Brett. I don't want to see what I've seen on television where you approach him and he's frightened. All we want is to find the car and Elijah, and we can take him to a hospital. He is really, really afraid of police.'

'It won't be a problem, Tracey,' Senior Constable Brett Allison repeated. 'We'll put the call out, we'll find the car, and call you or Jeremy straight away.'

'Don't call Jeremy. He won't be home. 'Lije doesn't have a licence; if you try to pull him over he could have an accident.'

Laura rolled her eyes. Her mother was repeating herself, but the police officer didn't seem to mind.

'I'll update the details as soon as we're finished,' Brett Allison reassured her. Tracey and Laura had brought him a photocopy of Elijah's passport photo.

Tracey talked the whole way home, testing Laura on what she had told Brett Allison.

'Did I give him my phone number?'

'I dunno, Mum. You must have. You would have for sure.'

'I don't think I did. Oh, how stupid! How are they going to contact me?'

'Relax. We'll call them when we get home.'

The officer who answered the phone promised to pass on Tracey's number; Senior Constable Brett Allison was still on duty, so it wouldn't be an issue. Tracey recited her mobile number.

'Mum, you forgot the last nine,' Jordan prompted from the kitchen.

'Oh. Nine on the end. Yeah, nine,' Tracey said.

4.

Jeremy was relieved to have Fiona in the car with him. They slowed at truck stops and strained through the dark for the Fairmont's boxy silhouette. Lorries roared past them, channelling ferocious wind. Jeremy pictured Elijah clinging to the road in his old car and flinched.

They found the ATM Elijah had used in Coonabarabran, but it offered no clues; so they carried on. Darkness fell, and town lights spread like scattered marbles — Gilgandra, Dubbo, Peak Hill, Parkes. They found a room in Parkes around midnight, and went to bed with unbrushed teeth. They hadn't thought to pack before they left. No one imagined it would take this long to find Elijah.

Jeremy lay beside Fiona, staring into the dark above the bed. His jaw and chest were tight; his eyes felt filled with grit.

I won't be long, mate, I'm just going to the post office and bank, and Elijah had nodded.

I won't be long. But he was. Lines in the post office, lines at the bank, and Elijah had slipped into another layer of the world. Elijah, who had no license. Elijah, who was scared and sick. The world was dull like a broken bell.

Elijah, Elijah, Jeremy's heart beat in his ears. *Where are you, mate? Tell me and I'll come and find you. Tell me. Don't be gone.*

Fiona lay asleep beside him. When he slipped bare-footed out the door, cold light had barely found the sky. Elijah had been missing for eighteen hours. Jeremy rolled a cigarette.

When Fiona woke, they left for Canberra. An hour down the road, Jeremy's mobile jittered in the console. It was Tracey. She had spoken to the uncle whose house they were driving to. Elijah wasn't there.

Allison had called, Tracey said. She thought someone was watching her apartment from the park this morning; did anyone know what Elijah was wearing? Allison had thought it might be him, but when she leaned over the balcony the person had walked away.

Jeremy closed his thoughts until they reached the edge of Canberra, where he texted Tracey.

Mobile battery low. Use Fiona's number if u need to. We r in Canberra.

Jeremy and Fiona went to his brother's house and checked the doors and windows. They circled the yard and looked up and down the street. No car. They could wait here for Elijah or drive to the apartment in Sydney. They decided to wait until noon in a park at the only entrance to the street. However Elijah arrived, if he was coming to his uncle's house, he would have to pass them. If he hadn't come by noon, they would leave for Sydney.

Fiona lay on the grass and stared into the dappling leaves above her. Jeremy leaned his back against the tree and broke twigs into tidy piles.

In Wee Waa, Tracey huddled on the couch. It was after midday; the girls were still in bed.

'Don't worry, Mum, Elijah will turn up,' Laura had said last night. He was just 'doing a runner' from all the stress, stretching his wings, she said.

'Be free! Run 'Lije, run!' Jordan had shrieked in reply, and chased her sister down the hall.

Tracey had slept with the phone beneath her pillow. Now she cradled it in her lap.

The streets around Elijah's flat were new and fresh, as though just released from plastic wrapping. Cobbled pedestrian zones led to brand new tennis courts, manicured parks, and outdoor restaurants. If Elijah parked the Fairmont here, it would be obvious, Jeremy calculated. There was no one at the apartment. Allison was still at work. It was 3.30pm.

Jeremy and Fiona walked to where the Parramatta River curved its drift past manufactured greenlands. They chain-smoked, staring at the river, their hands seeking warmth from their takeaway coffees. Jeremy explained in his summary how he had tried to decipher the logic behind Elijah's disappearance. While his son's decisions appeared random to others, his actions still followed discernible patterns for the Holcombes. When Elijah's delusional fears became too much, his pattern was to take flight.

Jeremy figured Elijah's $1000 withdrawal on the afternoon he disappeared was an attempt to avoid being traced through his bank account by living off cash for as long as he could. If their first assumption that Elijah was heading to an uncle's house in Canberra was wrong, why else might he have stopped in Coonabaraban? Had they said anything in conversation on the weekend that Elijah could have taken as a cue? Jeremy and Fiona had talked about going camping. Fiona offered Bellingen, while Jeremy suggested a site near Coonabarabran where they'd camped before. Perhaps Elijah was at that spot, sitting in the bushland waiting for them to arrive?

Elijah may have believed we were giving him secret plans of escape, Jeremy wrote, reflecting on the camping conversation.

Jeremy and Fiona decided to circle back to Coonabarabran. They rang Tracey to tell her; she was just off the phone from the Narrabri police — there were no reports of Elijah or the car.

Within minutes of hanging up, Fiona's mobile rang. Jeremy watched her face as she spoke.

'He's right beside me. I'll put him on.'

It was a female officer from Narrabri Police Station.

'Mr Holcombe? We have some news for you regarding Elijah, but we'd like to tell you in person. Can we come over and see you?'

Jeremy's ears began to ring.

'I'm not in Narrabri. I'm in Sydney, looking for Elijah. I'm outside his apartment.'

Jeremy could hear a hand cover the phone at the other end. There were muffled words, and then a deeper voice came on the line. It reached through a long, dark tunnel towards him.

'Jeremy?'

'Yes.'

'Mr Holcombe, it's Inspector Ridley speaking from the Narrabri Police Station. We've been trying desperately to contact you. I would like to speak with you in person.'

'Well, that's not possible; I'm in Sydney.'

'I have some bad news for you.'

'Is it about Elijah?'

'Yes.'

'Give it to me straight.'

'Mr Holcombe, your son is in Armidale. There has been an incident. Your son has been shot by the police and he has passed away. I'm sorry, Mr Holcombe. I'm sorry to have to give you the news this way.'

Jeremy fell. His own voice echoed in the tunnel.

'How do you know it's Elijah? Are you sure? What happened?'

Fiona screamed.

'Mr Holcombe, I don't have the information to answer your questions. I have Detective Inspector Stier on another line. Can he ring you on this number?'

Detective Inspector Greig Stier from Armidale called immediately. Jeremy heard a stream of sound. Elijah had presented to police at Armidale station. They took him to hospital. He left. Police found him walking down the street. Elijah ran away. Police chased. Elijah ran through a café and picked up a knife. He threatened police with the knife. Police shot him. Elijah was dead. There would be an investigation. Homicide detectives were on their way from Sydney.

'Get off my fucking phone, you pack of gun-happy, trigger-happy cunts!'

Jeremy clutched at the ground, ripping grass in handfuls, saliva running from his mouth. He wanted to block his ears and mouth with earth. A coffee cup lay by his face. A bent straw. People in the park were watching. Fiona clutched the skin of her face and screamed. Jeremy swayed as he pulled himself up. Dirt and grass clung to his face and clothes.

'We have to tell Tracey.'

Laura answered the phone in the kitchen. The sky was darkening outside.

'Hey, princess, how are you?'

There was a quality to her father's voice she had never heard before. Laura locked eyes with Jordan, sitting on the kitchen bench.

'We've found Elijah.' Her father's voice was hoarse. 'He's in Armidale and they've shot him.'

'What?!'

Tracey wrenched the phone from her daughter's hand.

'Jeremy?'

'I'm so sorry, it's the worst possible news,' she heard before the floor fell away beneath her.

Fiona took the wheel for the drive home to Narrabri. Jeremy slumped in the passenger seat. Tarney, whom they'd collected from university, sat like a mountain, still and solid, in the back. Their sobs merged with the throbbing of the windscreen wipers. Fiona fought to hold simple things in her mind: chips in the windscreen, the cigarette between her fingers. She could see, in the rear-view mirror, a sprinkling of rain on Tarney's hair.

When they reached country roads, it was late and dark. Guideposts floated, white lines broke and slipped away. Disappearing, reappearing, gone.

It was 1am when Fiona pulled into a tiny service station. The pumps were locked, the lights were out; the slam of the car doors splintered the night. She watched Jeremy and Tarney crunch across the gravel. When she tried to get out of the car, she couldn't move. Shock landed like a punch in the stillness. She shook and gagged, searching for Jeremy, mute with panic. She clawed through the dark and found him sitting on the kerb. The sky was crystal clear and cold. Tarney stood at a distance. Fiona watched their bodies turn to gold in a sweep of lights. A familiar car pulled in, and two men stepped out towards them, heads low. Jeremy's cousin David Phelps and a friend had come to accompany them home. They formed a knot of bodies in the dark, tears flowing, arms entwined.

The group of mourners reached Jeremy's house at 3am and stumbled through the door. The men fell into chairs, and Fiona checked the phone for messages.

'Fuck! Fuck! Fuck!! Those bastards!' she screamed.

The men shrank in their seats. Fiona cowered against the wall. David Phelps replayed the messages.

Both had been left the previous day, when Elijah was still alive: one at 11.30am, the other an hour later. One message was from the Narrabri police. The other was from Armidale station.

Both were telling us that Elijah had just presented himself to the Armidale Police Station, Jeremy's statement said. *We were devastated. Tracey and I had both specifically asked the Narrabri Police to call Tracey, yet she had heard nothing from the Police even when she called them. We also realised we had many options of people on the ground in Armidale. Any one of them could have intervened and cared for Elijah until Tracey or I could get there.*

The grief in Jeremy's timeline left a mark on me. If what he claimed was true, if the police had followed the Holcombes' instructions and contacted Tracey instead of him, Elijah would be alive.

Four Corners wanted to uncover what happened between those messages being left and Elijah being shot in Cinders Lane. I talked to anyone who would take my call, starting with the local press.

Lu Danielli freelanced as a TV cameraman and worked at the *Armidale Independent* — a rival to the *Armidale Express*.

Lu was in Cinders Lane within minutes of Elijah's shooting. He filmed a stream of uniforms pouring through the lane, chequered police tape rolling out, Elijah's body being covered in a blanket, and detectives with clipboards talking on mobile phones. He interviewed eyewitnesses on the spot, and when I rang three months after the event, Lu shared everything he knew with me. It might not all check out, he warned, but this was the story doing the rounds in Armidale — a version of Elijah's last day stitched together by witnesses and locals since the shooting.

Elijah was depressed. He visited his father in Narrabri on the Sunday and asked to borrow his car. He then drove to Armidale and parked at the hospital. No one knew where Elijah spent the night, but he had an aunt in town — maybe he had planned to stay with her? Elijah's father called the police at some point and reported Elijah missing. He asked the police to look out for his son and told them Elijah was depressed.

On Monday morning, Elijah returned to Armidale Hospital's Emergency Department and asked for help, but he was turned away. He went to the police station and begged to be taken to hospital. The police obliged, but Elijah waited in Emergency for more than an hour, so he left. The nurses called police to say Elijah had absconded. Two officers in uniform went out to find him. They spotted Elijah in the street and followed him on foot into the shopping mall. A cop in plainclothes was also in the mall, maybe off-duty or having a coffee, it wasn't clear. No one could explain why the cop who ended up shooting Elijah had chased him, but everyone said the guys in uniform had been left behind in the chase.

I scribbled down everything Lu said, knowing already that some of the details were wrong. Elijah had run away on Monday, not Sunday, and he'd taken the car, not asked to borrow it.

Lu promised to send me a copy of the filming he'd done in Cinders Lane. He rattled off names of witnesses; the people he had interviewed were all in the lane when Elijah was shot. No one from the hospital or local police was talking, he said.

I split Lu's list of a dozen names between the producer, Ivan, the reporter, Quentin, and myself. It took us a week to reach them all. What did they make of what they saw in Cinders Lane that day, we asked. Did Elijah threaten the police or others? What was he doing when he was shot? Few people who spoke to us agreed to be named or quoted.

There were crucial points of difference in their stories, but a common chain of events emerged.

Just before 2pm on Tuesday, Elijah had run through Beardy Street Mall, Armidale's open-air shopping strip. A man in a baseball cap was chasing him. Elijah ran into a café called Caffiends. He rushed past customers, down the hall, and into the kitchen where he swiped a bread knife, then he walked out the back door into Cinders Lane. The man in the cap followed him, entering the kitchen as Elijah slipped out the back. Café staff and people in the lane said Elijah held the knife loosely at his side. He wasn't waving it or threatening people. There was broad agreement Elijah was trying to escape the man pursuing him, but by the time the man in the cap got to Cinders Lane, Elijah was walking slowly.

Four witnesses we spoke to heard the man in the cap yell repeatedly: 'Put down the knife!', but Elijah ignored him and walked away up the lane. The man in the cap unholstered his gun, yelled to Elijah again, and then raised his gun and repeated the command. 'A change came over Elijah' before he stopped and turned around, one person said.

This was the point at which stories diverged. Some people said Elijah was shot as soon as he faced the gunman. Others said he moved, but it wasn't clear in what direction or how far. One account, seen from a window overlooking Cinders Lane, differed from the rest.

'From when I saw them, the officer had his gun out and was pointing it at Elijah. Elijah started running towards the officer. He took maybe two steps, had covered a metre, maybe two, when he was shot. It appeared Elijah was going straight for him. I've heard others have said Elijah wasn't running towards the policeman; that's not what I saw,' the man who had watched from the window said. He declined to go on camera.

At the end of the week, I flicked through my notes of scrawled-out conversations. None of the witnesses reported being frightened of Elijah. Only one picked the man in the cap as a cop. I scored the page with thick neon lines:

'… it didn't seem to be a dangerous situation … I think the officer could have de-escalated the situation. He didn't try … Elijah didn't have a chance … our mental health system is failing us … Nobody in the car park felt frightened because of Elijah … The weirdness is … why didn't [the policeman] pull out his phone earlier and get backup? … The system has let the coppers down. It's the way he's been trained, I feel sorry for him … It was all very surreal.'

Four people agreed to go on camera: Judy Tennant, who saw the man in the cap pursue Elijah up the lane; Sonia Stier[1], the owner of Caffiends Café, and her apprentice chef, Sean Miller, who were in the kitchen when Elijah swiped the knife; and Leanne Thomas, who ran from a café to give Elijah CPR.

The rest of the *Four Corners* team left the office on a two-week filming trip across the country. At almost eight months pregnant, I was grounded. No airline would let me fly.

Alone in the office, I fed Lu Danielli's DVD into my computer and watched the screen come to life. SES workers in fluoro-banded trousers,

---

1 No relation to Greig Stier

clumps of police, Elijah's body, and, above it all, grey, windblown skies. This was Cinders Lane on 2 June 2009.

'Look, normally, mate, I'd be happy to help you but not this one,' someone said off-screen. Lu slipped with his camera under blue and white tape, nosing for images like a dog for scraps. The off-screen voice broke in testily.

'Lu, I said get back.'

I fast-forwarded through the footage, searching for Rich. Would I know him instinctively if I saw his face? I scoured the lane for a white baseball cap.

The crime scene was fifteen minutes old. Through the chassis of a paddy wagon, I glimpsed Elijah's body beneath a sheet. The frontline cops had the physical innocence of a gathering of large animals.

An inkblot hung in the branches of a tree behind the van that guarded Elijah's body. The bottom of a sleeve bobbed with the breeze. Someone had lifted Elijah's jumper from the ground and placed it in the sky. At the end of the disc was a sit-down interview in what looked like a living room, carefully lit for television.

The interviewee was Leanne Thomas, the woman who had given Elijah CPR. Leanne ran a pub in Armidale; she had close-cut hair and gold-hooped earrings, pearled nail polish and a fairy-floss-pink fleece. She was calm and stoic in the middle of the screen.

I was at a café with a friend who was a nurse, Leanne told Lu.

'We noticed some people over at the window, so I hopped up to have a look. There was a man lying on the ground, his head half on the gutter, the rest of him lying on the laneway. There were people around, but there was nobody at the body. So we started to go over.'

Leanne's friend felt for Elijah's pulse, and a third woman came to help them.

'My friend started CPR on his chest. The other girl got the mask and put it onto his mouth and started blowing, but she couldn't get a seal properly. So she held it, and I blew into the mask, inflated his lungs, and my girlfriend pumped on his chest. She had blood all over her hands and on her jumper.'

'What happened next?' asked Lu.

'Well, when I was down on the ground, blowing the air into this man's lungs, I noticed on the ground, a knife — it was just lying there on the footpath, and at that stage I didn't know what was wrong with him. I didn't know he'd been shot. I thought he might have been stabbed. There was no blood on the knife but ... I've got a knife here that is similar, which is just a bread knife that you'd have at home in your kitchen.'

Leanne looked down at the knife lying in her lap, but I couldn't see it.

'There were bits of food — and I didn't know at that stage that he'd run through the café and grabbed the knife but when I look back now, it was probably bits of melted cheese [on it] and he'd just grabbed the knife off the counter.'

Her face was blank, but muscles twitched beneath her skin.

'Um, I think that the police ...' She paused, her voice choked.

'They're given capsicum spray, but I don't sort of think this knife would — you know — I'm cutting myself fairly hard there ...'

I watched, mesmerised, as Leanne dragged the serrated knife across the pale-pink fleece. Its blade could get no purchase on the fabric.

'I, I do, I know it's a weapon. I understand that. But I just think, you know, that young boy is somebody's brother and somebody's son, and he's not here tonight because he got banged straight in the chest.'

I was holding my breath. Leanne shook her head and looked down at her lap.

'If this man, which is what I've heard them say that he was — is mentally unwell, then no amount of reasoning is going to make him drop the knife. The only option they've got at this point is to shoot him and I don't think that's a very good option, not if it was my son.'

'Do you feel at all for the police?' Lu asked. 'Obviously, they've reacted for good or for bad in a very difficult situation.'

'I feel very sorry for the man that shot him. I'm sure he didn't want to shoot him but he probably wasn't left with too many options …'

'So why do you feel it's important for you to speak out on this?'

'I just think there are too many police shootings in Australia and we need to give the police alternatives so they can deal with violent people, but not kill them.'

She lifted the knife into frame and ran her fingers across the serrated blade. Light bounced onto her face and her composure broke.

'I think I'm still in shock …'

Jeremy and Tracey were standing at Elijah's grave. Jeremy had a mobile face. A breeze blew Tracey's hair against her forehead. It was the first time I had seen their faces.

The crew was back from their two-week trip, and I was spooling through their tapes.

Tracey reappeared in a living room, blonde and vibrant in a hot-pink blouse. She sat forward on the couch, leaning in to Quentin's questions. When she talked about Elijah, she smiled, but her voice shook whenever she said the word 'police'.

She was Picasso's ravished woman from *Guernica*, anguish streaming from her eyes and throat. I watched with my fingers pressed against my lips.

'Ah, nightmares, dreams, trying to piece it together, ah, the children, my other children, family, friends. Our wonderful, beautiful friends are just so confused. And I can't judge, except that I know Elijah. And it's wrong. He was treated like a criminal and he was ill and he went for help and this is how he was treated. He was shot in the street. And he's a beautiful boy … You've got to be able to tell the difference between a criminal and young man that's ill.'

'Is there any evidence you've heard that [the police] tried to defuse the situation?' Quentin asked.

'I hear from people that were there that he was yelled at to get to the ground, drop the knife, drop the knife, bang. Shot in the chest … We went to them when we were in need of help … I don't know what that police officer's going through, but I know he didn't get up in the morning and say, "I'm going out to shoot Mrs Holcombe's son." So it's gone wrong for everyone.'

Jeremy replaced Tracey on the couch. He had springy curls and deep-brown eyes. He looked younger than he sounded on the phone, but the intensity I'd come to know was visible.

'Why do you think the officer shot Elijah?' Quentin asked. 'Should he be criminally liable for what he did?'

'I'm sure this guy is going through his own personal hell at the moment and I feel for him, I feel for him and his family,' Jeremy said evenly. 'You know, this guy is someone's son, too, and we don't know anything about him. I don't know if he has a wife or kids or whatever — all I know is he made a terrible mistake, and good people make mistakes, too. It's for someone else to decide whether his mistake was of a criminal nature.'

The anger that pulsed through the document Jeremy had written about Elijah's life was absent on the screen.

'When you look at the actions of that final detective, he is a product of our society,' Jeremy said. 'Threat is a very subjective thing, I think … We could look at any given situation and depending on our own state of mind we can interpret it as a threat or not. Obviously, I know more about Elijah than that officer did, and I would know that Elijah is no threat to anyone under any circumstances. Obviously, the officer didn't have that information, even though we made all that information available to the police.'

What he couldn't accept was how the police appeared to have escalated Elijah's situation.

'At every point along the way, you know, they pursued Elijah when we specifically asked them not to,' he said to Quentin.

The Holcombes had heard, as we had, that the shooting officer was still on duty.

'If that is true, then they're underestimating what these sorts of events can do to someone's psychology. I fear the culture within the police force may be if you were having any sort of psychological difficulty, you would keep it to yourself for fear of showing some sort of weakness. There are so many things about that that are wrong, not least of all that it demonises the mentally ill. You know, we really don't need any more of that.'

I watched the final edit of the show before it aired, and called Jeremy and Tracey to prepare them for what was coming.

'Jeremy, it's Kate. I've called to read you the script of Elijah's story.'

I blamed the fact I was eight months pregnant for my trembling voice and the shortness of my breath, but a few pages in, the only sound at my end of the line was sobbing, and on Jeremy's, steady breathing.

'I'm sorry, Jeremy. I'm so sorry for what's happened to you all. I'm sorry I'm crying, this is terrible, it's not my place …'

'That's OK.'

'Are you OK with what's in the script?'

'Yes. Thank you.'

'I'd better call Tracey now,' I said.

Four Corners aired, as always, on a Monday night.

The response from police was explosive. Serving and former officers flooded *Four Corners*' feedback page, 'outraged', 'disgusted', and 'appalled'.

> As a current frontline Police Officer I am DISGUSTED at the attitude displayed by both Four Corners and the general public … If you don't want us to deal with situations in the community … don't call us.
>
> As a serving Police officer I issue a challenge — before you criticise, join the cops, wear the uniform, carry the gun and all the responsibility that brings. Experience the adrenaline, the split-second

decision-making, the danger, the responsibility, and the reward of doing a job well. Then come back and lodge your report …

Criticising from the safety of an armchair was easy — people who 'spent their lives studying the issues … have never been face-to-face with a psychotic drug-affected individual brandishing a weapon and intent on doing serious damage to themselves or others,' another officer raged.

Some said *Four Corners* had damaged police morale by suggesting officers were reckless in their use of force.

I thought I might write about the hundreds of violent mentally ill people I have managed to control without force (most of whom are let out of hospitals) or the numerous times that my colleagues and I are assaulted on a daily basis (with very little support from our useless legal system) however I don't have all day. What I will simply say is this: police are there to protect themselves and the community … Do not blame the police for the failure of the mental health system … It is not the police officer's job to stand there while dealing with a violent person and decide whether the person is mentally ill or not. We are not psychiatrists.

Other responses were more reflective.

As a frontline Police Officer for 20 years, I can tell you that you get to experience a lot of the bad things in society that most people just don't see. I attended a violent incident in which I almost shot a mentally ill/drug affected male who tried to stab me with a kitchen knife. He was only a metre away at the time, whilst I had my pistol pointed at him yelling at him over and over to drop the knife. He did not do this and kept advancing on me. Your body just reacts automatically when your life is threatened at this level. I still think about the incident a lot and know that if I shot the male it would have been justified. As a result I can relate to the incidents that were shown on this Four Corners program.

Of all the criticism, what stung was the accusation that *Four Corners* had failed to show the perspective of frontline police in these situations.

The program made no effort to explore the agony and stress felt by the police involved, the maths and physics involved in reaction times, the time it takes to die when stabbed, the time it takes an armed offender to reach you, the numerous examples where violent mentally ill people have been taken into custody without the loss of life. No mention was made of these.

I had contacted media units and unions for police forces in NSW, Victoria, Queensland, the Northern Territory, and Western Australia, seeking interviews with officers who had dealt with people in psychiatric crisis. Serving or former, male or female, identified or in silhouette — whatever it took, we needed their point of view, I said. We wanted to hear what it was like for an officer embroiled in one of these situations.

Not a single person had either raised their hand or offered a reason for refusing, and police blamed us for not acknowledging their vulnerabilities? I was furious.

One week after Elijah's story aired, Tracey and Jeremy Holcombe marked Elijah's twenty-fifth birthday; their first without him. Two days later, I gave birth to my daughter.

2010

From: Kate Wild
Sent: Sunday, 10 January 2010
To: Jeremy Holcombe
Subject: Floods

Dear Jeremy,

I've been thinking about you and your family for weeks, hoping you enjoyed Christmas together even with the sadness that must be part of your first without Elijah. Also hoping that you survived the reported floods OK?

Jonathon and I had a beautiful baby girl Stella on the 5th of November and we're loving the new experience of being parents. It was particularly nice to take Stella home to my family over Christmas.

Have you heard any more about dates for Elijah's coronial hearing? I would like to stay in touch with you about it even though I'm not at work for the next 12 months or so. I'd like to come to the hearings if at all possible. The legal process moves very slowly but I think of you all very often.

All my best wishes to you and the family for 2010.
Kate

From: Jeremy Holcombe
Sent: Wednesday, 13 January 2010
To: Kate Wild
Subject: Re: Floods

G'day Kate!
It's good to hear from you. We're all doin' ok, thanks. We were determined to enjoy Christmas and we did. My sister and her husband have been hosting the family Christmas in Armidale for a few years. We decided to put the 'geography' to one side and just enjoy the day. We had our moments of course but mostly it was all good. We have more than our fair share of musicians and amateur singer-songwriters in our ranks so we all played for each other and of course Elijah featured as inspiration for us all.

Tracey, Tarney and Laura decided to have Christmas in Wee Waa with Tracey's sister visiting. They had a quiet but enjoyable time with a lot of support from the locals.

Great to hear Stella arrived safely. Congratulations!! And of course you don't need me to tell you to enjoy every second you can with her.

We have no news regarding the inquiry. The last advice was that 'this matter is listed for mention at the Glebe Coroner's Court, on Friday 15 January 2010 for full service of the brief', which is this Friday. I will certainly keep you in the loop.

Anyway Kate — I wish you and yours a very Happy New Year — and thanks again for writing.

Cheers,
Jeremy

5.

I had left *Four Corners* behind but not the Holcombes. My days were filled with my baby's needs, and it hit me with force as we became acquainted: Elijah was this precious. This much a person from the very first moment, and his parents didn't have him anymore.

I had faith that a coronial inquest into Elijah's death would reveal the facts and circumstances of his shooting.

Of all the jurisdictions in Australia, the Coroner's Court is the most revelatory. It eschews the reductive practices of adversarial law used in criminal courts, where two parties fight for control of the evidence by weaning out truths inconvenient to their case and limiting argument to the smallest line of questioning.

The Coroner's Court is inquisitorial. It involves itself in the *investigation* of a case; hence the brief of evidence that police had prepared for the Coroner on Elijah's death. The Coroner and their appointed counsel assisting are participants in the search for truth, unlike magistrates in a criminal or civil trial, who adjudicate between the defence and prosecution's cases.

In my experience, the Coroner's Court was uniquely capable, for this reason, of bringing a sense of justice to proceedings. Although its purpose focused on the manner of a person's death, it was a jurisdiction rich with life. Discovering the reason for a death meant diving deep into biographies to examine the life a person lived before they died.

In his notes on Elijah's life, Jeremy had revealed why he decided to speak to *Four Corners*: *To show that Elijah was innocent of any wrongdoing and 'armed' himself as a response to being pursued by an unidentified man with a gun. To ensure that if anyone is held responsible for this tragedy it is not merely placed at the feet of the shooter. In our opinion, other people acted at best incompetently, at worst criminally on that day. To see change, both in how the police deal with the mentally ill and how they deal with the family following fatal interactions.*

Those hopes for a form of justice for Elijah now sat with the Coroner overseeing Elijah's inquest.

A coroner has the power, and sometimes an obligation, to investigate certain types of deaths. Violent and unnatural, sudden death, where the cause is unknown or where a death certificate has not been signed — if the person died in custody or during a police operation, or where the person died in a mental health facility or residential centre for people with a disability, for instance. Not every death that qualifies justifies investigation, but because Elijah was shot by a police officer, his inquest was compulsory. That was why detectives from Sydney had driven to Armidale to begin investigations as soon they were informed about his death. The NSW homicide unit was responsible for gathering the evidence that a coroner would examine to understand and make rulings on a death. Their Critical Incident Investigation Teams (CIIT) established a timeline of events leading up to a death, collected witness statements and medical records, and did anything else a coroner requested.

Establishing the date, place, time, and circumstances, plus the medical cause, of a person's death is the sole remit of the Coroner's Court. A coroner does not declare guilt or innocence, and no one faces charges in a Coroner's Court. The theory is that this allows more room for facts and systemic issues to be identified, and for unnecessary deaths to be guarded against in future.

The Coroner's Court listed Elijah's inquest for dates in September and October 2010, one year and three months after his death. It was an ordinary length of time to wait. Preparing a brief of evidence for the Coroner was a long and detailed process for police.

Jeremy's lawyers received a summary of the evidence in March of the same year. It included the name of the shooting officer: Senior Constable Andrew Rich.

Jeremy posted me the summary, and asked if I would scrutinise it.

I am attempting to do the same myself and making notes as I go, but I am afraid I am finding it very tough emotionally, he said in the note that accompanied the document.

I slid the document from its envelope, and Armidale's wintery mist entered my bones.

The police had done an incredible job. Their account of Elijah's movements on the last day of his life began at 6.30am.

The first person who noticed Elijah that morning was the caretaker of the Autumn Lodge retirement village. When he opened the front gates at 6.30am, the caretaker spotted an old grey Fairmont parked across the road. He knew every car that parked in Trim Street, and he'd never seen this one before. Wondering whose it was, he dropped the gate pin into its hole and walked inside out of the cold.

Around 7am, a pensioner noticed moisture on the windows of a grey sedan on Trim Street. Concerned, he cupped his hands against the glass. There was a man on the back seat, facedown, covered in a heap of towels or clothes. When he noticed the shadow of the pensioner and looked up, the young man looked as if he had been crying.

Later that morning, the older man walked back past the car again. This time, the back door was open, and a man in his twenties was climbing out, dishevelled and unwashed. The young man ducked below the door and hid when he saw the older man. The pensioner decided to call the police when he got home, but then changed his mind once he arrived. It was none of his business; he would leave it be.

Police offered no explanation for why Elijah's next destination was the Armidale police station, but at noon he appeared at the public counter 'to make a confession', the summary said. What he had confessed to was a mystery.

The station officer in Armidale made a phone call to police in

Narrabri, and returned to tell Elijah he was not in trouble. His parents didn't want him charged; they wanted him to get help. The officer asked where he had left the car, and Elijah gave vague directions. When Elijah asked to speak to a psychiatrist, the officer arranged for a car to take him to the hospital and told the driver of the paddy wagon that turned up, '[Elijah]'s come to the station to hand himself in for stealing a car, but he told me he needs help for some psychiatric problems he's got. He's supposed to be on medication and told me he wants to be assessed … He's not under arrest for anything.'

Elijah needed reassurance before he agreed to climb into the wagon's cage.

At the hospital, the triage nurse led him to a gurney. The summary said her name was Robyn O'Brien.

In her evidence to police, O'Brien said Elijah looked well. His clothes were old but clean, and he didn't smell.

'I don't feel any emotions,' Elijah told her.

'What happened?' O'Brien asked.

Elijah shrugged.

'Have you lost your job or had a relationship breakdown?'

Elijah was silent for a long time, then nodded.

'What, a relationship breakdown?'

'Yep,' he said.

'Are you suicidal, Elijah?'

'I was. A few days ago.'

'So you're not now?'

'No.'

'Did you have a plan?'

'No.'

'Do you have a weapon, guns, ropes, or a stash of pills somewhere?'

'No.'

O'Brien knew the doctor and mental health nurse would have more questions, so she didn't push.

'Have you been eating normally?'

'No.'

'What about sleeping?'

'No.'

Elijah said he hadn't taken his medication for a few months, but had started back on it a couple of days ago. O'Brien assessed him as depressed but not psychotic. He was softly spoken, alert with good insight, and no evidence of hallucinations or delusions. She informed the doctor and called the mental health nurse, Carla Rutherford.

Rutherford read Elijah differently when she saw him twenty minutes later. Her impression was of a dishevelled young man in dirty clothes, who wouldn't make eye contact or answer questions. She took Elijah to an assessment room and asked him why he had gone to the police. Someone called the Boongalaree were after him, Elijah said. Who were they? Carla Rutherford asked.

Elijah didn't answer for a long time.

'Am I a voluntary or involuntary patient?' he finally replied.

When Rutherford said he was voluntary, Elijah announced he was leaving and walked out of the Emergency Department.

The mental health nurse was upset. She hadn't had time to assess Elijah properly; he showed symptoms of psychosis and he should have been triaged higher, she told her colleagues.

A police officer in plainclothes walked in moments after Carla Rutherford had left the room. He introduced himself as Senior Constable Andrew Rich; he was looking for Elijah.

'He's gone,' Robyn O'Brien said. 'We have concerns for his safety, so if you find him can you bring him back?'

The document skipped five pages at this point. Events at the hospital gave way to a street in Armidale's CBD.

A council ranger writing a parking ticket saw an orange car make a U-turn and park across the road from him. He picked it as a police car, despite the lack of markings. A man I now knew was Senior Constable

Rich stepped out and walked towards a young man on the footpath. Rich took a set of keys out of his pocket. The council ranger heard him call out, 'Hey mate, you've dropped your keys!'

The young man looked back at Rich across his shoulder.

'You've dropped your keys. Do you want them?' Rich repeated.

The young man kept on walking.

'He doesn't want them. He's not stopping,' Rich said to someone in the car and chuckled, the ranger told police.

Rich reached towards his hip, where he wore a pistol in a holster. The young man bolted and Rich chased. They each crossed the road and turned the corner at full pelt. A second officer in plainclothes got out of the car and jogged behind them. The ranger heard him sigh.

Various people in the summary recounted the two men running through Beardy Street Mall. Elijah pushed past outdoor tables and slipped through the front door of Caffiends café. Staff and customers told police Elijah walked straight through the café towards the kitchen. The owner of Caffiends, Sonia Stier, was in the kitchen when he walked in. She asked him who he was, but he ignored her. He swiped something off the kitchen bench and left through the back door. The apprentice chef saw what it was — a bread knife. Elijah seemed dazed, the apprentice chef told police, as though he might be on drugs.

Rich was only seconds behind. The first thing the apprentice noticed about Rich was the pistol on his hip, and then his white baseball cap.

Rich headed for the back door, following Elijah. Events moved quickly from there.

The summary listed evidence from sixteen people in Cinders Lane. It was impossible to fathom how they could all see and hear such different things; from Elijah shouting and running at Rich, to Elijah remaining stationary and silent.

I searched the document for a statement from Rich. There wasn't one. But other officers who were interviewed revealed what police had understood as events unfolded in Cinders Lane.

Rich had called the police station from the back door of Caffiends with a short, sharp message:

'I'm chasing a bloke in Cinders Lane, he's got a knife,' Rich said.

Backup calls went over the radio, but before there was time to respond, Rich called again. His message sent a flood of police pouring out the front door and running to their cars.

Detective Senior Constable Windred was one of them. He drove the three hundred metres to Cinders Lane and found Rich standing on the footpath ashen-faced, his right hand bright with blood. Rich was taken to Windred's car.

'Are you injured?' Windred asked.

Rich shook his head.

'What happened?'

'I had no choice, I had no choice.'

'Did you shoot him?'

'Yeah, I had no choice, mate. I had no choice,' Rich said.

Windred took his colleague's gun and drove Rich to the station. He photographed the blood on Rich's hand and clothes, and sent him to the bathroom to clean up. Rich returned sobbing. Within half an hour, Rich was told Elijah had died, and he broke down completely. Someone called a counsellor, and Rich was taken for breath and drug tests.

I realised, reading these fresh details, that the story had changed narrators. Elijah's family owned the story of his life but the police owned the narrative of his death now. This was the work they did every day.

Twenty minutes after the fatal shot was fired, Detective Inspector Greig Stier watched paramedics pull a blanket over Elijah's face. A black-handled knife lay on the ground not far away. Stier walked the length of Cinders Lane giving directions: CCTV vision from the lane needed to be collected. Rich and and his partner, Dufty, must be kept separated to avoid them talking.

As the rain moved in over Cinders Lane that night, the SES raised a bright-blue tarp to cover Elijah's body. At midnight, Stier handed the investigation over to homicide detectives who had driven straight from Sydney. The Critical Incident Investigation Team (CIIT) would run the case from here.

The summary of the evidence took a different direction when it reached Acting Inspector Peter Davis from Weapons, Tactics Policy and Review, the unit of the NSW Police Force in charge of training.

Acting Inspector Davis had been given a brief 'to review the circumstances and provide opinion regarding the actions of police at approximately 1.55pm on the 02/06/2009 at Armidale NSW, involving Mr. Elijah Holcombe'.

Elijah, Davis wrote, 'was considered unstable in a public place with innocent bystanders nearby, armed with a large bladed knife'. He was not under police control when he had the knife, and 'at no time did he comply with directions from police'.

Davis described bystanders as 'innocent' twice in the space of five sentences. 'Large bladed knife' appeared three times in four lines. I fumed. What was a knife unless it was bladed? Did a serrated bread knife even qualify as a 'blade'? Davis failed to quote any innocent bystanders who'd felt threatened by Elijah and his bladed knife.

According to police forensics, the knife they received in an evidence bag was a black-handled Victorinox–Fibrox. Its overall length was thirty-four and a half centimetres, with a twenty-centimetre blade and a serrated cutting edge. Foodstuff stained the left face of the blade.

Acting Inspector Davis 'asserted', 'outlined', and 'indicated' his way through Elijah's shooting. 'The discharging of Senior Constable Rich's firearm was considered a last resort predicated by the actions of Mr Holcombe,' he said.

Acting Inspector Davis was of the view that Rich unholstered his gun because 'he feared for his own safety and the safety of other innocent bystanders'.

Elijah refused multiple commands from Senior Constable Rich to drop the knife, he wrote.

'Further, Mr Holcombe armed with the knife — charged towards Senior Constable Rich, at which the Senior Constable feared for his own safety, indicating "I thought he was gonna stab me" … I am of the opinion that Senior Constables Rich and Dufty acted professionally in what can only be considered as a most profound life-threatening situation.'

The head of the CIIT, Detective Inspector Chris Olen from Homicide, agreed.

In Olen's opinion, 'Senior Constable Rich was justified in discharging his firearm as there was an immediate risk of serious injury to him or to his life and there was no other way of preventing that risk.'

Plenty of people quoted in the brief saw the bread knife in Elijah's hand. Not one said they felt threatened.

The brief did concede one weakness on Rich's part.

He had not completed his mandatory defensive training for the year in knife defence. It was scheduled for June, the month he shot Elijah.

Evidence from Elijah's doctors made the saddest reading of all the material police had collected for the Coroner.

A registrar at Concord Hospital's mental health unit, where Elijah had spent a month receiving treatment, told police Elijah felt 'overwhelmingly guilty' most of the time and believed the Turkish mafia wanted to kill him. He had responded well to medication, but because of 'ongoing stressors relating to his relationship with his wife and deterioration in his mental state whilst on periods of leave', Elijah's admission was prolonged. He returned after one weekend stay with Allison with superficial cuts to his wrist, telling hospital staff he had hurt himself after 'a disagreement with his wife about his treatment'.

'He seemed torn between wanting to continue his admission and focus on his recovery and concern that his admission would impact negatively on his relationship with his wife.'

'His main problem was his wife,' another doctor wrote, which

I took to mean two things: that Allison was still the fulcrum of Elijah's delusions, and that her insistence that Elijah leave hospital wasn't helping him. Jeremy had hinted in conversation that Allison's own mental health was fragile.

If Allison's own health was tenuous, the push to have Elijah by her side made sense. Elijah was her rock, she was a long way from home, she needed him to be well for her. With the burden of guilt he already carried for having kissed another woman at a party, I could imagine Elijah doing anything to please his wife and make reparations.

Jeremy and the Holcombes remained protective of Allison, but Jeremy had elaborated on the relationship in his summary of Elijah's life.

It seemed to me they had very different sensibilities and priorities in life. The Elijah I knew had very little regard for the material things. He was interested in the arts, music, knowledge, and various sub-cultures away from the mainstream. Allison seemed to be more of the upwardly mobile young professional type. I know that many of Elijah's long-term friends believed the same. They regarded Elijah and Allison as a mismatch. I had many conversations with Elijah about this. He did not refute it.

Elijah 'hated' the unit he shared with Allison; it was a 'horrible, fake enclave', he told his father. When he checked out of Concord Hospital, he planned to 'get back to the things he believed were important', Jeremy had written. Elijah wanted to try and work things out with Allison, and if they couldn't, he would leave the relationship, he told his father.

Perhaps because of his own experience, Jeremy could see things from Allison's side as well.

I also recognise that the situation must have been extremely difficult for Allison. I am not sure how one is supposed to respond when the person you love and live with believes that you want to destroy him.

Convincing her husband to leave residential treatment when she was the psychological focus of his illness struck an odd note. What was Allison's experience of Elijah's illness? By all accounts, she appeared ill equipped to help him, but who came equipped at twenty-three for their husband to develop paranoid delusions?

Allison was an easy scapegoat. If she hadn't convinced Elijah to leave hospital, none of this might have happened.

But Elijah was not a child — he was unwell. A psychologist who treated him at Concord said that Elijah could still make rational decisions. 'His insight and judgement were appropriate for his stage of therapy,' the psychologist wrote in observation notes. Elijah could make decisions for himself when he checked out of hospital and went home to his wife.

6.

In the midst of digesting the police report, I broke the news to Jeremy that my husband and I were moving north.

'Our move doesn't change my interest in following what happens in Elijah's coronial inquest; I will still follow every step from the Northern Territory. I'm sorry it means I won't be there for the inquest and won't be able to come to the hearings. But one step at a time; I'll get on with reading the brief,' I wrote to him.

Our Sydney farewells went on for weeks.

The last goodbye was a long drive to my parents' place. Seven hours after leaving Sydney, we turned off bitumen onto dirt, where the timber mailbox stood. Fresh gravel lined the creek crossing; the paddocks were water-coloured green. From a kilometre away across the plain, I could see that the trees around the house had grown.

Nothing else had changed.

I nudged the back-gate open with my hip and walked up the path towards the house, holding Stella. To my left across the burnt-out lawn was the Hills Hoist, a rainwater tank, and a dip in the lawn where a jacaranda tree used to be. Up the back steps, over the bleached verandah, through the squeaking door, and the house had swallowed me. The pantry was full of homemade cakes; Mum had put flowers beside our beds. The house smelled like a linen closet.

We set up Stella's cot in my old room. When she woke each morning, I took her to my parents and tucked her in with them, searching their faces for memories to repeat, remembering weekends crowding their bed with my siblings.

I riffled through a trunk of childhood books and toys and claimed my share to take away. My mother gave me her grandmother's ring. Borrowed on my wedding day, now it was mine to keep.

My father drove me around the paddocks. Our elbows hung out the windows of the truck. He remembered almost rolling it when I was three and we were chasing pigs together. How I'd urged him to 'Go faster, Dad, go faster!' and he had. It was a happy memory of intimacy.

Outside conversations like these, I waited for an open exchange of feelings, but no one strayed from the agreed-upon script our family had used for years. The rhythm and rules of my parents' life turned like the massive stone wheel of a mill, predictable and resolute. Friends who visited my family with me had observed how quiet I was here compared to the personality I shared with the world. The air around my family was heavy with determined silence. It was part of my parents' history — and so became part of mine — that certain emotions and facts could be extinguished if you ignored them with enough force. The key to survival was banishing to unreality anything you could not face.

My mother's silence when I was young was so loud that it filled the house some days. The word depression didn't cross my parents' lips until they were in their sixties. My mother blamed her moody withdrawals and sudden rage on hormones and lack of sleep. When she slipped away in the afternoons and closed the bedroom door, I would go to the swing in the jacaranda tree, daring myself to soar above the gutters, over the roof to the garden on the other side. I learned without a word being spoken that her silence could not be talked about.

My father went to school in the middle of our backyard, just a few metres from the jacaranda tree. He and his sisters did lessons each day in a one-room schoolhouse with a governess. My father lost his father to polio when he was five. No one told him what had happened because people didn't talk about death to children then, even farm kids who killed birds and rabbits. My father developed a stutter, which appeared when he was tired or stressed. He overcame it as a teenager, but the silence of his father's loss shaped his life.

As a kid, I harboured fantasies about a cottage near our house. I dreamed of trudging across the plain and sneaking into its haunted rooms. It sat in a paddock on the neighbour's property, abandoned, like a doll's house in the grass. Grown-ups mumbled about darkness in the family blood; they said a relative of ours had shot himself there. I thought if I was quiet enough I could sneak up on his ghost. When I asked once, in my twenties, about the cousin who had shot himself, the answers skipped away and disappeared like stones on the surface of the creek. Again and again as I grew older, I noted what was left unsaid. I watched at school, and church, and social gatherings, and realised that this 'unknowing' was all around me. The silence that hung over our landscape lived first in people's mouths.

I kissed my parents at our visit's end and fled.

We flew above the dry brown centre of Australia and entered the wet heat of the tropics in June.

My legs swelled like an allergic elephant's from midgey bites. Heat rash mottled Stella's skin. We slept for hours in the afternoons, drugged by humidity, under the smoke of mosquito coils. Darwin smelled like heaven. Frangipani trees with hands of deep, round leaves threw perfume everywhere. Ginger plants waved at palm trees, bougainvillea draped over cyclone fences like scarlet feather boas. Gardens were dotted with pot plants, as though the soil could not be trusted.

In the street, on buses, in knots of cross-legged figures under trees, people spoke languages I had never heard. Buildings were cement and squat or teetered on skinny timber legs. New apartment blocks looked like candles on a birthday cake. Floors were tiled, furniture was plastic, everything new was cheap and ugly, exotic and parochial. I loved it.

When our boxes arrived, I tore them open. I joined a mothers' group, bought a bike, and got a dog. My phone filled up with new contacts — GP, electrician, babysitter, vet. I soon added the old couple on the corner, whose house our dog escaped to every day.

I walked to a park the size of a suburb every morning, pushing the pram and pulling the dog over footpaths shaded by tamarinds. I lay in bed with my husband each night and listened to the scrub fowls' noisy copulations. We were quietly self-congratulatory. Our life was fresh, enlivening. Dizzying.

Eight weeks after we had settled in, an email arrived from Jeremy.

From: Jeremy Holcombe
Sent: Thursday, 29 July 2010
To: Quentin McDermott / Four Corners; Kate Wild
Subject: Tracey

Hi Guys,

Sorry to bring you bad news but I thought you would want to know that Tracey has just been diagnosed with an aggressive form of cancer. She is currently in Sydney and will shortly commence chemo followed by surgery to remove part of her stomach and oesophagus.

The symptoms commenced shortly after Elijah's death. I am sure she would welcome any contact from you guys.

Jeremy

'How big is it? How advanced?' I asked on the phone.

Jeremy's reply fell in loops at my feet, heavy and rough like rope.

'I believe the words the doctor used were "aggressive and terminal". She's had trouble eating since Elijah died but we didn't think anything of it — none of us have been good. She saw the specialist last week. He said the tumour's probably only twelve months old. She thought it was an ulcer.'

His laughter was bitter. Tracey's GP had told her that extreme stress was a common factor in this type of tumour. Worry over-activated the gastric juices. Her tumour had grown where the excess acid pooled. Tracey was convinced Elijah's death had kicked it off, and Jeremy agreed.

He urged me to call her.

I'd hardly spoken to Tracey when we prepared Elijah's program. Now I felt like a vulture circling a broken animal. What would she think if I called? What would I say?

In early August, our next-door neighbour announced himself with heavy footsteps on the timber stairs. He knocked on the flyscreen and peered inside.

'Are you alright?'

'Yes. I'm fine, thanks. Why?'

He scanned the room with a professional eye. Dave was a police officer with the dog squad.

'Well, is that your car out the front?'

Dave raised an eyebrow and tilted his head towards the street.

I peered through the louvres. Our car had rolled from where I parked it, had crossed the road and mounted the kerb. Its nose was an inch from a concrete fence.

'Shit! I must have forgotten to put the handbrake on — God. Imagine … Thanks — Oh God.'

I'd never had a car accident in my life. I was breastfeeding, I had baby brain; it was so damn hot, I told myself. But I might have known then there was more to the vagueness that had started to wash over me.

I raced down the stairs and, my hands shaking, backed the car down off the footpath.

'You ought to leave it in gear when you park,' Dave said through the window.

I pulled the handbrake hard this time and opened the door, bracing for a scolding, but Dave had plodded back to his yard, pulled the gate shut, and locked it.

Two days later I sat at an intersection, my hands an inch above the steering wheel. I indicated, accelerated, and turned — into oncoming traffic. Wheels screeched, a horn screamed, and a carload of young hoods swerved to save all of our lives. They tailgated me through two sets of lights, screaming obscenities out the window. I kept my eyes on the road and turned the music up, drowning their horn beneath chirping children's CDs.

'I'm sorry, I'm sorry … Jesus. Fuck.'

I stepped out of the car in our driveway into air that wobbled like liquid mercury. Objects floated just beyond arm's reach, fading in and out of focus. I stumbled upstairs, locked the door behind me, laid my daughter in her cot, and crawled beneath the sheets. This was how it always started. Space and distance distorted first, and then my memory of regular rules and the meaning of different signals vanished. After that, fear and anger set in.

Why was it back? Why now when life was so full of promise?

In the months that followed, the dark spores spread. Wherever life touched me, I left or collected wounds. Physically, I existed. Emotionally, I was evaporating.

September arrived, the season of madness in the tropics. One night, I threw myself out of bed and woke with the impact of the boards. The bruises took weeks to fade. The memory of who I was went with them. After eight years at rest, my shadows had emerged to devour the light that illuminated life.

7.

From: Quentin McDermott
Sent: 12 October 2010
To: Kate Wild
Subject: Hi

Hi Kate,

Have you spoken to Jeremy since Elijah's inquest started?

Q

Quentin's email punctured my malaise. While I struggled through days devoid of feeling, blindsided in turn by bouts of rage and deadening pain, the legal process had delivered the Holcombes to the door of the Armidale Courthouse for Elijah's inquest. With all of my energy turned inwards to survive, they had vanished with the rest of the world.

I searched for news on the inquest proceedings.

'Dad visits the street where Elijah Holcombe was shot', *The Daily Telegraph* headline read. Below it was a photograph captured in early light. A cluster of black-suited men in conversation weighted the top left of the picture. In their midst, a full foot shorter than the group, with her hands interlaced, stood the Coroner, Mary Jerram. She gazed with furrowed brow at a spot ahead of her, perhaps picturing whatever the man beside her was pointing at.

In the right foreground stood Jeremy and Fiona, puffy-faced and stunned. Fiona, in long leather boots, clutched her arms beneath her breasts. Jeremy stood beside her, hands on his hips. The colours they wore were lighter than the lawyers', and they inhabited a different plane. Like actors peering through the fourth wall, their focus was attached to a point beyond the Coroner's, somewhere at the far end of the lane.

I emailed Jeremy tentatively. I was thinking of him and Fiona and the kids, I said. I wished I could be there to offer them more support. I hoped they were being treated well 'and that through all the pain of the next 2 weeks there will be some answers for you'.

The inquest was only in its second day when Quentin's email had arrived. *I could still get to Armidale. I'd hardly missed a thing.*

I would have to take Stella; she was too small to leave. What if she cried during crucial evidence? If she came to court, how would I take notes? Who would help me? Where would we stay? The effort of creating answers was beyond me.

Rich's actions were clearly mistaken; the whole thing would be over soon. The Holcombes would move on and so would I. *Just let it go.*

The inquest was listed for two weeks of hearings, with a recess of a week between two sittings. I read newspaper reports on the proceedings each day, but there was nothing in them I didn't already know until the day counsel assisting the coroner read directly from Rich's statement to police.

> Counsel assisting the coroner Chris Hoy SC read excerpts from Constable Rich's statement in which the officer asks Holcombe to 'Drop the knife, drop the knife, drop the knife'.
>
> Constable Rich said Holcombe replied, 'F..k you, shoot me you f..king c...'.

The plain-clothes officer said he then asked Holcombe twice again to drop the knife, but he just 'let out a roar' and said, 'You can go ahead, f..king shoot me you c..., shoot me'.

The Australian.[2]

Not one person in the summary of evidence had reported hearing this.

The uncorroborated claim came to light on the Friday before the inquest went into recess. When hearings recommenced on 25 October 2010, the first witness called by counsel assisting contradicted Rich's claim.

Andrew Strudwick, a council employee, 'heard no talk or yelling between Holcombe and Senior Constable Andrew Rich before the fatal shot was fired', *The Australian*[3] reported.

'Elijah Holcombe did not have a chance to negotiate as a NSW police officer fired his pistol almost instantaneously when the mentally ill man turned to face him, an inquest has heard.'

It was impossible to tell what direction things were moving in, but the tone of reporting in the second week suggested counsel for the police were pushing back.

Judy Tennant, who had spoken to *Four Corners,* was the thirtieth witness in a list of seventy-one who had been called to give evidence at the inquest.

'During two hours of cross examination, which ran from yesterday afternoon until this morning barrister Ray Hood, acting for the NSW Police, suggested Ms Tennant had fabricated her testimony,' *The Australian* reported.[4]

The paper hinted that, having only heard from half of the witness

---

[2] Minus, Jodie (2010) 'Armidale man "unarmed" when cop shot him', *The Australian*, 15 October.

[3] Minus, Jodie (2010) 'No words spoken as cop shot man', *The Australian*, 26 October.

[4] Minus, Jodie (2010) 'Don't shoot, Elijah Holcombe witness begged officer', *The Australian*, 27 October.

list, the inquest was likely to run overtime.

Then, on the second-last day of hearings, the Coroner dropped a bombshell.

'Having heard the evidence that I have to date, I must say that my view has formed more strongly with each passing hour that an indictable offence has been committed,' Coroner Mary Jerram told the court.

A coroner does not have the power to determine criminal responsibility for a death. But if, during an inquest, a coroner forms the opinion that the evidence before them might satisfy a jury that a crime has been committed, and there is a reasonable prospect of conviction, they are obliged to refer the matter to the Director of Public Prosecutions (DPP).

At that point the case, in this instance Elijah's, leaves the Coroner's jurisdiction and enters the criminal legal system. The coronial inquest is suspended, and the DPP must determine whether the evidence from the Coroner's Court is strong enough to justify charges and if it is, what those charges might be. If the DPP proceeds with charges, the coronial inquest might not re-open. Some inquests will resume once criminal matters have been heard and settled. If the DPP decides that the evidence does not warrant charges, the inquest may be re-opened and run its course.

Mary Jerram had reached the opinion that shooting Elijah in Cinders Lane may have been a criminal act. On the final morning of the inquest, she suspended Elijah's case and referred the matter to the DPP.

'It is very important that you understand this isn't a criminal court and I lay no criminal charges, it will be for the DPP to decide,' *The Australian* newspaper quoted Jerram.

I scanned the paper for Jeremy's response.

Holcombe's father, Jeremy, who attended every day of the inquest, told *The Australian* today he was relieved by the Coroner's decision but said there were no winners in the story of his son's death.
'We all knew Elijah and we knew he just wasn't capable of any sort of violence, no matter how delusional he might have been and we

really came here because it's like his assumption of innocence had been denied,' Mr Holcombe said.

'The police kept saying he was guilty of these things and he somehow brought it on himself and we never accepted that and you could see that with her honour's decision, we certainly feel that it vindicates Elijah.

'He did nothing to provoke what happened to him and we don't really care who is guilty of what, it's just that Elijah wasn't guilty of anything.'[5]

On top of a suppression order banning the publication of any image that identified him, it was now illegal to publish Rich's name. With the temporary suspension of Elijah's inquest, Rich was transformed into 'a known person', invisible and silent.

The pressure on the Holcombes lifted immeasurably, and the stakes for Rich became far higher. The DPP would decide if Elijah's death justified a charge as serious as murder or manslaughter against Rich.

'The known person, who had been at the inquest since day one, did not react when the Coroner made her comments,' wrote *The Australian*.

Four days after the inquest closed, the Holcombes marked Elijah's twenty-sixth birthday, and the year reached for its finish line, exhausted.

The waiting room at Darwin Private Hospital was cold and white and ugly. It was just before Christmas.

The specialist called my name from the doorway, closed the door, and opened my file. We talked for twenty minutes.

---

5   Minus, Jodie (2010) 'Family of Elijah Holcombe say they feel vindicated by coroner's referral of case to DPP', *The Australian*, 29 October.

'So what would you like me to do for you?' she asked.

'I want you to test my hormone levels.'

She was round and wrinkled, a 70-year-old baked apple.

'Is there a history of depression in your family?'

'Some.'

'And you have a history?'

'Yes.'

'There's nothing wrong with being medicated for a lifetime if it's what you need. It's the only way some people hold onto any quality of life.'

My heart thumped out of time. She leaned across the desk and spoke with force.

'It's a legitimate choice and it's no one else's business.'

'I still want hormone tests,' I said. 'My mother said her hormones went crazy after she had each baby. Maybe that's all it is.'

'We can test your hormones but here's the number of a good GP.' She handed me a slip of paper. 'I want you to see her and talk about medication while we wait for the blood results.'

2011

8.

We spent New Year's Eve with friends in Sydney: Ivan, a six-foot-four Irish-Dutchman, and his architect-fashionista wife, Tash. Ivan had produced Elijah's story for *Four Corners*.

When it was time for our 14-month-old daughter to go to bed, Tash pulled a wicker wash-basket out and we stashed her in the living room. Dinner was olives and cold quiche. Their eccentricity renewed me.

We snatched conversation around children's cries and didn't reach the core of any topic, but I felt the layers fall away nonetheless.

Ivan poured wine, and Tash asked for New Year's resolutions.

'Get a job!' I piped thinly. 'Before I go crazy.'

'Why don't you write a book?' said Tash. 'There's no one left in this country to write good books — everyone's working in television.'

'The only thing I want to write about is the story I did with Ivan on Elijah Holcombe. But I missed the inquest; it's too late.'

I turned to Ivan. 'Have you spoken to Tracey?'

'You know she's sick, don't you?' he replied.

The conversation drifted away, but Tash gripped me in a bear hug at the door when we were leaving.

'You should write that book,' she whispered across my shoulder.

When I woke on New Year's Day, the ferries were honking on Sydney Harbour, and Elijah was sitting on the edge of the hole, leaning down to pull me out.

The number you have dialled is disconnected. Please check the number before trying again. The number you have dialled is disconnected —

It was the end of January 2011, three months since my last conversation with Jeremy. I sent out a search party via email.

'I think he's moved totally off grid,' Ivan responded.

Did 'off grid' mean off the power supply or off the rails? I asked. He offered to check with Tracey, and sent back a mobile number.

'He's not in range much. She says he's building a hut up on a friend's place,' Ivan wrote.

When the crackling line connected, Jeremy's voice was tight. Fear stripped away all grace, and I launched straight in.

'Jeremy, I want to write a book about Elijah. How he died — everything that happened. Would you be OK with that?'

He hardly paused before replying.

'It depends what you want to write, Kate. I don't want a witch-hunt. He's flesh and blood like the rest of us.' Jeremy's voice pulsed with familiar anger. 'We shook his hand at the end of the inquest and he isn't a monster.' He was talking about Rich.

'I want to try and work out why things ended the way they did. For everyone,' I said.

'There's no black and white here, just a lot of grey,' he warned. If I got Tracey and the kids' permission, then I had his, too.

Tracey was home in Wee Waa, after months of chemotherapy in Sydney. I apologised for not calling her after Elijah's story had aired or when Jeremy told me about her diagnosis.

'I didn't know if you'd want a journalist you hardly knew barging in at such an awful time,' I said.

She laughed. 'Considering how we know each other, you needn't have worried.'

I took a deep breath.

'I want to write a book about what happened to Elijah.'

When Tracey spoke again, her register had changed.

'Until the inquest started, and we got the result we did, I thought it didn't matter what other people believed about Elijah. But this huge weight lifted when they said he wasn't a bad person.'

'What would you write about?' she asked after a long pause.

'About what went wrong. Elijah's not the sort of person who normally gets shot by the police. He hadn't hurt anyone. He wasn't on drugs. I want to know why the police thought he was dangerous,' I said.

'I need to talk to the kids,' Tracey replied.

'Of course. I'll call back in a couple of weeks,' I said.

But Tracey's tumour was in a hurry. Ivan rang again before Tracey could get back to me to say the doctors had sent her back to Sydney for another round of chemotherapy. He had seen her by chance on the street. If I wanted to see her, I should do it soon, he said.

I walked from the city through Sydney's Hyde Park down to a wedge of no-man's land between William Street and the Domain. Tracey was staying with an old friend close to the hospital.

I stopped at a corner shop and bought plastic-wrapped roses heavy with scent. Showroom windows glistened with sports cars. Pollen, gardenias, and the smell of piss choked the air.

I rang the bell at a three-storey townhouse with the nameplate 'Sweeney Tiggemann Solicitors'. A reedy figure poked his nose through the security door.

'Yes?'

'I'm here to see Tracey. Tracey Holcombe?'

In a single move, the man swung the door open and grasped my hand to shake it.

'David Sweeney,' he declared, pulling me into a narrow hallway.

I learned in subsequent conversations that Tracey had been Sweeney's personal assistant when he ran the office of a legal firm in Wee Waa.

'Tracey and I just laughed all the time. I think I offered her the PA's job one day in the supermarket. Jeremy was on suicide watch, and it was one of the few times she got out of the house,' Sweeney told me when I asked how he knew the Holcombes.

He had moved to Sydney by the time of Elijah's shooting, but it was Sweeney who organised a legal team to represent the Holcombes at Elijah's inquest.

Sweeney pointed me up a steep flight of stairs.

'She'll be up there. She's expecting you. Go up, go up.'

The room upstairs was a cream cocoon, a sanctuary in the building's aged body.

Tracey lay in pale light on a couch, under a blanket, her hair shorn. Cushions were banked around her back. Her teeth were shadowy, her skin was grey. The brightly coloured woman from the *Four Corners* interview was gone. The warmth in her weakened voice was all the colour that remained. Tracey held out her arms to me.

'You look just the way I imagined!' she said, folding me into her huge soft chest and pulling me down onto the couch beside her.

'You're so tiny. And flowers! For me? Those are the exact colour I've chosen for my funeral — how did you know? Ruth, can you put these in water for me? Kate, this is Ruth, my cousin.'

A round-shouldered woman with a home haircut was chopping potatoes at the kitchen bench. A saucepan bubbled on the stove beside her. Ruth shuffled to the couch for the flowers and banged through kitchen cupboards for a vase.

'Fix yourself some tea if you want, I won't get up. The kettle's over on the bench,' Tracey said.

The chemotherapy gave her crippling nausea, she explained.

'I don't think I've eaten today. Terrible for the big fat person I used to be.'

Her lack of appetite had tipped the doctors to the fact her tumour was growing again — hence the new round of chemotherapy, she said.

'Because I couldn't even swallow properly — they went to put a stent in last week and it was closed up to about half the width of my little finger!'

Tracey held up her pinkie.

'I'm not going to be cured — it's a type of cancer they can't knock on the head — but they said, "If we can maintain your health, you can have a lifestyle for years to come".'

Words spilt from Tracey, rushing through the narrow doorway in her throat. I knew from watching her interview with Quentin that Tracey was a talker, but her eagerness now carried with it the knowledge that time was running out. She still had so much she wanted to say, especially about Elijah.

'When did they diagnose you?' I asked.

'In May.'

'I had a heart-attack pain in my chest whenever I tried to swallow. We thought I had probably worked my way up to a stomach ulcer from worrying about different things — mostly Elijah and Jeremy. Then the doctor told me it was terminal. How do I go home and tell my kids this after everything they've been through? That was my first thought.'

She coughed weakly.

'I asked the friends I was with to give me twenty minutes on my own. Then I sat in the park across from the doctor's rooms and I had a chat to God. "OK God, if you're in control of this, what do you want me to learn?"' Tracey laughed. 'I said, "Can we just talk about it and get it over and done with?" And then it was just like, OK, you either lay down and die or you take whatever comes and the moment you die you die, and until then you live and do the best you can.'

Ruth picked up her handbag, her eyes downcast.

'I'm going to the shop. See you in a while.'

I took out my dictaphone. 'Are you OK if I use this?'

Tracey nodded. I wedged it beneath a cushion on the couch.

'You not going to Elijah's inquest — was that because you weren't well enough or for other reasons?' I began.

'I wanted to go. I wasn't well enough, and the doctors said, "You're not to go". As the days went on, I felt that I had to be there. I rang Jeremy and spoke to David Phelps, his cousin that was there helping, but they said, "There's no need for you to be here". I just felt that I'd let Elijah down a little bit. Jeremy said, "No, it's going so well".'

Tracey sighed.

'It wasn't necessary in the end anyway, but I can't envisage myself ever going there again.'

'To Armidale?' I asked.

'Going there is not going to fix anything,' she said. 'It's not going to answer questions; it will just be sad. I don't know why that moment in time had to happen, I probably never will, and that's what we live with.'

She picked at the tassels on the pale-blue scarf wound around her throat. Trying to understand had made her sick, she said.

'I didn't sleep, I would just go over and over it. Every night I would leap in front of that gun and take the bullet instead of him — anything I could do to try and change the scenario I knew. "Oh, if we'd only done this, oh, if we'd only done that", and I would actually get to the stage where I could hear the phone ringing or really think I could change something to make it not work out the way it worked out, and Elijah would be saying to me, "Mum, I'm dead. I'm OK, but I'm dead. Mum, I'm OK, but I'm dead. Stop doing this".'

Tracey was back in the torturous dream — my child, my skin, my responsibility. 'And the psychologist I was seeing, she'd be saying to me "He's trying to get in, he's trying to talk to you, but you've got your head down under the covers and you're not letting anyone in. You're just making yourself sick with your grief. Listen to him. Listen to what he's saying — that he's OK and there was a reason for it." He said, "Mum, there's a reason for it, let me do what I've got to do".'

'Do you talk to Elijah much?'

'All the time.'

She beamed.

'I was going in to have the final camera down to see about this ulcer, and Elijah was standing there beside my bed, as alive as if he was just standing there. I was saying to him 'stay with me', and he was looking off towards the surgeons looking really worried. He said, "Mum, they're going to tell you really bad news, but you're going to be OK. I'm going to be here with you". I mean, I have these little moments — you never know whether they're real or not — and you've got to believe. I think you are what you believe, and maybe what you believe is what happens. I believe that even if it is memories and flashes of Elijah — I do see him.'

Tracey broke off to check my reaction.

'I had a bit of a crash-and-burn this morning,' she confessed, smoothing the scarf's end flat with her palms. 'My girlfriends came over and said, "Well, it's about time you had a bit of a cry and a bit of a sook for yourself". I hadn't seen Elijah for a couple of days, and my two favourite Van Morrison songs came on the radio: *There'll be Days Like These*, and then *A Beautiful World*, and I thought thanks 'Lijah for trying to help cheer me up.'

Tracey seemed to be weighing up whether to go on. She drew a quivering breath and plunged in.

'I remember Elijah was missing and it was the second day. We'd slept all night on and off, and had people waiting to hear if the phone rang or anything and that afternoon, must have been about … it was after he was dead anyway. About 3 o'clock, I walked past my mother's photograph, and I said "Nan—"'

Tracey fell silent for a long stretch.

'"— do you know where my boy is? Can you find my boy? Can you keep an eye out for my boy?" 'Cause I thought, you know, she's dead, she can see everything.'

She laughed.

'And straight back, she said "I've got your boy". And I thought, oh, she's got his back, she can see where he is, what town he's in, whatever. 'Cause I thought he's driving around somewhere. Straight back, she said,

"I've got your boy", but he'd been dead for about two and a half hours then, I found out.'

Tears made dark blots on the blue scarf. Tracey looked up, struggling to pull air into her ravaged throat.

'I mean, I don't know whether that makes sense to anybody else but me, and I've turned it into whatever I want to turn it into, but *why* — why would that message come through from everything that could come through? Because I can look back now and think, she meant it. She's got my boy. He'd been dead for hours.'

I asked if she thought it would help to speak to Andrew Rich or see him. Tracey shook her head.

'It must have been so technical for him. I don't think even hearing his explanation will give me any satisfaction."

'Do you think if there *was* an explanation it would …'

Tracey broke in, 'Justify it?'

'No, that it would feel any different, give you any peace?'

'Nuh. Because I know in my heart there's no reason. There's no reason he should have been shot. That man could have done a whole lot more before he even thought about … it should be the last thing in the world that anybody would even think to do to anybody, after you've exhausted everything.'

She fired off alternatives.

'I mean shoot him with a fire hose, just let him stand there 'til the sun goes down. There just must have been so many other options. There were other police coming; he'd called for assistance. I think he really took the easy way out for some reason. I would exhaust every avenue before I pulled a gun on someone and pulled the trigger.'

'Are you angry at him?'

She sighed and twisted on the couch.

'If he was standing there right now, I'd feel a lot of compassion for him. I'm sure that man didn't get out of bed in the morning as a police officer wanting to protect and serve the community, and then shoot my son just to cause heartache and misery. I'm just angry that it's a choice he made. I'm angry that it happened.'

She had trusted police to bring her boy home when she asked them for help, and they had said they would. It was one of many betrayals in the last two years, I thought. The police, her body, her husband of thirty years. The grief began when Jeremy left, but there was no distinction anymore between one tragedy and the next, Tracey said.

'I would never have envisaged after having such a happy life for the first half of my life, to think well, bang, here you go. You've had all the good stuff, now you are going to experience all of this …'

She lay on the couch, fighting to speak through heavy sobs.

'I just want it to stop. I want to be normal and at home, hang the clothes on the line, put the tea on. And I hate feeling sorry for myself, but I thought I would be out of here by now, but I just keep getting sick.'

Whichever way she turned for comfort, the door was closed, and no matter how many times she reviewed her life, Tracey could not find what she had done to set it tumbling.

'All I ever wanted to do was be married and have children. I just wanted to be a housewife. It didn't worry me whether I worked or not. I just wanted to stay at home and play with the kids. I still can't believe that he's dead. I just feel like I'm going to wake up one day and he'll walk back from university or he'll come back on the train.'

'I couldn't believe when Jeremy told me on the phone, "The worst, worst possible news," he said. I said, "that means he's dead?" Half joking, you know.'

She lay back and took a deep breath, her eyes closed.

'He's saying right now, "they're going to put my picture on the book, Mum".' Tracey smiled at me. 'You know the thinker photo, the one we had on his coffin?'

I nodded.

'That was him and Allison messing around,' she said. 'I said to her I don't want him smiling happily on the coffin, and she said, "That was his author picture for the back of the book he was going to write".'

Tracey had opened a door to a hitherto forbidden room, and I slipped in.

'Did Allison go to the inquest?' I asked.

Tracey shook her head.

'Do you think their relationship affected Elijah's mental illness very much?' Tracey straightened against the pillows. Caution surfaced.

'She was very frightened by it, but I don't believe any of it was her fault. I said to her, "We would have gotten through all of this. We were doing the best we could at life, and we would have gotten Elijah back to you; if it didn't work out, it didn't, but it was life". And she said, "Did I pull him out of hospital too early in the first place?"'

Allison wasn't responsible for Elijah's death, Tracey said emphatically, and I wondered how many times she had needed to give Allison this reassurance, too.

'That man, the moment he pulled that trigger took away all ours and Elijah's options. He finished it, pulling that trigger.'

Feet slapped on the stairs, announcing Ruth's return. She plonked a bag of vegetables on the counter and turned to the potatoes on the stove.

I shifted the conversation to safer ground.

'When Elijah was paranoid, was he still Elijah or was he quite a different person?'

Tracey answered with a story. The Easter before he died, Elijah was sitting on the verandah of the cottage where his mothers and sisters lived, smoking. Laura and Jordan had scolded him and nagged him to give it up.

'And I said, "Yes, Elijah, your beautiful lungs, what are you doing smoking cigarettes?" and he smiled his beautiful smile and he looked at me across the table and said, "Mum, cigarettes aren't going to kill me. A policeman's going to shoot me." We're on the verandah, being absolutely normal, and he just smiled and said it so matter-of-fact, like he was a prophet. We went, "Oh, Elijah, that's your mental illness talking, you're not going to be shot by a policeman, blah blah blah".'

Ruth handed Tracey a mugful of pureed potato with a straw.

'And then he'd just go back to being normal, but he believed it and he didn't know why.'

Tracey could usually tell if he'd stopped taking his medication.

'He must have only done it three or four times, and there might have been other times that we don't know about,' she said. 'He would call me at two o'clock in the morning and he'd say in this flat voice, "Hi, Mum", and I would just freeze. And he'd go, "Um, I've just sort of come to", and he would have been hiding at a train station with his passport and a thousand dollars, which is what he had on him the day that he died.'

It happened often enough for Tracey to see a pattern. Something would trigger his paranoia and an episode would build.

'How long would the episodes last?' I asked.

'Twenty-four hours, six hours, all different. If he was here today, he'd introduce himself and he'd sit here and talk to you, and when you leave he'd say to me, "Now what's she got to do with everything? Who sent her?" He wouldn't be suspicious of you. There'd be a *them*, are *they* going to talk to you later and get information about him?'

The dim light of the afternoon added to the feeling we were roadtripping in heavy fog. I looked for landmarks one of us might recognise. What about Jeremy's illness, how did that come on? I asked.

After Elijah's teenage diagnosis, Jeremy had a complete breakdown, Tracey said. When Elijah described how he felt to the GP — dark hopelessness and a complete lack of emotion — Jeremy said, 'Sounds like me. You know, I don't feel things.'

Tracey's voice fell to a dull whisper.

'I'd known Jeremy since I was fifteen, sixteen. To me it was just Jeremy, but when I look back now, it wasn't normal behaviour; things we tolerated and he struggled with. He would constantly be paranoid.'

Jeremy was in and out of hospital and clinics for two years after Elijah's diagnosis. He was in his forties by then. Tracey said his illness was far more chronic than Elijah's.

'For Elijah it was mostly anxiety, although his paranoia was definitely more bizarre.'

She criss-crossed the state to find help for them both.

'I used to wait. I'd be out in the waiting room crocheting rugs, just to be there with them as long as I could. "Don't leave me", they'd say. I stayed as long as I could. I would just wait in the waiting room or sit in the lounge while they slept, so they wouldn't be alone. Until I had to go home or the other children needed me or I'd spent too long away — I used to hate leaving them 'cause in their minds it must have been so confusing and scary.'

Tracey looked fragile beneath the blanket, like a small, hairless animal.

I listened to my recording of our conversation in bed that night. The reflection of the Harbour Bridge floated like a half moon on the water.

'A lot of people, once they knew we were having mental illness issues, they would secretly come to me after dark or ring me on behalf of a "friend". "Tracey, so-and-so is having trouble with her husband or her mother", and whether it was them or someone else it didn't really matter. I'd go, "Yeah, I'll give you a number for someone, tell him I sent you",' Tracey said through my headphones.

All the things they couldn't say out loud, people had whispered to Tracey in the dark, because the Holcombes owned what others couldn't face. Tracey was a life buoy in an ocean of need that no one would admit existed. It was what made the Holcombes so remarkable to me.

I had grown up in the world they lived in, but no one I knew would admit that their family carried the blemish of mental illness. Public health campaigns made a regular circuit of country towns like ours, loaded with information posters, but their visits rarely broke through the surface. I'd been to one of their workshops with my mother before we left NSW. It was held in the hall where I'd learned ballet as a five-year-old. Girls I'd gone to primary school with fussed over Stella when we arrived, impressed I'd finally had a baby. I added our plate of sandwiches to the slices and instant coffee on the table and filed into the hall with all the other women. It was a ladies-only 'wellbeing' event.

The workshop facilitator handed around a clipboard.

'There are two lovely women down the back here to pamper you. Put your name down for a hand massage or a manicure. I've had mine!' she said, waggling her lacquered nails in the air.

Judy — on her nametag — wanted us to know we were 'in a safe space'. We could talk about anything. Fifteen women smiled at her politely.

'Why don't we draw the raffle to start with?' She held a battered ice-cream container above her head, shook it, and drew a ticket.

'Jenny? Jenny B is the winner!'

A weather-chaffed woman in the front row turned bright-red.

'Go on, Jen, go and get it!' the rowdier women barracked.

The facilitator held a basket wrapped in cellophane towards her. Jenny whispered in her ear and ran from the room in tears.

Judy touched her hair and turned to flick the projector on. 'The ladies down the back are waiting for their first customers — who's up next for the manicure?' she trilled.

The afternoon stumbled on. We learned how to check our breasts for lumps and how to stall diabetes with daily exercise.

'Can I see a show of hands from anyone dealing with mental health issues?' Judy asked after a coffee break.

The room fell silent. No one made eye contact.

'What about in your family or friendship group?' she prodded.

A couple of women left the room to check on children. Judy pushed on.

'I'll begin by sharing my own experiences, shall I?'

Someone followed with a confession that they had once called Lifeline. Where could she go for more substantial help when she lived 260km from the nearest psychologist? the confessor asked Judy.

'Be innovative. Think outside the square,' Judy offered. 'There are some wonderful online courses in managing anxiety these days.'

No one raged. No one called bullshit. The women nodded politely, had their manicures, ate their sandwiches, and took their unexamined pain back home. It was their silence that destroyed me. But what choice did they have? No one was really listening.

'It is such a personal battle,' Tracey whispered through my headphones.

9.

The only record of Rich's explanation for why he shot Elijah was in the brief of evidence police had prepared for the Coroner.

The brief was now with the Director of Public Prosecutions, to determine whether Rich should be charged over Elijah's death.

Fortunately, Jeremy Holcombe had a copy of all five folders. When Elijah's inquest was suspended, he had sent it to *Four Corners* — Quentin was interested in a follow-up story.

If *Four Corners* would give me the brief, I could have it, Jeremy told me in a phone call.

'You're very welcome if you can come and pick it up,' Quentin said when I rang. 'I'm afraid I can't mail it to you; it's too big.'

I'd only been back in Darwin for six weeks since seeing Tracey, but there were other reasons to return to Sydney. Philip Stewart, the lawyer who represented the Holcombes at Elijah's inquest, had transcripts of the Armidale proceedings: the key event in Elijah's story that I'd missed my chance to be part of.

'You can come into the office and I'll set you up with them,' Philip offered when we spoke. 'But you can only take notes — no copies. I'd be breaking the law.'

Philip Stewart was a partner at Nyman Gibson Stewart, a law firm whose office phone number was 1300 NOT GUILTY. The firm shared a building with the NSW Philatelic Society in an alley squashed between Surry Hills and Darlinghurst.

A young receptionist behind a worn desk nodded when I gave my name and walked me to a small room stacked with folders.

'If you need anything, talk to Katie.' She pointed to a well-dressed girl across the hall. 'She's Phil's PA.'

The room smelled like dust and methylated spirits. The receptionist thumped a fat manila folder on the desk.

'Start with this one. Phil's in court. He's due back about two o'clock for a Channel Seven interview.'

I had five days to read and copy two weeks of legal examination. I wiped the dust from the surface of the desk.

A concert of phones rang throughout the morning. Shifts of bright young men, hair heavy with product, and women in tight suits trafficked in and out. They spoke brashly and laughed loudly, sharing stories of their mornings in front of different magistrates.

At 3pm, a boom mic appeared at the doorway of my cubbyhole, followed by a crew and trussed-up journalist. They trooped into Phil Stewart's office to set up. The lift doors pinged, and Phil's voice boomed out.

'See you did your hair and makeup 'specially, Katie,' he shot at his PA, and then grinned as her colour rose. 'Channel Seven here yet?'

He strode into his office and closed the door. Muffled laughter and something about high-speed police pursuits floated out. The door re-opened, and the boom and camera headed to the lift, followed by the stutter of high heels.

'When'll it be on? Tonight, you think? Alright,' Phil shook hands, grinning broadly. 'You sure you don't want a shot of my PA before you go?' The lift doors clanged shut.

A huge head with bulging blue eyes swung around the doorframe.

'And how are you doing, Miss Wild?'

A meaty hand reached out towards me from six-foot-three of grey suit.

'You got what you need? Katie fix you up with everything?'

'Yes, thank you. There's a lot to get through.'

'I think we're still waiting for the last week to come through.' Phil swivelled. 'Katie, have we got all those transcripts yet? Can you call the court and find out where the rest are?'

He patted the edge of the doorframe briskly.

'Let's get a coffee tomorrow before court. No copies remember — only notes,' he reminded me, pointing at the folders on the desk.

I stayed at Nyman Gibson Stewart late into the night, typing, reading, and scribbling notes. I listened through the thin partition to the rasping tones of a lawyer on the other side. She was talking someone through a drink-drive charge.

'Yeah, we can fight it. We might be able to get you off, but if you want us to take your case you have to listen to me first … Are you listening? Stop talking for a minute, would you? You need to come in tomorrow for a meeting. No, it won't cost you for the first one.'

A phone crashed into its cradle.

'Jesus fucking Christ! Some people are fucking unbelievable.'

Phil Stewart drank two short blacks in quick succession and settled into the vinyl seat across from me. Why did I want to write about this case? What was I going to say about the cops? Had I met the Holcombes? Jeremy was pretty intense, wasn't he? Good person though, good family. If I wanted an interview with him for the book, he'd be happy to help. When I was finished with Elijah's story, he had plenty more that needed telling.

'Why did *you* take the Holcombes on?' I asked.

'Someone had to help them,' Phil said, his eyes on his cup. 'They didn't have money for a lawyer. It's a disgrace that young bloke was shot. Absolute disgrace. No reason for it to happen, the cop stuffed up and he gets all the legal representation in the world to get him past it. You can't let the cops get away with it.'

He pushed himself out from behind the table and pointed his head towards the door.

'Gotta go. You going back to the office?'

'I'm going to drop in on Tracey Holcombe. I'll be back after lunch.'
Phil nodded and waved, his mind in court already.

Tracey and I met on the footpath outside Sweeney's place, coming from different directions.

'I had a bit of energy this morning, so I've been walking in the park,' she said, obviously pleased.

We tramped upstairs. The curtains were pulled back, the window was open, and a fresh rug lay folded on the couch.

'I didn't expect to see you again so soon,' she said. It was a gentle question.

I boiled the kettle and told her why I was back.

'I've been reading the transcripts of Elijah's inquest. There were so many moments when a tiny thing could have gone differently and changed what happened. Do you ever think about that?'

I handed Tracey a ginger tea. She cradled it and nodded.

'I try not to because that's part of the reason I got so sick. "Oh, they rang Jeremy's answering machine but he was out looking for Elijah"; "If someone had stayed at Jeremy's house",' she mimicked. 'If, if, if. The more information you find out, the more peace of mind you get, but it doesn't change the final outcome, and I have to be at peace with the fact Elijah's not here anymore leading a life.'

She shifted on the couch to face me squarely. Her features sharpened briefly.

'Really, the only thing that annoys the crap out of me about this whole thing anymore is the policeman. I didn't get to hear what he had to say and why he did what he did. I haven't read his statement, I just got that way where I couldn't do it anymore.'

On the walk from Nyman Gibson Stewart to Tracey, I had passed a scatter of homeless men sprawled in the sun on the steps of a church — a mass of matted hair and swollen trunk-like legs that smelled of urine.

None of them were over forty. Could this have been Elijah one day if he'd survived Rich's bullet? Had Tracey contemplated that?

She batted the question away with a flap of her hand, and snorted.

'Oh gosh yeah. I don't think it would have gone away! But I was optimistic, and his therapists were optimistic. I always thought he had more good life than troubled because of his intellect, but that's no guarantee he wouldn't continue to suffer these things. All the shooter did was take away our options. We'd dealt with mental illness for a lot of years. It was like, "Yeah, he's still got leukaemia",' she said drily.

There was a long pause.

'You know, the grief is changing,' Tracey said.

'How?'

'I couldn't think of Elijah before without being traumatised. I'd well up with this feeling of devastation. I wanted to be able to think of him and just go, "Oh, my Elijah was a beautiful person who did this and did that", and I can do that now without crying.'

She smiled at me proudly through tears.

'That's a big leap since the last time I saw you,' I said.

She nodded and pulled a tissue out of her sleeve.

'I didn't think I would ever get over Jeremy leaving, and then I got a phone call to say "Your son has been shot", and then they told me I had cancer!' Tracey laughed, still shocked by the train of events and her own survival. 'It's like it sort of picks you up and moves you to another building, you know?'

She put on a voice like an announcer calling the next train into a platform.

'"You're in the cancer-dying building now, not in the loved-your-son-who-was-tragically-killed building or the husband-left-you-for-another-woman building",' she said. 'It's physically like they pick you up and put you in another environment. I couldn't believe I could change so dramatically to "Oh, not really that worried about Elijah anymore, I'm gonna die"!'

We laughed together.

'But it was! It was like that!' Tracey insisted, her face wide with amazement. She slapped the couch for emphasis. 'How your mind does that I have no idea, but it did. The wisdom and the knowledge you gain along the way really do make you stronger for something else that comes along. I'm more at home now with the idea that he's gone. That's all out of my hands. I'm terminally ill. I've got to take care of myself now.'

The next three days flew as fast as my fingers on the keyboard. I sat at my desk at Nyman Gibson Stewart, trying to swallow the transcript with my eyes.

On Friday afternoon, I set off down Elizabeth Street to Central Station and bought a soft black wheelie bag at a crappy shop. I crumpled it beneath my arm and walked the familiar path to the ABC.

Quentin greeted me with a hug. There were shadows beneath his eyes.

'Scripting week — usual hell,' he murmured with British understatement. 'Footballers and head injuries. Brutal stuff.'

We reached his office.

'That's what you're after.' He pointed to a tower of folders in the corner. 'I've had a look, but I won't get back to it for a while.'

I counted five binders. Quentin held the mouth of my new bag open and I pushed Elijah's brief into its saggy belly.

'You sure you'll be able to get all this back to Darwin?' Quentin asked politely.

We stared at the misshapen bag.

'I might be up for some excess luggage,' I replied.

I pulled the bag behind me like a fat black calf, back to Nyman Gibson Stewart, where I poked my head around the door of Phil Stewart's office.

'How was court?' I asked.

'Good. Last day, eh? Did you get what you needed?'

'Yes, I did. Thank you.'

'Have you got a minute? I want to show you something.' He waved me to a chair, pulled a DVD out of a plastic sleeve, pushed it into the computer, and turned the monitor towards me. CCTV images appeared in a tiny box. I pulled my chair forward.

'What is it?'

'Watch. You'll see.'

The picture was over-exposed and grubby, like opening your eyes under river water. The camera was obviously mounted high on a wall. People moved like objects in a flicker book.

Phil hit the fast-forward button. 'There's a bit I want you to see.'

On the screen, a man in a baseball cap stepped out from behind a wall. He leaned down with one hand on his knee and pressed a mobile phone to his ear then straightened and moved in long steps across a lane. There was a gun on his hip and he wore a goatee. The camera moved ahead of him, but the man was walking quickly.

It was Andrew Rich in Cinders Lane. In seconds, he was back in frame, below a woman in a bright-red jacket walking past a jumper on the ground. She looked around then stopped to watch Rich.

He was chasing someone. He drew his gun. The woman in red could see his target. She turned, and I followed her gaze to a young man in the car park walking between two parked cars. He was holding something in his hand.

A woman and teenage boy walked into shot together. The boy was in a school uniform. The pictures had no sound, but there must have been a loud noise in the laneway, because the teenager and young man both turned as if they'd heard their names called. The teenager ducked behind a car and the camera pulled away. The scene shrank. In a second, Rich's cap was a fluorescent spot on the horizon. The camera swung to the beginning of its arc, one hundred and eighty degrees away. Asphalt and brick walls filled the screen. Fifty-three seconds ticked over on the time code before the white cap reappeared on screen, crouched over a body in the gutter.

'From when he comes into the lane to when he fires is not even two minutes. Not long to decide you're going to shoot someone, is it?' Phil said with a twisted smile.

'Can I have a copy?'

Phil shook his head.

'You've hardly left that little office all week, come for a drink. It's Friday. Meet some people before you go.'

We walked to the pub on the corner where Nyman Gibson Stewart's bright young things had already started. The girls tapped manicured talons against their glasses and flicked straightened manes over their shoulders. The boys mixed amongst them in skinny ties and highly polished shoes. They swapped court stories and football tips, resilient with youth. Phil elbowed into the huddle to introduce me. He praised their wins, brushed over their losses, and ribbed anyone who left an opening.

When the DJ started, I headed for the back end of the room. Phil followed, grinning.

'Feeling old?'

'How long have you been a lawyer?' I shouted back over the music. We found a table and slipped behind it, beers in hand.

'Since I stopped being a cop,' he replied.

I raised my eyebrows. 'Really?'

He savoured my surprise.

'I was a cop for fourteen years, got bashed one night by seven cowards. Screwed up my jaw and half my teeth, left me with PTSD and agoraphobia. I went into police prosecuting after that to avoid having to wear the uniform. Did a law degree, resigned from the cops at thirty-five, and moved to Narrabri with my wife and child to start again. That's where I met Sweeney — have you come across him yet?'

'David Sweeney who Tracey's staying with?' I asked.

'That's him. Sweeney gave me my first job as a lawyer,' Phil said. 'He hated going to court; I didn't. Home and court were the only two places I felt comfortable for a long time; outside that, every day was a nightmare.'

Phil took a swig of beer from his schooner.

'Narrabri was an opportunity to recover away from the rat race. Sweeney gave me that opportunity, so when he moved his legal practice to Sydney, I referred non-criminal work to him to help him re-establish himself. He did the same for me when I moved back here. Sweeney's the one who got me involved in Elijah's case.'

10.

My study had become a cityscape. Folders, transcripts, and notebooks sprawled like suburbs across the floor. Our tangled garden pressed its face against the louvres and reached inside to touch them. It was build-up season; even the furniture sweated.

I lifted the cool white binders of the brief from the belly of the crumpled bag and lined them up on my desk.

Rich's statement was in Volume 2. It was fifty-three pages long. He'd made a second statement five months later, but they each began the same way. A detective told Rich that he was not under arrest; this was not a criminal investigation. Did Rich agree to being interviewed? He didn't. The detective warned if he refused to answer questions Rich could be subject to discipline by the police force.

Rich responded woodenly.

'You have advised me that you are investigating the death of Elijah Holcombe … You have also told me that I am not alleged to have committed any criminal offence and you do not intend cautioning me.'

I read the paragraph three times before I realised Rich was reading from a statement.

'I wish it known that any answer I give or anything I say or do hereafter is not given or done of my free will but because I am compelled to do so by the direction to me,' he continued.

'I also wish it understood that I will object to this record of interview or anything that derives from them being admitted into evidence or otherwise being used in any criminal, disciplinary, civil or any other proceedings taken against me. I'll take the same objection in any such proceedings at which I am called as a witness … I also reserve the right to take the same objection at any coronial inquest which may be held in relation to this matter.'

I sat back in my chair, heat rising in my face. Rich objected to his evidence being put on the legal record. His job was to protect the public, but he was protecting himself instead. I imagined him in the same situation with someone he had pulled off the street. *I don't care whether you want to answer questions, mate. I want to know what you did. If you're clean, there's nothing to worry about, is there?*

Where was it written that Rich could decree how his evidence could be used? Not in a criminal, civil, disciplinary, or coroner's court if he had his way. Was this a privilege reserved for police? How could Rich or any officer be allowed to object to giving evidence? It was the bedrock of policing.

After reading out his list of objections, Rich told detectives his version of events.

When he walked into the station around midday, the duty officer Joel Aiken said a young man had come in to confess to stealing a car. Aiken told Rich the car had been left on an Armidale street somewhere; could Rich give him a hand and look for it? Rich went looking, but couldn't find the car. He searched again with his partner, Senior Constable Greg Dufty. Together they lapped the streets for half an hour. They called Aiken two or three times for more information. In one of these calls, Aiken told Rich and Dufty that Elijah was at the hospital '… to be scheduled, I think, to be scheduled,' Rich told detectives.

In a different call, Aiken told them Elijah had left the hospital. Rich and Dufty went up to Accident and Emergency; Rich said he spoke to two nurses.

'I said I was looking for a young man who was up here for a psych evaluation or scheduling. They said, "Yes, he's just absconded about ten minutes ago". They said, "He hasn't been seen by a doctor. We've got concerns for his safety. Can you bring him back?"' Rich recalled.

Rich and Dufty were both in plainclothes. They found Elijah within fifteen minutes, near a camping store in the CBD, on Rusden Street.

'Elijah, it's the police!' Rich yelled out.

Elijah stopped and looked at him.

'I said, "Mate, it's the police. I just need to talk to you for a minute". I walked a bit closer with my badge out. I said, "Mate, it's the police. I just want to talk to you about the stolen car",' Rich recorded in his statement.

Elijah told Rich to throw him the keys, but Rich refused and said to him instead, 'We've been up to the hospital and they want you to come back.'

Elijah started to edge away, so Rich walked towards him.

'Mate, you need to go back up to the hospital,' Rich said.

That was when Elijah sprinted across the road, Rich claimed. So he gave chase. They rounded a corner and ran into the pedestrian mall on Beardy Street.

Rich said he called out, 'Stop, come back to the hospital', but Elijah ignored him and walked into a café. Rich followed Elijah inside the café and down the hall towards the kitchen. He judged he was thirty seconds behind him.

'There were three or four people working at the kitchen at the time. They sort of looked shocked and looked at him and [as] soon as I lost sight of him I heard metal on metal. I could hear a scraping of metal and then I saw him come around back to the left towards the back door and I saw that he was holding a knife in his hand at that time. So I just wanted to keep a safe distance.'

'Were you saying anything to Elijah?' a detective asked.

'No, I was more focused on the people. I wanted them to get out. I said, "Look, get out. Come on, he's got a knife".'

When Rich saw Elijah had a knife, he reached for his capsicum spray, also known as OC spray. It wasn't in his pocket, so he rang the station to ask for backup. Rich told the operator, 'He's got a knife. I need someone up here now. He's armed himself with a knife.'

He said he also told a girl in the kitchen, 'I'm a police officer. Call Triple-0.'

The detective asked Rich to describe the knife.

'It probably had a thirty- or forty-centimetre silver blade. It looked serrated on one edge.'

Rich followed Elijah out the back door of the café and up to the thoroughfare of Cinders Lane.

'[Elijah] started to jog again,' he said. 'As I started to move towards him, I said, "Elijah, stop mate. Put the knife down, this is enough. You need to stop". I wasn't yelling at him at that stage.'

Elijah didn't stop. Rich intimated to detectives he was worried about the safety of other people on the street.

'So I challenged him, yelled at him: "Stop. Drop the knife". He started to slow down, turned my way. I'd drawn my firearm by then, had it down by my side.'

Rich's speech fell into shorthand.

'Yelled at him, "Mate, drop the knife. Drop the knife. Police, drop the knife". I continued to follow him. "Elijah, drop the knife." He turned and faced me, I drew my firearm, pointed it at him.'

Rich said he was about ten metres from Elijah.

'I closed the distance a bit. He turned and faced me. I pointed my firearm at him and then started to give him verbal commands. "Drop the knife. Drop the knife, drop the knife", yelling at this stage.'

'He said, you know, "Fuck you, shoot me, you fucking cunt". And then I said, "Drop the knife, drop the knife" I can't recall how many times, several times. And then he just yelled. He didn't say anything, it [was] just sort of like a roar and he started to run at me and then took two to three steps if that and then I, I fired at him.'

Sweat trickled down my sides beneath my shirt. *Bullshit*. Where were the witnesses who corroborated Rich?

I dragged out my notes from Phil Stewart's office and riffled to pages stiff with highlighter that captured an exchange from day two of Elijah's inquest, between counsel assisting the coroner, Chris Hoy, and Acting Sergeant Joel Aiken from Armidale Police.

Aiken was the officer Elijah had 'confessed' to and the one who asked Rich to find Elijah's car. When detectives interviewed Aiken for his statement, he'd recalled a conversation he had with Rich in the hours after Elijah's shooting.

Chris Hoy read Aiken's recollection to him in court.

'I just said to him, "Mate, what happened?" and he said to me [Elijah] had got a knife and he called on him to stop and yeah, he turned and that was it, that's all he told me,' Hoy read out.

'That's right,' Aiken confirmed from the stand.

'Just clarifying, is that what Mr Rich told you about the end of the incident — "He turned and that was it"?' Hoy said.

'Yes.'

'And that relates to the explanation as to the shot then being fired?' Hoy checked.

'Yes.'

'Was there any commentary given to you by Mr Rich as to Elijah swearing at Mr Rich?' Hoy asked.

'No,' Aiken replied.

'And being precise and not meaning to be offensive, "Fuck you", words like that, or "Shoot me, you fucking cunt"?'

'No, there wasn't.'

Hoy compared Rich's statement against Aiken's memory, line by line.

'Was there any recount that he [Elijah] was yelling and then started "like a roar"?' Hoy asked.

'No, he didn't tell me,' Aiken said.

'Never told you anything like that?'

'No, he didn't.'

'He made no mention of a roar?'

'That's so, no, he didn't.'

'And he made no mention of [Elijah] starting to run at him or taking two or three steps?'

'No, he didn't.'

There was another point on which Aiken and Rich's evidence differed significantly.

Half an hour before the shooting, when Rich and Dufty were looking for Elijah's car, Rich recalled being told by Aiken that Elijah was at Armidale Hospital 'to be scheduled'.

'Scheduling' refers to detaining someone involuntarily in order to assess their mental state. In NSW, the power to schedule someone is legislated under the *Mental Health Act*. Scheduling is regarded as a last resort and it can only be done by a doctor or accredited mental health worker if a person is mentally ill or disturbed, and a less-restrictive option is not appropriate. Less-restrictive options include the person agreeing to voluntary admission, or releasing the person into community care or to their family.

If Aiken believed on 2 June 2009 that Elijah needed to be scheduled, it suggested he thought that Elijah could be dangerous.

Phil Stewart cross-examined Aiken on this point during the inquest.

'I think you've agreed earlier with counsel assisting that you had told Senior Constable Rich that Elijah had gone to hospital for the purpose of being scheduled?' Phil Stewart asked.

'No, for the purposes of see[ing] a doctor, not scheduled,' Aiken corrected him.

'Are you saying at no time did you tell Senior Constable Rich that Elijah was going to the hospital for the purpose of being scheduled?' Stewart clarified.

'I don't believe I did. I don't remember,' said Aiken.

What behaviour did Elijah exhibit, Stewart asked, that made Aiken believe it was *not* necessary to schedule him?

'Elijah was not displaying any signs of wanting to harm himself, me for instance, or harm anybody else in the public. He was quiet, but he would respond when I asked him a question,' Aiken said.

If Aiken didn't see Elijah as a threat, where did Rich get the idea of scheduling from? And why was Senior Constable Greg Dufty also under the impression that Elijah was being scheduled?

'I thought he was being assessed, um, as a possible, um, schedule. Because the conversations we'd had in the car is he'd been taken to the hospital because they believed he had some mental issues,' Dufty told detectives.

The only reasonable explanation I could muster for this conviction was that Rich and Dufty assumed, without anyone saying "schedule", that Elijah's mental state was grave because police were the ones who took him to Emergency.

Senior Constable Peter Shelton, who drove Elijah to hospital, described his passenger as 'calm and quiet'. Robyn O'Brien, the triage nurse who met them on arrival, said Shelton told her expressly that Elijah had not been scheduled.

'He did not at any time threaten my staff or me, and we all felt quite safe with him in the unit,' O'Brien said at Elijah's inquest.

The hospital's mental health nurse, Carla Rutherford, claimed she felt the same. There was no reason to schedule Elijah.

The point seemed settled until the barrister representing Rich, Brent Haverfield, pointed out in cross-examination that Rutherford's view of Elijah on 2 June 2009 was quite different to the one she was presenting to the Coroner.

'This is a discussion you've had after Elijah has left the hospital,' Haverfield said, and he read from the statement she gave police. 'You say, "I told [other staff] that as I did not have the power to schedule him he'd been able to walk out, yet I was concerned that he could harm himself or others." Why did you have that concern at that time?'

Rutherford told him she was not concerned; she'd simply wanted Elijah properly assessed.

I found Rutherford's statement in the brief and read it for myself.

I was actually worried about him leaving as I believed he may be acutely psychotic … I repeated that I strongly felt that he should have been triaged higher and seen by the doctor. I told them that as I did not have the power to schedule him he had been able to walk out, yet I was concerned that he could harm himself or others.

In the middle of Rutherford's conversation with her colleagues, the Armidale police rang to tell the hospital that Elijah had stolen a car the day before. Rutherford told detectives:

I said this information might indicate psychosis as it showed thought disturbance … I advised the emergency department staff to make sure the police were notified of him leaving against medical advice and that the police should bring the patient back for further assessment if apprehended. I advised Dr Murphy and Robyn O'Brien that if he did return that he should be seen immediately with the possibility of scheduling him …

What basis did police have for returning a voluntary patient like Elijah? Haverfield asked.
Rutherford seemed unable to grasp the principle of the question. So Elijah could be assessed, she repeated.
What Haverfield wanted to know — and so did I — was what *power* police were being asked to exercise under Rutherford's petition that they bring Elijah back. Did she think she was asking police to return a runaway patient as a favour? Or did she believe the hospital had authority to engage the police's force because her clinical view was that Elijah might be dangerous?
As far as I could tell from his statement, before Rich reached the hospital, all he knew about Elijah was that he'd stolen and dumped a car. Whether or not Aiken used the word 'scheduling', Rutherford's perspective complicated the story, because she told staff in the Emergency

Department that she was very concerned about Elijah's mental state. By the time Rich came in looking for Elijah, Rutherford had gone. It was Robyn O'Brien who asked Rich to bring Elijah back. How much of Rutherford's anxiety did O'Brien relay to Rich? It was hard to know.

The *Mental Health Act 2007* (NSW) was less than crystal clear on where the balance of power lay in the situation Rich found himself in. Section 49 of the *Act* says that 'an authorised medical officer may request' that police apprehend someone and bring them to a mental health facility. But the section only applies if the medical officer believes that apprehending the person will be unsafe unless the police are there to help.

It seemed to cover what O'Brien had asked of Rich based on Rutherford's perception of Elijah — except that O'Brien was not 'an authorised medical officer'. Neither was Rutherford for that matter. So why had Rutherford thrown the idea around that the hospital should ask the police to bring Elijah back? Why not just call the doctor over, who had the power to make the call?

Perhaps the answer was the one she gave in court — because she knew that Elijah didn't qualify to be held in hospital against his will.

Returning my focus to Rich's statement, three points in his retelling of the afternoon bothered me: his approach to Elijah outside the camping store; the events in Caffiends' kitchen; and the minutes that elapsed from the back door of the kitchen to shooting Elijah in Cinders Lane.

Rich's approach to Elijah on Rusden Street was witnessed by two people.

Willow Grieves, who worked at the camping store, told the court he saw a bright-orange Commodore, bristling with antennas, parked outside the shop when he rode back from lunch. Grieves picked the Commodore as a police car straight away.

He saw two men on the footpath near the shop. One wore a gun clearly visible on his hip, and Grieves assumed he was a plainclothes police officer.

Grieves weaved between the two men on his pushbike. He heard the police officer say to the second man, 'Do you want your keys?' or 'Do you want the keys?'

The second man slowed, turned around, and then backed away a little. He looked like he was about to run. Grieves told the inquest he considered for a split second jumping off his bike to tackle the second man, but he resisted the urge and kept riding instead. When Grieves reached the corner, he heard pounding footsteps.

'I had a glance over my shoulder and I saw Elijah running with an undercover cop sprinting after him,' Grieves told the court.

Counsel assisting the coroner, Chris Hoy, asked if he heard Elijah say anything. Did he swear, perhaps, or ask Rich to throw him the keys? Did Grieves hear anyone yell, 'Elijah, it's the police'? or, 'Mate, it's the police, I just need to talk to you for a minute', 'I just want to talk to you about the stolen car', 'We've been up to the hospital and they want you to come back'?

Grieves had not heard any of those things.

The second witness to events was a parking inspector, Bernard Maurer, who was writing a ticket across the road. He saw Rich take a set of keys from his pocket. He 'jingled them about' and yelled out to Elijah, 'Hey mate, you dropped your keys,' Maurer told the court.

By Maurer's account, Elijah turned around and looked at Rich, and then slowly backed away. Rich chuckled and said, 'He doesn't want them, he's not stopping,' to someone in the orange Commodore, and then called out to Elijah, 'I'm an undercover cop, mate, you're obliged to stop.'

Rich put his hand near his hip, close to his gun, and Elijah ran. Rich chased him, Maurer told the Coroner.

He said another man — who we knew was Dufty — got out of the car at this point. Maurer said in his statement that Dufty let out a sigh as he jogged past, 'as if he was annoyed that he had to run'.

Counsel assisting the coroner, Chris Hoy, repeated the questions he'd put to Willow Grieves.

Did Maurer hear anyone say, 'Elijah, it's the police' or 'Mate, it's the police, I just need to talk to you for a minute', or 'I just want to talk to you about the stolen car', or 'Mate, I'm not going to throw you the keys, I need to talk to you about it', or 'We've been up the hospital and they want you to come back'?

Maurer said he didn't, and Rich's barrister, Brent Haverfield, jumped to his client's defence.

'There could have been conversation you didn't hear from your positioning across the road,' he suggested.

'I heard it loud and clear,' Maurer replied.

Rich told detectives in his interview that he chased Elijah from the camping store to the mall, a distance of about three hundred metres.

He said he called out, 'Stop, come back to the hospital', but Elijah ignored him and jogged into Caffiends café. Witnesses agreed that Elijah headed for the kitchen, with Rich in close pursuit.

Rich lost sight of Elijah at the kitchen door, but he said that from the hallway, 'I heard metal on metal'. He linked the sound to his next sight of Elijah walking out the back door of Caffiends with a knife.

It was a tiny thing, but I couldn't let it go. Anyone in the kitchen might have made that noise. A stainless-steel tray or a pot on a pan could create the sound of metal on metal. Why assume or infer it was Elijah picking up a knife? The flourish was conspicuous next to details I had no trouble believing — Rich stumbling on the steps, almost dropping his phone, for instance.

I cross-checked Rich's claims against those of other people in the kitchen.

The owner of Caffiends, Sonia Stier, was standing near the fridge when Elijah walked in. He was moving quickly, she told police. He brushed right past her, took an object from the bench, and walked out the back door without answering her question — 'Who are you?' Sonia didn't see what he'd taken.

Her apprentice chef got a closer look. It was 'a large serrated-edged bread knife', Sean Miller told detectives.

'He sort of concealed it. I'd say he held the handle in his hand and sort of held it down by his side without showing too much of the blade at all. He seemed very anxious,' Miller said at Elijah's inquest.

'Were you worried or anything, about the fellow?' Hoy asked.

'No, wasn't worried about myself, I felt pretty comfortable.'

'Even though he had a knife?' Hoy asked the teenager.

'Yeah, it happened pretty quick, eh, and he didn't have the knife out, he wasn't waving it at us. He wasn't trying to hurt any of us and it happened within ten seconds, so yeah, I wasn't frightened at all.' Elijah didn't make eye contact, Miller said.

Hoy wanted to know how soon the second man came into the kitchen after Elijah left. Within a second, Miller said. Sonia Stier thought it was longer. She only noticed Rich when he stood up from behind a freezer in the hall. Elijah was a metre out the back door by then, she said.

Sonia Stier asked him who he was; Rich turned and said in a quiet voice, 'police'. It was the only thing she heard him say during the minutes he was in the kitchen.

Rich told detectives he warned Stier and the others: 'Look, get out. Come on, he's got a knife.'

'I wanted them to get out,' he said in his statement.

No one in the kitchen remembered Rich's warning. The dishwasher, Peter Hunt, thought Sean Miller had said the same words to Rich — 'Look out, he's got our knife.' Miller denied saying anything.

Rich described Elijah standing at the back door of the kitchen, holding a silver serrated knife with a blade that was thirty to forty cemtimetres long. The sight of the knife made him reach into his pocket, which was when he discovered his OC spray was gone.

Other statements in the brief said police had searched for Rich's spray between the camping store and Cinders Lane after the shooting, and again the next day, but it was never found.

Phil Stewart had a theory about the OC spray, based on a request Rich made after the shooting that Dufty retrieve his sports bag from the car. Rich suffered migraines and carried medication for them. One came on after Cinders Lane, and Rich asked his partner to get his bag from the Commodore on Rusden Street — that's where his tablets were. Phil Stewart guessed the spray was also in Rich's bag and he wanted to dispose of it. The theory wasn't tested at the inquest, though, because the case was referred to the DPP before Rich or Dufty were called for evidence.

The back door of Caffiends was a ten-second walk from Cinders Lane.

Chris Hoy did the sums based on the CCTV vision and presented them to the Coroner at the inquest.

'At 13.57.21 ... we see Senior Constable Rich looking east down Cinders Lane with what appears to be a mobile phone to his left ear in his left hand ... At 13.57.43 we see Mr Rich has his gun drawn ... The next photograph is 13.58.49 and at that stage we can see Elijah on the ground and Senior Constable Rich over him with other personnel.'

Rich drew his gun twenty-two seconds after leaving Caffiends. Less than a minute later, he shot Elijah.

There was a copy of the CCTV vision in Jeremy's copy of the brief. I pulled the disc out of its plastic sleeve and carried it to the kitchen.

Our magnetic knife rack sat above the stove. I studied the curve of the carving knife and the square nose of the cleaver while I waited for the kettle. The bread knife sat between them like a middle finger.

Tea in hand, I moved to the couch and pushed the disc into the machine.

The picture opened on a rural scene. A mural of rolling hills and cockatoos, horses with legs like logs of wood, and a bearded man (a farmer or bushranger?) painted on a wall. The camera couldn't choose what it captured; there was no one behind the lens. It filmed whatever came before it in sixty-second automated circuits of the lane.

I watched a woman and teenage boy lurch out of a narrow passageway. The boy was in school uniform. The camera moved left and Rich stepped into frame — this was the part Phil Stewart had shown me. Rich talked into his mobile phone, leaning on his knee, and then strode quickly out of shot. The camera continued on its circuit and caught up with him across the lane as he passed Judy Tennant in her bright-red jacket. A car began to pull out of the car park but paused before it reached the lane. I watched Rich draw his gun.

I searched for Elijah in the grainy picture and found him by following Judy Tennant's gaze. There he was, between the cars, stepping back onto the footpath by the road.

The mother and son from the passageway had reached the car park, where the camera picked them up again.

The boy and Elijah turned almost in unison and looked across their shoulders. The boy ducked down behind a car. Elijah did nothing, and the camera pulled away. The scene grew distant as its eye returned to the brick wall covered in rolling hills. I counted the seconds it took to move across asphalt and trees, street bins, and jerking bystanders. Sixty-six seconds later, Rich reappeared, crouched in the gutter beside Elijah's body.

A man in riding boots charged up the road — it was Dufty. Faces clustered around the passageway turned like great white dinner plates to follow him. The camera jerked through another circuit. The first police car appeared on the scene. Another revolution, and there were people kneeling, pumping at Elijah's chest. By 2.01pm, police were pushing people back and stringing chequered tape between trees and poles.

I clomped back downstairs to the study to interrogate witnesses who had seen the missing minute.

More than one witness used the word 'surreal' to describe events in Cinders Lane that day.

One woman assumed it was all a training exercise. In a session on hold-ups at her own workplace, an instructor had used the exact same words as Rich — 'Get down, get down now.'

'I thought to myself, how ridiculous is that to be doing your training exercise out in the public gaze. Someone might think it was real,' the woman told the inquest.

When she heard a gunshot from the back step of the library, she stubbed out her cigarette and went inside.

Kim Blomfield, who appeared in the CCTV vision with her son, said she craned her head to find the movie cameras when she saw two men, one with a knife, one with a gun, walking ahead of her in Cinders Lane.

Lisa Moor said she stopped her car as she was trying to leave the car park because a man with a gun crossed the lane in front of her. She thought of leaning on her horn to break the moment, but instead she reached for her phone and pre-dialed Triple-0.

Moor described Rich pointing his gun at a young man on the footpath. She saw the young man make a movement — it might have been a step backwards, she said. He mouthed some words, but she couldn't hear them. Then she heard a gunshot.

Phil Stewart pushed Moor further on the stand.

'Do I take it that what you saw was a single step?' he asked.

'Yes. It was a slight movement, yep.'

'You were asked whether the young person ran towards the policeman and you said "I didn't see it". Did it happen, is my question.'

'Not that I ever saw, it did not happen,' Moor replied.

Another witness, Matthew Schaefer, heard shouting when he stepped out of his girlfriend's car, 'Put the knife down, Elijah, put the knife down!'

He noticed a young man walk into the car park and duck between some cars.

'He looked like he was running away from something or scared of something. He was walking along at quite a pace, looking over his shoulder,' Schaefer told the inquest.

Schaefer could see the person the young man was scared of, at the entrance to the car park. This second man walked into the middle of Cinders Lane, pulled out a pistol, and pointed it at the young man, yelling, "Put the knife down", over and over.

The young man turned, and both men stood still. Schaefer estimated they were five metres apart.

'After [Elijah] stopped, he put his arms out in the crucifix fashion. His arms out to his side. He had a knife in one hand, facing back towards the gentleman with the gun,' Schaefer told the Coroner.

'Had he said anything at that stage, the younger man?' Hoy asked.

'That's the first time I heard him, and he was saying, "Shoot me, shoot me." They were both just eyeballing each other, if you like … The man with the gun was yelling at him to put the knife down and get onto the ground. The man with the knife was still yelling out to shoot, he was saying, "Shoot me."'

'How many times do you think he said that?' Coroner Jerram interjected.

About six, said Schaefer. He remembered silence for a couple of seconds, and then the young man stepped off the footpath and onto the road, towards the gunman. It seemed like Elijah was lunging towards Rich; he might have started to run, Schaefer said. The movement Elijah made 'definitely wasn't slow'.

'There's some material before us that is suggesting that the younger man said words along the lines of — and pardon my language — "Fuck you, shoot me, you fucking cunt" — yelled out. Did you hear …' Hoy asked, but Schaefer cut across him:

'I didn't hear those words.'

'There is also material before us to suggest that the younger man made a roar or some type of noise like a roar, a verbal roar just as he moved forward. Did you hear that?'

'No, I didn't hear that either, I can't remember that,' said Schaefer.

'From your position it was silent, there was a pause and silence?'

'Yes, that's what I remember,' Schaefer said.

The witness after Schaefer was Ian Greenhalgh, a librarian.

Greenhalgh had walked down Cinders Lane parallel to Elijah. He noticed a bread knife in Elijah's hand, and he heard Rich shouting.

'I felt no cause for concern from the young man — he certainly was making no urgent or violent movements to get away from anybody, he wasn't interfering with the progress of other people who were walking through the car park, and I had no expectation of danger from him,' Greenhalgh told the Coroner.

He described Elijah's reaction when Rich took out his gun.

'He wasn't intent on making a run. He wasn't dropping the knife. At some stage in the repeated command to put the knife down, it was as though this change of mind came over the young man and he turned back towards the man with the gun and took two, maybe three loping steps,' Greenhalgh explained.

The turn was 'like a turn made as a result of a decision: "I'll move back towards this man." Not an urgent movement.'

'In those steps, were there any words said by the younger man?' Hoy asked.

'No.'

'What happened?'

'Well, the gun went off, and a man dropped to the ground ... Almost simultaneous with the gun going off was that command again, "Drop the knife", but it was like the words were still in the air after the man had fallen to the ground.'

Hoy asked Greenhalgh if he heard Elijah roar.

'In all of his actions, he did them in silence. He certainly wasn't running hard towards the man with the gun and he had not raised the knife in any way,' he replied.

Greenhalgh said he did not hear swearing or see Elijah take the crucifix position.

Lisa Moor, Matthew Schaefer, and Ian Greenhalgh's evidence all came out in the first week of the inquest. Between them, they claimed Elijah moved a few centimetres, possibly away from Rich; that he ran at Rich; and that he 'loped' towards him. Moor said Elijah's lips moved, but she didn't hear if sound came out. Greenhalgh said Elijah didn't say anything, and Schaefer heard him shouting, 'Shoot me, shoot me.'

When the inquest reached its second week, counsel assisting the coroner, Chris Hoy, persisted with his line of questioning. Did Elijah move in the seconds before Rich fired? Did he swear and roar or taunt Rich to 'Shoot me, you cunt, shoot me'? Was Elijah holding the knife when Rich fired?

Andrew Strudwick said Rich and Elijah were walking along the lane when he first saw them. Strudwick worked for the Armidale council, and was heading towards Rusden Street. Elijah held a knife 'forward of his body with a straight arm … pointing to the ground,' Strudwick said.

Rich held a pistol in a two-handed grip and walked behind Elijah, pointing the gun at him. Strudwick heard Rich yell repeatedly, 'Put the knife down, get on the ground', but Elijah kept walking and held onto the knife. He looked over his shoulder a few times then pivoted on his heel. When Elijah faced Rich, Rich fired, Strudwick said.

Hoy asked if Rich fired as the turn happened, as it finished, or as Elijah faced him.

'As he faced him. I didn't see him take any other steps. I saw him turn and face the second male, who fired his pistol.'

Was there talk or yelling as Elijah turned — any words along the lines of 'Fuck you, shoot me, you fucking cunt?' asked Hoy.

Neither man uttered a word, said Strudwick.

What about something like a roaring? continued Hoy, and did Strudwick hear Elijah swear at all?

'Did you see him raise his arms out in what has been described a crucifix position? Take a lunge?' Hoy persisted.

Strudwick said he witnessed none of these things.

Ray Hood, the barrister for the NSW Police, asked Strudwick if it was possible that Elijah raised his arms crucifix-style, and Strudwick didn't see it because his line of sight was marred by bins and trees?

Strudwick agreed it was possible.

Hood took Strudwick to Ian Greenhalgh's evidence. Greenhalgh claimed that Rich's call to 'drop the knife' was still in the air after Elijah fell, Hood said, and arranged the order of his following words with care.

'It would be wrong to describe this — that the words of [Rich] were still in the air, to coin a phrase, when the shot was fired. Because [Rich] had said nothing immediately before the shot was fired. True, on your account?'

Correct, said Strudwick.

'Might you be wrong?' Hood asked.

Strudwick said it was possible he was.

The story tangled around itself like fence wire discarded in a paddock.

Elijah ran, Elijah walked, Elijah stood stock-still. He roared, he swore, he didn't say a word.

How was it possible for people who were there to see and hear completely contradictory things?

Ambrose Hallman, who also worked for council, described watching what looked like a play from his office window. A man on the street wearing a baseball cap asked a man on the footpath to get down on the ground.

The man on the footpath 'moved towards the man in the cap and that's when I heard the bang,' Hallman told the inquest.

Hallman's window was on Faulkner Street, on the first floor of a building that looked down along Cinders Lane as if it was a runway.

Hoy asked him how the man on the footpath had moved towards the other man on the street.

'In my statement, I said he sprinted ...' Hallman began, but the

Coroner pushed that recollection aside.

'I want to know now, when you really give it some thought now; what was it? Sprinting, running, stepping?' Jerram asked.

'It was an urgent movement towards the man with the cap. At the time, I said two steps, and I would still say there was at least two steps. They were not normal steps, not a standard pace.'

The distance between the men was about nine-and-a-half metres before Elijah moved, said Hallman. The whole thing lasted less than a minute.

Phil Stewart asked Hallman in cross-examination if Elijah fell forward onto the road when he was shot. Hallman said he did.

'Prior to that he'd been on the footpath? So the falling motion was onto the roadway — it wasn't as if Elijah was on the road and simply fell down where he stood?' Stewart clarified.

Hallman confirmed that that was correct. It appeared to him that Elijah had fallen from the footpath onto the road.

He did not witness Elijah roar or swear, or take the crucifix position, he told the court.

I started a tally card of witnesses as I worked my way through the brief and inquest notes. People who said Elijah moved versus those who said he was standing still. Those who believed Elijah was silent versus those who said he spoke before the shot.

By the sixth day of the inquest, there were four people in the column, 'Elijah moved'. Their evidence ranged from a possible step backwards to a lunging 'sprint' at Rich. The two men who said Elijah 'sprinted' or 'ran' reduced their assessment under cross-examination to two or three 'urgent' or 'fast pace' steps. There wasn't time for more than that, they decided on reflection.

There was one person in the 'Elijah was stationary' column. This person claimed Elijah did no more than pivot before Rich fired.

Three people said Elijah didn't make a sound. One saw his lips move but didn't hear words, while the fifth said Elijah shouted "Shoot me" half a dozen times.

Four moved versus one still. Three or four silent versus one shouting.

Joan Whitburn managed the Armidale office of the NSW Department of Premier and Cabinet. The building she worked in had just one entrance, through a pair of glass doors facing onto Cinders Lane.

On the afternoon that Elijah was shot, Whitburn heard angry shouting outside.

'It was loud enough to cause me concern and I thought someone was perhaps being abused', so she looked through the front doors. She saw two men in the lane, Whitburn told the inquest.

She hurried to an adjoining room and pulled the phone along the desk to a window where she had a clear view of the men. She told the Coroner she had a feeling she might need to call emergency services.

Whitburn judged she was ten metres away from the two men through the glass. Elijah faced her at ten or eleven on an imaginary clock face. Rich was at one o'clock, with his back to her on an angle. Rich stood with his legs apart and gun at chest height, poised to fire, she told the inquest.

When Hoy asked her to demonstrate how Elijah was standing, Whitburn raised her arms above her in a Y.

'You've indicated in your statement that there was shouting still going on,' Hoy said. 'Are you able to recall any of the words?'

The only thing she could remember was 'Stop', which came from the man holding the gun, Whitburn replied. She didn't hear anything from Elijah. What she remembered of the young man was his face.

'I just remember thinking that he had this, I don't know, it was a strange look on his face. It's difficult even now to put words to it, I just remember thinking it was an odd response, that's all I can say.'

'There's been some suggestions in material before us that [Elijah] said some words.'

Hoy apologised for what he was about to utter.

'The words were along the lines of, "Fuck you, shoot me, you fucking cunt". Did you hear anything [like that]?' he asked.

'No, I didn't.'

'There's a suggestion that he let out a roar and then advanced upon the police officer?' Hoy proffered.

Whitburn didn't hear the roar.

'Did you see him move at all towards the police officer?'

'No.'

Hoy read from the statement Whitburn gave police: '"I couldn't make out what was being shouted but it was loud. At that moment, the guy that had his back turned away from me fired the gun." Can you just describe what you saw at that moment?' Hoy pressed.

Joan Whitburn's words came out in clumps.

'Yes, and the gun was fired and I looked down to the phone, because I was still trying to call the emergency services and I had the phone to my ear — looked up and I saw the blood spreading at the front of the victim and then the victim fell.'

Counsel for the NSW Police, Ray Hood, suggested Whitburn could have missed what happened when she looked down at the phone to dial. Whitburn had already admitted that on her first attempt she misdialled Triple-0 and had to try again.

'Precisely at that time when your focus was so directed, what [Elijah] was doing at that point you would not be able to say conclusively?' Hood put to her.

Whitburn agreed. She told the court she did not notice Elijah's hands.

Hood suggested if her view of Elijah from the window was clear, she must have been able to see 'the totality of his body'.

'His face was what I was concentrating on. I saw his arms, and all I remember is his face and his torso and the black gun being held and saying out loud, "Don't shoot" to myself,' Whitburn replied. 'That's why I can't remember what he had in his hand.'

Phil Stewart told me later that the atmosphere in the court was thick with horror by the time Whitburn stepped down.

Stephen Swain spoke after Whitburn. He was fifty years old and worked for Armidale Council.

Swain sat around the middle of the list of seventy-two witnesses expected to give evidence. He told the court that on the day Elijah died, he stopped for a cigarette in Cinders Lane before he went back to work.

'Is there a particular spot that you ordinarily go to, to have a cigarette?' Hoy asked.

Near a tree on the south-eastern corner of the car park, Swain said, and he circled the place on a map handed up to him.

Swain's attention was taken by a male voice yelling, 'Elijah, put down the knife'. He looked in the direction of the voice and saw a young man walking towards him across the road. The young man dropped a jumper on the ground and veered through the car park back onto the footpath. This was when Swain spotted Rich behind Elijah. Rich called out at least three times, 'Elijah, put the knife down,' Swain claimed.

Elijah stopped and turned around. Rich yelled again, 'Get down on the ground; get on the ground now.'

Hoy asked what Elijah was doing at that stage.

'He just turned to face the police officer, and as best I can remember he was just standing there,' said Swain.

Hoy prodded him on, 'And what happened then?'

'Well, the police officer raised his pistol and he asked him twice to get down on the ground. And then he raised his pistol and fired a shot.'

Neither man moved before or after the shot, Swain said. He did not hear Elijah swear or roar or speak. It was Swain who lifted Elijah's jumper off the ground and hung it in the tree above his body.

The final tally of credible witnesses[6] was: Elijah moved two or three steps towards Rich — five people. Elijah turned to face Rich but did not move — four people. Elijah may have stepped backwards — one person. Elijah turned and ran at Rich — one person.

Nine people said Elijah did not speak. Two saw his lips move but didn't hear words. One swore Elijah shouted, 'Shoot me, shoot me'.

'I wonder if I could see my counsels assisting and perhaps Detective Inspector Olen as well?' the Coroner said when Swain finished speaking.

I imagined the looks that travelled the room. The barristers' beetled brows. The detectives' dry hands rasping against blue trousers. The dull patter of men's shoes, the rustle of Jerram's skirt, if she wore one. A line of dark suits leaving the room like mourners behind a coffin. The heavy wooden door closing on their backs. Darting glances, stifled coughs. The squeak of a door, and a procession of solemn faces returning.

From her position on the bench, Coroner Jerram addressed the room.

'Gentlemen at the bar table and everybody else in the courtroom — on the witness list which we began with there are witnesses from whom we have not heard. But it is my view that it isn't necessary at this point.'

Had his lawyers had time to warn Rich what was coming?

'It gives me no pleasure at all to say this, but having heard the evidence I have to date, over the last few days my view has formed more strongly, with each passing hour if I may say that, that an indictable offence has been committed.'

Mary Jerram explained her obligation to pass to the DPP any evidence she received that she believed was capable of convincing a jury that a serious offence had been committed. She was prepared to suspend Elijah's inquest and refer Rich to the DPP but 'as a matter of fairness'

---

[6] The Coroner indicated during hearings that a particular witness's evidence could not be afforded a great deal of credibility. A second, separate witness was unable to identify Senior Constable Rich from CCTV stills, and went on to ID another person as the shooting officer. The accounts of these witnesses are not included in the tally. Nor is the account of Mr W Browning, whose evidence that Elijah ran 13–15 metres towards Rich the Coroner ultimately found, 'was contradicted by all other evidence'.

she would give his legal counsel the opportunity to convince her not to. Brent Haverfield had until the following morning to gather and present his arguments.

At 9.30am the following day, Brent Haverfield told the Coroner he did not think there was a reasonable prospect a jury would convict his client, but he would not oppose the matter being referred to the DPP. His client believed it was in everyone's interests if the matter was dealt with as swiftly as possible.

With that, on 29 October 2010, Coroner Mary Jerram suspended Elijah's inquest and passed responsibility for what might happen next to the NSW Director of Public Prosecutions.

I made my first call to the Office of the Director of Public Prosecutions five months after the suspension of Elijah's inquest. Had a decision been made regarding charges against the officer involved? I asked. Not yet, said the woman who took the call.

We spoke almost weekly after that. Her manner was always friendly, but the answer never changed. When was a decision due? I asked one day.

The Office of the DPP didn't set deadlines, she said politely.

I slept for hours some days on the bed in my study, amongst the documents of Elijah's life and death. When the words began to blur or I couldn't bear Armidale's bleakness any longer, I would let the white sheets and heat remove me. I escaped my own pain in Elijah's story; sleep was all that erased them both.

I couldn't hurt or be hurt by anyone, when I was asleep. I couldn't disappoint or fail people. Unconscious, I was innocent. My internal loop of blame, of bitter hatred of people I normally loved, switched off. *They think I'm making it up to get attention, they wish I would snap out of it. They're all contributing to the world, where I'm just an angry, ugly scar. They must wish that I would disappear and leave their happiness undisturbed.*

I saw the world through a magnifying glass that only picked up on pain and failure. The single way to escape what it told me was to close my eyes and stay very quiet, so I kept friends and family at arms' length with the one technique I knew — silence.

11.

At the end of April 2011, I composed a letter to Rich, via his barrister, with Jeremy Holcombe's words ringing in my head: *I don't want a witch-hunt. He's flesh and blood like the rest of us.*

My reading of the evidence so far was that Rich had made a terrible mistake, but Jeremy was right: it didn't make him a monster. I had no idea how Rich was coping; how he felt about his decision to draw his gun now the chaos was over and he'd had time to reflect. What could Rich add to the picture in my head to help me understand his actions? Was he as certain now as he had been then that his life was in danger in Cinders Lane?

I told Rich I was a journalist. I had Elijah Holcombe's family's permission to write a book about the circumstances of Elijah's death, and I wanted to meet with him. I knew Rich's family would be grieving his experience as much as the Holcombes were grieving theirs; no story like this was simple, I wrote. If he were willing to speak to me, I would come to New South Wales to talk to him face-to-face; no strings attached.

A response arrived ten days later from Walter Madden Jenkins, Solicitors Conveyancers and Attorneys.

> As you acknowledge in your letter there are unresolved legal issues around Elijah's death and in the circumstances, it is not appropriate for our client to contact you.

It was signed by a partner of the firm, Ken Madden.

12.

A red balloon on Facebook showed I had a message waiting from Jeremy.

'Can you reacquaint me with your phone number, or give me a call?' it said.

It was 12 July 2011.

I leaned against the verandah rail, watching birds flit through the pandanus, while we talked. Tracey was seeing the oncologist in Sydney tomorrow to decide whether to have more chemotherapy. If the decision was yes, the treatment would take a few weeks. If it was no, she would move into the hospice straight away. The kids would go down and stay with her until the end.

'Can I call Quentin and Ivan and let them know?' I asked.

'Yeah, sure. She'd love to hear from you, too.'

'I'll definitely give her a call.' I was numb.

'Try her tonight or tomorrow afternoon — she's not good in the mornings,' he said pragmatically.

Tracey still saw Elijah's death and her own as 'part of one big sorry story', Jeremy told me. It was good to hear his voice. Strong and still edged with impatience.

I spoke to Tracey once before she moved into the hospice. Her Facebook page became the only way to send messages after that. Her sister Nira wrote daily updates. Friends and family left well wishes, and the kids posted photos of her in the hospice garden. Quentin and Ivan said that when they visited, Tracey was grey-skinned and heavily sedated.

When Quentin rang on 10 August to say Tracey had died that morning, I went straight to her Facebook page.

Tracey Stove-Holcombe
Tracey passed away this morning at around 4am at Sacred Heart Hospice. Tarney & Jeremy were with her & the girls had been with her during the day. She slept most of the day & was without pain or anxiety. She was aware of the outpouring of love & well wishes from you all.

An image flashed across my eyes of Tracey and Elijah in a joyful embrace. They pulled back to hold each other at arms' length and smile before gripping the other to their chest again.

David Sweeney called thirty minutes later. Tracey's funeral was in Wee Waa on Monday.

13.

I sat squashed beside my daughter in the back seat of my parents' car. The number of road trains roaring through the landscape increased the closer we drew to Wee Waa. My parents had offered to come with me and take care of Stella, so I could go to Tracey's funeral unencumbered.

A string of coloured lights between the front fence and a single row of rooms announced the Cottonfields Motel — Wee Waa's second-best accomodation. Cars were nosed up at nearly every door.

We dumped our bags and wandered down the pebble drive to ease the car-cramp from our bodies.

Sunday-evening quietness cloaked the town. The few cars that passed roared like jets against the stillness, straining as if they wanted to fly. Stella dawdled, picking dandelions and leaves. Paddy melons covered empty lots. Everything around me was familiar.

On the verandah of one fibro cottage, a couple sat staring at two tree stumps. There were moats around the stumps, filled with water. A love song blared from the radio of a truck trussed to each base with chains. The couple was waiting for the earth to soften so they could pull the tree roots out like worn teeth.

That night in our threadbare room, my parents formed the double bow they had made for forty years. Stella lay like a swaddled brick in her cot. I looked out the window at the coloured lights, listening to my family breathe. Tomorrow I would say goodbye to Tracey and meet Jeremy for the first time.

'Are you going?' the waitress asked, pen poised. She nodded at the church across the road and raised a thin-plucked eyebrow.

I was filling in time ahead of Tracey's funeral with a mug-a-chino in a main street cafe.

'I made the decision not to go,' the woman she was serving answered piously. It was a considered choice. Something about this funeral was undeserving or she was rationing her attendances, I wasn't sure which.

'Looks like we'll have another one soon,' the waitress stage-whispered and named another ailing local.

In the corner, near a fish tank, a husband and wife shared a pot of tea and glanced at their watches without speaking. When they stood and straightened their tie and skirt I followed them across the road.

The church was washed in bright winter sunlight. Men dressed in black talked in the shade of trees and smoked. Women gathered at the steps in stiff skirts, wafting a mix of perfumes.

I sidled into a pew behind men and women shaped like Tracey. They had to be her siblings; their broad backs and faces bookended clumps of freckled children.

A violinist started ABBA's *Dancing Queen* and laughter rippled through the crowd. Across the aisle, a few rows up, I recognised Jeremy's mop of hair. The woman beside him must be Fiona, and next to her would be Tarney, Laura, and Jordan.

Tracey's coffin lay before the altar, covered in white and scarlet flowers.

The woman beside me tapped my arm and smiled.

'I think I got the last one,' she whispered, handing me a funeral program. On the back was a photo of Tracey and Elijah, their arms around each other's necks, beaming.

Two years ago, the coffin up there was his.

Six hundred people chanted the Mass, singing and praying in one voice. Tracey's sister Nira gave the eulogy. She mapped Tracey's life from eight years old at Narrabri pool to the teenager who fell in love with

Jeremy. I was reminded of something Tracey said on our first meeting. She was lying on the couch after a round of radiation.

'I would never have envisaged after having such a happy life for the first half, to think, well, bang! … Now you are going to experience all of *this* and learn something from it,' was how she described the grief that had come to her.

Nira reached the second half of Tracey's life, the part when things 'went bang'. In the space of a few years, her mother died, her marriage collapsed, and her eldest son was shot.

'Two years ago, the devastating blow of Elijah's tragic passing was almost too much for Tracey to bear, and as strong as she tried to be, the sadness and stress and the uncertainty and confusion around the circumstances caused her so much pain, something had to give. The rest, as we say, is history and now we are here to say goodbye …'

Nira left the lectern, and one of the girls sitting with Jeremy walked down the aisle to the middle of the church. I checked the program; it was Jordan.

'Mum only asked for a couple of things today, and me singing this song was one of them,' she said into a microphone.

A clear, pure voice filled the church with a soaring *Over the Rainbow*. Jeremy hung his head and shook it from side to side. Tracey's brothers met Tarney at the altar. Together they lifted the white and scarlet coffin and carried Tracey out. The congregation formed a single line behind them and spilled out onto the steps and lawn.

Jeremy and Fiona were alone near the hearse when I got out. They stood close together, eyes wary, shoulders touching. Fiona smiled whenever people came near, and then smoothed her dark hair or ran her palms over her skirt. Jeremy was solid, like a woodcutter in a fairytale. People approached them occasionally, but they were mostly left alone. I took a deep breath and walked across the lawn.

'Um, hi Jeremy, I just wanted to introduce myself, I'm Kate. Kate Wild.'

Jeremy's face blanked then flooded with recognition. He held out a thick square hand.

'It's very good of you to come, Kate. It's great you're here.'

Would I join them at the cemetery, he asked. I flinched. If I wasn't imposing.

Of course not, he said. I was welcome.

I left with relief and joined the drift of people walking to their vehicles. The town clock chimed midday, and a line of cars snaked towards the cemetery. Half a block on, children from Elijah's old primary school bubbled along the footpath. A police car passed in the opposite direction.

The plot beside Tracey's was a riot of plastic flowers. My mind flew to scenes *Four Corners* had filmed of Jeremy and Tracey visiting Elijah's grave. The artificial flowers, the pink dirt, and the wooden cross were in front of me now, next to Tracey's open grave. Clods of dirt thudded against the coffin lid. A woman cut loose a clump of helium balloons tethered to a chair. They soared up, bobbing and dancing, and became a flock of shiny birds. No matter how high they rose, I could still make out their tails and wobbling heads.

Tracey was gone.

The dark assembly parted, and knots of people drifted off to visit relatives and friends, buried years before on similar days.

The bar of the Wee Waa Bowling Club was surrounded by poker machines and people. Women ferried cups of tea and men signalled relief in barks of laughter. Close-clipped greens lay like a picnic rug on the other side of wall-sized windows. It was every wake I had been to in a country town.

Jeremy and Fiona sat at the far end of the room with the woman who had played the violin. I clutched a lemon squash and scanned the crowd. Fiona walked towards me.

'Will you come and join us?'

I nodded, blushing.

She directed me to the seat beside Jeremy, and a screen lit up behind us with photos of Tracey. A skinny, flat-chested girl squinting in front of a garage; a young mum with her hands on the shoulders of a little boy; a woman in her forties, clowning in a long blonde wig. Jeremy turned in his chair and narrated each photograph, drawing me in to the circle at the table and further into the story of his family. He and Tracey grew up in front of us, and as the montage ran, Elijah appeared. Jeremy pointed him out each time.

The photos faded, and the afternoon became a swirl. Every conversation opened on Tracey, but they all turned to Elijah in the end. No one could separate Tracey's death from his.

Jeremy guided me towards his older sister, Liz, and left me with her near the bar.

'Sometimes I wonder if it's such a bad thing that there are people in that cemetery over there who only one or two people knew were mentally ill,' she said when the conversation turned to her nephew.

'The way we treat mental illness now is the same thing we did with sexual abuse twenty years ago — this whole thing of talking about it, telling everyone. We thought we would de-stigmatise the victims by getting it out of the shadows.'

Social workers, doctors, nurses like her thought it was a great idea at the time, Liz said. Why should the victims have to hide?

'But we had no idea how many people would come out and say "it happened to me". It was chaos. There weren't enough people with the training to know what to do.'

Mental illness was just the same. Talking about it didn't translate to enough help for everyone who needed it, she said bluntly.

'We're fucking it up, and you have to ask — since we decided disclosure was the way to go, have outcomes improved? If you look around and you look at Elijah's story, you have to say no.'

Was she saying it was better to stay quiet about mental illness than risk what might happen if people knew? That if Jeremy and Tracey hadn't told police about Elijah's mental illness he might still be alive? Or was she saying that Elijah's death was not just Rich's fault; that there were other failings?

Jeremy re-appeared. He wanted to introduce me to Laura. I followed him into the crowd, glad to escape the train of thought his sister had set running.

Laura was at a table of friends and cousins near the bar, drinking rum and Coke. She was short and buxom, with long dark hair and the inscrutable eyes of a madam in a saloon.

'Laura, this is Kate,' Jeremy said.

Laura looked me up and down and raised three fingers from her glass.

'Hi Laura, how are you?'

I cringed. *Fucking stupid thing to say.* Would it be too creepy if I friended her on Facebook to stay in touch, I asked to cover my stupidity.

'No, that's fine,' Laura said, turning back to her friends.

The room was emptying. I hadn't planned when or how I would spend time with Jeremy during my visit — I had just assumed it would happen after Tracey's funeral. Surrounded by grieving friends and family, I realised how small my claim on his time was.

'Jeremy, I know this might not be the right time, but I want to talk to you more about — everything,' I stumbled.

'What's wrong with now, while you're here?' he said. 'Give me a call after lunch tomorrow.'

I used the morning before meeting Jeremy to find a rental car. My parents were going home, and I would need my own transport for the next few days: I planned to drive to Armidale.

The nearest place I could rent one was in Narrabri. Mum and Dad offered to give me a lift before they left.

The woman behind the counter pointed to an electric-blue V8 Commodore with a spoiler parked out the front.

'It's one of our large cars, but we've given it to you for the price of a small one. We put a car seat in the back for the little one.' She smiled.

'Thank you. That's very generous. Really … kind,' I replied.

Dad put our luggage in the Commodore and handed me a tattered road map.

'Should get you back to Wee Waa pretty smartly,' he said, nodding at the spoiler. 'Safer than a small car.' His eyes twinkled.

We stopped at the bakery for a final coffee and sat at a table in the sun. Stella toddled on the footpath then bolted with a gleeful shriek. Dodging pedestrians on pudgy legs, she looked back to check that I was chasing.

I swept her up into my arms at the kerb. The ANZ bank stood across the road. Opposite it was the post office. It was the corner where Elijah had taken off in Jeremy's car almost two years ago. My heart clenched. Stella slipped from my grasp and lit off in a new direction. I caught her at the back steps of the bakery. A dark-haired police officer in uniform smiled and held the door for us. My eyes flicked to his badge: *John Ridley.* The officer who informed Jeremy that police had shot his son was buying his morning coffee and bun.

'Nice wheels.'

I was back in Wee Waa at the Cottonfields Motel. The young, beanie-d road worker walked around the Commodore in open admiration.

'Is that yours?'

'No, it's a hire car. It was all they had,' I mumbled.

I buzzed the tinted window down when I met Jeremy.

'I feel like an undercover cop.'

'You look a bit like one, too,' he laughed.

We met at the top of a sandy lane. Jeremy walked me to its end where Tarney, Jordan, and Laura lived in a cottage they called the Little Crooked House. It was a timber cubby half-sunken in the ground, with a simple garden and solar panels on the roof. Tarney played a steel-stringed guitar on the verandah. The girls were somewhere inside.

Jeremy pointed out a beautiful timber home next door, with sprawling verandahs and walls of windows that drew in light and air.

'That's where the kids grew up. Tracey and I built that house. She moved into the cottage when we sold it after we separated,' he said.

My image of the Holcombes changed in an instant. The homestead was a masterpiece. You could only look with pride at a structure that beautiful, particularly if you'd built it. I tried to imagine Elijah punching holes in its walls or Jeremy confined to one of its bedrooms, paralysed by depression. It was a struggle to conjure the images against the talent and love that had built what was in front of me.

'Come around the corner,' Jeremy said. 'I'm staying at Mum's house; we can talk there.'

Mary Holcombe welcomed me inside. She deposited Stella with a roomful of grandchildren and sent Jeremy to boil the kettle.

'You go downstairs into the garden,' Mary said, shooing us towards the door. 'We'll take care of the little one.'

We sat at a lace-metal table on the lawn. Jeremy rolled a cigarette. The corners of his eyes creased in calculation. His hair was longer now than in photos from the inquest. Dark, greying curls touched his collar. He vibrated like an animal hiding in the open, every muscle tensed for escape.

'I'm still waiting for the world to stop turning,' he said when I asked how the last twelve months had been.

He and Fiona were living in a tent in the mountains above Narrabri. They'd set up camp on New Year's Day, with plans to build a cabin and get back to what was essential.

'Plus we were broke and we didn't have anywhere else to go,' Jeremy quipped.

Fiona had quit her job before Elijah's inquest, and he hadn't worked for months, he said. When the rent on their house went up before Christmas, they figured they had nothing to lose.

The first eighteen months after Elijah died were pure survival, Jeremy said. He had three other children who needed him, and Fiona and her kids, too, plus family responsibilities. He had retreated to the mountains to survive.

'I'm quite a selfish person in a lot of ways. I like to spend a lot of time thinking. I like calmness and order. Tracey was the opposite. Chaos and colour, that was Tracey's life. Her greatest love was her children.'

'Who are they like — your kids?' I asked.

'Elijah used to tell Tracey, "I'm Dad, aren't I, Mum? I'm just like Dad" and in a lot of ways I s'pose that's true. But he was a more exaggerated version of me. Smarter than me, more musically talented than me, and to the extent of the parallels in our illnesses — certainly there are elements of paranoia in my thinking, but his brain was more exaggerated with that. I was out of action for a couple of years at one stage. I owe Tracey a great deal — she did everything.'

'How's your mental health now?' I asked.

Jeremy narrowed his eyes against the smoke of his cigarette.

'It was really bad at the second anniversary.'

David Sweeney was helping him and Tracey bring a compensation claim against the police, he said.

Sweeney had told me Tracey was suing, but he hadn't mentioned Jeremy. My stomach dropped.

'Part of the claim is you get a forensic psychiatric assessment,' Jeremy continued. 'Tracey did hers early for obvious reasons, and I thought about it and thought about it and I wasn't going to go.' But he did.

Jeremy leaned back in his chair, warming to the story.

'I sort of went there thinking, nah, I'm alright, you know? I'm not going to tell him I'm a victim, I'll just tell him the truth. I said, "We've moved out of town, and I'm squatting on some bloke's place, and I'm living in a tent, and it's not as romantic as it sounds." He said, "It doesn't sound romantic at all".' Jeremy laughed.

'He told me at the end I was a complete write-off. Apparently, I have all the symptoms of PTSD. I don't carry a phone, but when there's one there I'm constantly checking it for messages and checking Facebook to see what the kids are doing. Hyper-vigilant.'

I asked if he worried more about the other kids now.

'Constantly. Jordan went missing off Facebook for twenty-four hours and — God.' He shook his head. 'You're just scared all the time something else is going to happen. Waiting for the next one, which is a terrible way to live.'

I danced around the subject knotted in my stomach. Jeremy had sworn he wanted justice not retribution. Now he was suing.

'Do you think a particular outcome on the legal side of things will change anything for you?' I asked.

The legal process was so slow it was too frustrating to think about, he said. He just wanted people to know the full story.

'Which is why this story chose you, Kate,' he said, pinning me with a fierce gaze. 'And it did choose you, didn't it?'

I threw the dregs of my tea into the garden. White noise buzzed in my head.

'There were so many details that didn't come out even in the part of the inquest we had,' he said. 'The police stuffed it up from one end to the other. That's another reason I have consideration for Andrew Rich. The police made a victim of him, too, through laziness and lack of professional integrity.'

I reached towards safer ground.

'What were the biggest mistakes they made?'

Calling him instead of Tracey when Elijah walked into the Armidale Police Station, Jeremy said. 'Even though Tracey and I both told them to contact her if Elijah turned up anywhere. They made no attempt to call Tracey. Ever.'

Jeremy pushed his point home on the table with a stubby finger. He told Senior Constable Brett Allison at Narrabri station that he was driving to Canberra to look for Elijah that night. He said he might be out of range on the road; the police should call Tracey if they spotted Elijah or the car. Tracey gave Brett the same message twice, Jeremy insisted. Once in person and once in a phone message.

'But they didn't call her. Ever. That's the biggest thing. When Elijah turned up in Armidale, they called my home number and left a message that we got the next day when it was all over. Now that was like eleven o'clock that morning when he came into the police station, and my sister Priscilla lives in Armidale. She was right there. She could have gone around and picked him up and kept him safe until we got there. That's all that had to happen but they rang me and I wasn't there — they made no attempt to call Tracey.'

I checked the brief weeks later when I got home to see if he was right.

A timeline of calls from Narrabri station showed five attempts to reach Jeremy's mobile between 11.07am and 4.31pm on the day Elijah died. They all went through to voicemail; Jeremy's phone had run out of batteries by 10am that morning. Two calls were made to Jeremy's landline from Narrabri station, one at 11.08am, the other at 11.22am. But there was no record of an attempt to call Tracey Holcombe. The brief contained Elijah's COPS report as well, the internal police record that gave officers across the state access to information about Elijah's disappearance. It contained no instructions to call Tracey rather than Jeremy if Elijah or the car were found.

The person who would know for certain if anyone in Narrabri had tried to contact Tracey was Senior Constable Brett Allison, the officer who took Tracey and Jeremy's statements when they reported Elijah missing. When I checked his evidence from the inquest, I felt sick.

Chris Hoy showed Brett Allison a page of notes.

'That's your handwriting on that page?' Hoy asked.

'It looks similar to my handwriting, yes,' Allison replied.

'Anyone else at Narrabri that writes like you?'

'I hope not.'

'So that's your handwriting and your notes. No criticism, but it seems evidence [sic] the number was incorrectly noted as to Mrs Holcombe? Did you understand that?'

'No, I didn't, sorry', Allison replied.

'Did you understand that, in fact, after Elijah was located, efforts were made to contact Mrs Holcombe with the number that was recorded — her mobile number — and it was apparently, with great respect to you, incorrect, and she was therefore unable to be contacted?'

'Sorry, you're saying that I've —'

'Written it down wrong? Yes.'

'Well, I —'

'That's the first you've heard of that?'

'Yeah, exactly.'

'Well, I am sorry to be the bearer of that news.'

According to Chris Hoy, police couldn't contact Tracey because Brett Allison took her number down incorrectly. I couldn't find any evidence in the brief that police from Narrabri *or* Armidale had tried to reach her, so why Hoy was so certain it was Brett Allison's fault, I didn't know. In a town the size of Narrabri, where Tracey had lived since she was a kid, if police knew they had a wrong number for her, it shouldn't have taken long to find the right one.

Tracey's home and mobile number were on Elijah's missing-person report, but they were redacted in the brief. Wherever the truth lay, Jeremy's point held. Police made little or no attempt to reach the person they were asked to call — Elijah's mother. Wee Waa's population barely topped 1600. A call to the pub or newsagency would have turned up someone who knew how to reach her. If the police had tried a little harder, if they imagined for a moment Elijah was their kid, he might still be alive.

Instead, when Tracey called the Narrabri station to check if they had any news on the afternoon Elijah died, they told her they had nothing. Elijah had been dead more than an hour by then, but the Armidale police hadn't let Narrabri station know.

Inspector John Ridley in Narrabri, the holder of the bakery door, had a call at 4pm to say Elijah had been killed by an Armidale police officer. Tracey Holcombe had barely hung up the phone, but no one called her back. It took Ridley fifteen minutes to reach Jeremy on Fiona's phone — a tactic no one else had thought to try all day. Tracey Holcombe did not receive a call from police until late that evening.

'What happened to Elijah was a catastrophe and catastrophes don't happen from any one thing, they happen from a chain of events,' Jeremy said in his mother's garden. 'And you know, I made some horrendous mistakes that contributed to that chain of events.'

It wasn't just Rich who let Elijah down, he pointed out. Rich was entitled to the presumption of innocence.

'But so is Elijah, and that's the bit I have trouble with.'

He looked to the sky and exhaled.

'There have been times I think where we were really naive.'

'About what?'

'Being seen to not be angry. Maybe people think that's because we knew Elijah was at fault or something. It wasn't that at all. We had to put out there what others didn't, and what they didn't put out there for Elijah was empathy and compassion. The world doesn't need any more anger and hate, it just needs empathy and compassion. So, you know, if you're going to talk the talk you got to walk the walk.'

So what is the compensation claim about? People don't sue out of compassion.

I quashed the thought.

'Did you really shake Rich's hand at the inquest?' I asked.

'Yeah, I did. Her Honour gave them the opportunity to make some sort of representation on why it shouldn't be suspended, and his counsel said that he'd directed them to not prolong it. That was sort of the excuse we had on the last day to go over, and I just shook his hand and thanked him for not extending it. But it was also about facing your monsters and facing your demons, and you know, he's not a monster, he's a living breathing human being. He's just another victim and product of this totally stuffed up society we live in, which is why I'm going to live on a mountain.'

'Your heart must have been racing walking up to him though,' I said.

Jeremy held my gaze. He reached into his tobacco pouch and didn't answer for a long time while he rolled another cigarette.

'No, I'm medicated,' he said finally. 'I've been on anti-depressants for ten years. I increased the dose to get through Elijah's funeral, and I've increased the dose to get through Tracey's funeral, and I increased the dose to get through the inquest. And I'm not very comfortable with that, but you've got to stay on your feet.'

A breeze sprang up, and birds left the tree above us. Was this offering of hands an act of true compassion or just a demonstration in a public place? Jeremy spoke about justice and forgiveness, but he was asking the police for money for his son's death. Riven with doubt, I pushed.

'It's got to be one of the most confronting things a person can do, approaching Rich like you did.'

'Yeah, shook the hand of the man who shot your son, I know all that. But I feel sorry for him. I've gone over and over and over this about the police, and I think the most honest criticism I can make of the police I have struck through all of this is they are dumb. They are indoctrinated with this blue culture and they just can't think for themselves anymore.'

'Was he there when you walked through Cinders Lane with the Coroner and lawyers?' I asked. 'I saw the photo of you and Fiona in the papers.'

Jeremy went still again. 'It was horrendous.' His voice was hoarse. 'I thought about it a long time. Eventually, I came to the decision that I had to do it.'

'Why?' I asked.

'I dunno. To see the things that were the last things he saw. I still wonder, too, you know, was he running down there — you got to know 'Lije to figure this out — was he running away in fear or running down there being sort of a cocky smart arse? 'Lije was sort of like that, you know.'

Ants marched in a crooked line across the table.

'The most horrible part to me was — and I was thinking about it the other day with Tracey when I was there when she died the other night — Elijah died alone with his head in a gutter. And there was never a person on this earth who deserved that less than Elijah. That's the bit that gets me,' he whispered.

'If things had turned out differently, do you think about the possibility his illness may have gotten worse?' I asked.

Jeremy nodded.

'I used to console myself that 'Lije had it all, but he didn't have it all very long; and he did. He had great friends, he was very talented, he was popular, and he mostly enjoyed life.'

The gaps between Jeremy's answers grew longer.

'His moments of despair were few and far between — of real despair, real unhappiness. But I think, yeah, it may well have been the best for him,' he said.

Mary came downstairs holding Stella's hand. She wanted an apple, sultanas, a story, a crocodile — whatever it took to have my attention back.

I turned the dictaphone off. Mary said something that I didn't quite hear.

'I'm actually finding it cathartic, Mary. It's my favourite subject,' Jeremy replied.

He agreed to come to the hotel that night once Stella was asleep, to see if there was anything left to say.

We sat at a table outside my room at the Cottonfields Motel and crossed our arms against the cold. We spoke of nothing but Elijah.

Jeremy thought about him daily. He saw Elijah everywhere: in crowds; in young men the same age; when a police car passed; and when he opened the kitchen drawer and saw the bread knife.

In summer, Wee Waa and Narrabri's cotton farms flood with uni students and backpackers making holiday money. A string of young Frenchmen had found their way up to Jeremy and Fiona's mountain campsite that year.

'All that age you know, twenty-four, twenty-five,' Jeremy said, shaking his head. 'And I often think — this is what you should have been doing, Elijah, travelling the world and being free.'

Memory was precious but painful. The second anniversary of Elijah's death had been far harder than the first.

'The anticipation leading up to it really caught me by surprise. In May, the Wee Waa show was on, and the way the light changes at that time of year, and the days are getting colder and shorter. It was horrible, anxious. I was a mess.'

He ground his cigarette into the soup tin ashtray and clamped his hands under his armpits.

'Sometimes now I worry that my memories of him, of our last conversation, are fading,' Jeremy confessed, and he told me the things he wanted to remember. Elijah as a toddler, pointing to a colourful parrot and telling his father he used to be a bird. The two imaginary friends, both called Billy, whom Elijah saved seats for at the dinner table and on car trips. The whip-smart teenager who regularly mispronounced words, including the name of his new hero, Socrates, which Jeremy said he pronounced 'Sew-Crates'.

'I said, "I think you might mean Socrates 'Lije," and that was the last time I knew more than he did.' Jeremy laughed. Our conversation petered out. Stella was asleep. The Cottonfields' weekend guests were gone.

Jeremy checked I knew the way to Armidale before he said goodbye. From my window, I watched his silhouette pass the string of coloured lights on the driveway.

14.

I buckled Stella into the bright-blue Commodore and waved goodbye to the Cottonfields. My father's tattered map lay on the seat beside me, too worn to follow, but I had found a use for it.

Two open-faced men in their twenties or thirties greeted me at the counter of the Narrabri Police Station. I unfolded the map and asked for directions. I was on my way to Armidale, I explained. Together we pored over various routes, comparing road conditions. A female officer joined the conversation. They were helpful and patient, young and strong and happy to repeat instructions, which I scribbled in the margins of the map. They were sure I would reach Armidale in four hours if I went over the ranges.

One of them might have been Brett Allison; they all could have known the Holcombes. But no one was wearing a name badge, and I didn't ask. I went because I wanted the police to be people in my mind, even if these weren't the right people. I wanted faces and voices in my head, and to know with my own senses that if I came to them in distress, they would help.

They would. I wrapped my daughter's pudgy legs around my hip, thanked the Narrabri police for their help, and left.

The Commodore growled up the Nandewar Range under the grey clouds of a cold snap. Lichen-spattered boulders turned their backs against the rain. I burrowed with them, hunkering deeper as I drove.

Armidale was bleak and prosperous. The cold had metal teeth. I drove the streets in search of the places that marked Elijah's last day. Trim Street by the nursing home, where he slept the night in Jeremy's car; the hospital; the police station; the camping store and Caffiends café. Then Cinders Lane, where everything had ended.

Trim Street was ugly. The trees were as bare as the day Elijah had parked here — I knew this from photos in the brief. The nature strip was nude, and the light-brick townhouses had aluminium attic windows peeping from their roofs like periscopes.

It was a poor place to hide and a bleak place to rest, whichever Elijah had meant to do. No canopy of trees or ramshackle gardens to look at. No sounds of a creek or playground nearby. Anything out of place would have screamed its presence. I pictured Elijah hiding, waiting for the street to clear before he stepped out of his father's car. The ground wet with dew, his breath visible in the air.

I swung the car around and followed Elijah into town.

The window of the camping store was filled with one-man tents and Gore-Texed mannequins. Rich offered Elijah the car keys here. The parking inspector said Elijah refused them, and Rich chuckled to himself and called out, 'I'm an undercover cop, mate, you're obliged to stop.'

Willow Grieves rode his pushbike along this footpath. He almost leapt off his bike onto Elijah. He almost broke the thread, but he changed his mind.

It took two minutes, walking slowly, to cross from the camping store to the muffler shop across the road, around the corner and into Beardy Street Mall: the path Elijah and Rich had taken. Running at the speed they had, it would take less than a minute. From the camping store to Caffiends and through to Cinders Lane was three sides of the same block: no more than five hundred metres, I guessed. I timed the walk twice, unable to comprehend how things had escalated so quickly in such a short time.

Caffiends was run-of-the-mill for a large country town. The sort of place uni students ate wedges with sour cream and waited tables on the weekend. I pushed Stella's pram past the outdoor tables and through the automatic doors.

The café was two thirds full on the day Elijah and Rich ran through, but today it was almost empty. Pine kitchen tables and chairs formed a clear corridor to the kitchen.

I asked the waitress if Sonia Stier still owned the business.

'She's gone to Tasmania,' she replied, plonking a sandwich with a side of hot chips in front of me. From what she was prepared to say, a breakup was behind the sale of Caffiends, not the fact it had been a crime scene.

I couldn't face asking her if I could walk through the kitchen, so I left and pushed Stella's pram through the mall. I found the alley that led to Cinders Lane. It was the same passageway I had watched figures emerge from on the CCTV vision in Phil Stewart's office.

Walking into Cinders Lane was like returning to a childhood landscape as an adult. Everything was smaller than the images in my mind. It was a pitiful patchwork of concrete and asphalt; the forgotten back-end of a collection of businesses. The place Elijah died was somewhere to park before you opened for the day, a service lane, a shortcut to other places. I walked its length in shock and fled to our hotel.

I stood in the shower until the whole room filled with steam. The staff had put out a cot for Stella, but I pulled her into my bed. The horror had seeped into my bones.

I woke in the dark. Stella rubbed a fist against her nose and her hand uncurled to rest against my face. I turned towards the force field of her warmth and tried to get back to sleep.

The next day was brilliant-cut. It had rained overnight. The sky was bright blue, and magpies chased worms in puddles.

I left the car at the hotel and set out behind the pram. Pushing hard in the direction of the police station, I had a flash of clarity. Twelve months ago, the Armidale papers had reported that Rich 'remained on duty'. What if he was still in Armidale? I could walk into the station and ask for him.

But wouldn't you leave in his situation? I thought, turning the corner into Faulkner Street. Imagine walking to the mall for lunch every day, past the alleyway to Cinders Lane. The surreptitious looks in the street and pub. Reminders everywhere. On the other hand, there was nothing to stop Rich going to work — he hadn't been suspended.

Armidale's new police station stood beside the old one on a corner block. The sleek, tall stack and the squat brick square were connected by a cube of glass, like mismatched conjoined twins.

The door in the towering facade was tiny. Black glass slid back on a flight of steep stairs. I imagined Elijah climbing them into the lion's mouth.

I want to make a confession.

I abandoned Stella's pram at the bottom of the stairs and hoisted her to my hip.

A single row of plastic chairs faced a polished counter at the top. No worn timber, no glass windows, just tile and concrete surfaces.

'Can you tell me if Andrew Rich is still working here?' I asked the woman behind the counter.

'Yes, but he's not on today.'

'Would you mind if I left a note for him?'

She pushed a pen and paper across the counter.

Asking was so simple. I might have been sitting in Rich's living room this morning if I'd made this trip a day ago. I retreated to the bottom of the stairs and wrote the date at the top of the page beneath the watchful eye of security cameras, 12 August 2011. I was in Armidale for the day, I said. I appreciated Rich's decision not to talk while legal matters were still in play, but I wanted to offer the chance to match a face to the person who had written once before. I left my number and encouraged him to call. I hoped he didn't mind me writing; I would be in touch again.

I had no idea of Andrew Rich's character. I had his words on a page from the statement he gave police, but without his voice behind them to signal meaning, we were both at a disadvantage. How could I judge him truthfully when the place in my head where his story should be was a silent, empty room?

15.

By the middle of the following month, almost a year after the suspension of Elijah's inquest, the Director of Public Prosecutions had still not decided whether Rich should be charged.

'I don't understand why it's taking so long,' I said in one of my regular calls.

'We take whatever time is necessary to treat each case with the seriousness it deserves. We follow a very thorough process,' replied the woman from the DPP who I spoke to every fortnight.

'Which is what?' I snapped.

My phone-friend explained with tight civility that a solicitor from the DPP would read the brief, the inquest transcripts, and a report on the Coroner's view of the evidence. When they were finished, they would hand the evidence and their opinion of it to a second solicitor, who would repeat the process. The third and final person in the chain was the Director of Public Prosecutions, who made the final decision on whether or not to recommend charges.

'You can appreciate, especially with a case like this, the process can take a long time,' she said.

'Which solicitor is it with now — one, two, or three?' I asked.

She wouldn't say.

'Maybe it's a sign that they're taking it seriously if it's going through three lawyers?' I said to Phil Stewart on the phone.

'Bullshit. It's a disgrace they're taking so long,' he replied.

Another coronial inquest began that month into the death of a different mentally ill young man shot by the police.

Adam Salter was shot in November 2009, five months after Elijah. The incident made headlines because the officer involved had shouted 'taser, taser, taser', but had pulled out her pistol instead and fired, killing the 36-year-old.

Police had responded around 9am to a Triple-0 call in Sydney's southwest. Adrian Salter said his son was in the kitchen, stabbing himself with a large knife.

Four officers attended the Salter's house. Adam's father and paramedics had taken the knife away from him and subdued Adam by the time they arrived. They walked into the kitchen to 'pools of blood on the floor and blood on the door and walls', police told the Coroner. Adam was on the kitchen floor, covered with blood from self-inflicted wounds.

The police took Adam's father out of the kitchen and left a young probationary constable in his place to 'keep an eye on' Adam while the senior officers went outside to talk.

Once they were gone, Adam made a lunge for the sink. Adrian Salter rushed in to stop him, but Adam brushed his father and the paramedics aside. He grabbed the knife and began to stab himself in the neck. Ambulance officers said they called for help, but it wasn't until a paramedic screamed, 'Can we get the fucking cops in here!' that Sergeant Sheree Bissett and the other officers came running, one paramedic said at Adam Salter's inquest.

Like the witnesses in Cinders Lane, accounts of what happened next fell into starkly different camps. Sergeant Bissett said she ran into the kitchen and saw Adam Salter at the sink, stabbing himself. Probationary Constable Aaron Abela was on Adam's left, and a paramedic was on Adam's right.

'[A]nd he's got the knife in his right hand … and Aaron is wrestling him,' Bissett told investigators. Constable Abela had hold of Adam Salter, she claimed, and they were struggling, getting nearer to her as they wrestled. 'At that stage [the knife] just swung around towards him [Abela] so I thought he [Adam] was going to stab him and kill him ... so I've just drawn my gun, gone "taser, taser, taser" ... and so I shot him ...'

Why Bissett cried 'taser, taser, taser' and then used her gun was a puzzle. Bissett swore she meant to use her pistol, and the call of 'taser' was a warning to other officers to clear the area. The Coroner concluded it was likely she chose her pistol by mistake, but there was no evidence to prove the point either way.

Paramedics who were in the kitchen said that, far from making an assessment of the situation before she drew her gun, Bissett responded to their calls for help by running in with her pistol raised ready to fire. They said Adam Salter and Constable Abela made no physical contact, and Adam's attempts at harm were directed only at himself.

Adam Salter's inquest ran for six days. Coroner Scott Mitchell released findings within a week.

'At best, the police intervention was an utter failure,' Mitchell concluded. 'Police killed the person they were supposed to be helping.'

'[Police] left Adam Salter in the care of a young, inexperienced and on the evidence of Adrian Salter and the paramedics, ineffective and unresponsive officer ... there is very strong evidence that [Sergeant Bissett's] description of the risk posed by Adam Salter is exaggerated, real doubt as to whether she gave any consideration to an appropriate means of dealing with Adam Salter, real doubt as to whether shooting him was justified and whether a less drastic means of appropriately dealing with him was not available. Most importantly there is a very strong flavour of confusion and mistake, and given her cry 'taser, taser, taser', I think it is more likely than not that Sergeant Bissett mistakenly chose her Glock having intended to employ her Taser.'

My heart curled in my chest as I read his words. It was the stuff of nightmares for everyone — Adam, his father, the paramedics, and police. How could anyone find their way back to wholeness after an experience like this and such damning findings?

Lawyers I knew gossiped freely about the case. Behind closed doors, police and some in the legal profession said Coroner Mitchell hadn't listened to the evidence; he had come to the case with his mind already made up. What was a police officer supposed to do when faced with a psychotic person wielding a knife in a tiny space? Adam Salter was dangerous; Bissett had done the only thing she could, police insisted.

In newspaper reports, Adam's sister described him as 'a genuinely great guy; loving, gentle, and kind.' His father said Adam had never been violent before the day he died. I believed Adam's family, but I couldn't think of a word other than 'violent' to describe a young man stabbing himself until blood covered the kitchen. If this 'gentle and kind' man had gone to such distressing lengths in his first-ever episode of violent behaviour, what did it say about how dangerous might Elijah have been in Cinders Lane?

I thought of Allison, whom I had found and lost in a single phone call. Elijah's wife knew him in a way his family didn't. She had noticed changes in his behaviour even before he called Tracey from the train station. What did she think about what he might be capable of when he was gripped by delusional fear?

I found her email address and sent a brief message. I believed she already knew from Tracey that I was writing about Elijah, and I would value the chance to speak to her to understand Elijah and his illness from her perspective, I wrote.

Elijah's diagnosis from Concord Hospital was in the inquest brief.

> A first episode of psychosis characterised by persecutory delusions and paranoia with possible psychotic depression and possible schizophreniform.

I looked up 'schizophreniform' in the bible of psychiatry, the

Diagnostic and Statistical Manual of Mental Disorders (DSM).

A schizophreniform diagnosis required at least one of four symptoms to persist for more than a month: delusions, hallucinations, disorganised incoherent speech, or a reduced ability to feel emotion. If any of the symptoms persisted for six months, the diagnosis automatically changed to schizophrenia, the manual explained.

I thought of Tracey's words to Jeremy when Elijah called her from the train station the first time. 'I think our boy might be a bit schizophrenic.'

Between his admission at Concord Hospital and taking Jeremy's car ten months later, Elijah's delusions and paranoia had persisted. His symptoms did not abate — they worsened. I needed more than a textbook to understand the complexity of a psychiatric diagnosis.

I contacted Dr Olav Nielssen, a forensic psychiatrist in Sydney whose doctoral thesis was on violence committed by people during first psychotic episodes. Nielssen had also recently given evidence in the trial of Antony Waterlow, a 42-year-old man with schizophrenia who had murdered his father and sister.

In late 2011, I stood at the base of a sandstone fortress in Sydney's eastern suburbs. I stepped into a glass lift and was carried to a house perched on the hill. The arresting figure of Olav Nielssen waited in the garden. Thick forearms, full lips, and thick dark brows beneath a shock of silver hair. He was a Norwegian herdsman dressed in board shorts. Nielssen led me to his study, where tea and slabs of dark chocolate waited on a tray. Sydney Harbour sparkled out the window.

I sketched Elijah's story for him. 'What I want to know is whether it's possible to predict someone's likelihood for violence based on their diagnosis and past behaviour,' I said.

Olav Nielssen leaned back in his chair and studied me with the gaze of a man who unpicked minds for a living. 'It's very hard to predict human behaviour because behaviour is always going to be an interaction between a person's tendencies and their circumstances. It's the circumstances that produce violence, which we can't predict.'

He offered me the plate of chocolate.

'For example, if you're paranoid out in the country and there's no one around, there can be no violence, but you might still be acutely frightened. Then if someone turned up you might be frightened of *them*, which could lead to violence. Fear is the main driver of violence by the mentally ill. Fear caused by frightening, delusional beliefs.'

I told him about Elijah's fear of police, how he took his father's car, walked into a police station, did a runner from the hospital, and picked up a knife in a café before he was shot.

'People who are paranoid — they jump to conclusions the rest of us wouldn't jump to. Often, it's informed by hallucinatory voices that conduct a narrative to explain things. What typically happens is that the hallucinations will inform you about the dangers you face …'

I interrupted. 'Elijah's parents said he didn't hear voices,' I said with confidence. 'I brought his psychiatric reports with me. If you looked at them, could you tell me what sort of behaviour you'd expect he might be capable of?'

Nielssen took the reports and scanned them, flicking back and forth between the pages.

'Well, it looks like he had bizarre delusions, so it's not just a transient drug-induced condition; it's the full syndrome of a proper schizophrenia-like illness. And I know you say he didn't have hallucinations, but quite often people don't recognise how they're reaching their delusional ideas. They don't recognise the way in which the ideas come into their mind. So again, I wouldn't rule out that he might have had evolving hallucinations,' he said gently.

Frightening delusions that evolved alongside events, and which incorporated people the person came in contact with, could be particularly dangerous, Nielssen said. The length of time Elijah was admitted to hospital and the level of medication he was on weren't insignificant, he added. Most people didn't stay in hospital for more than a couple of weeks, or require such big doses. I had thought of

Elijah's mental illness until now as mid-range in seriousness, but Olav Nielssen's assessment of the reports suggested I had underestimated how sick Elijah was.

'So what would you expect Elijah's behaviour to be like, and the path of his illness, from what you've read?' I asked.

He reached for the teapot and poured us each a cup. Nielssen based his answer on Elijah making a decision to stop his medication.

'You'd typically expect the same kinds of delusions to return once you stop the medication. But they can evolve according to your circumstances ... so you see events in your surroundings and you assume in your illogical way that they relate to you. You see a certain car passing by and you interpret it to mean you're being followed. As well as illogical thinking, there's emotional regulation. So people can get angry very easily, which you can understand if they believe you are a threat. The capacity for self-awareness is also impaired. So you try and explain, "You know, I think you're having a psychotic episode", but their ability to logically interpret what you're saying is diminished.'

I asked if that meant that descriptions of Elijah as calm and responsive earlier in the day had no real relevance to how he might have behaved by the afternoon.

Nielssen nodded. 'You do see that a lot. People who are psychotic can be quite labile, depending on how they interpret what is going on around them.'

'Which means it isn't fair to say "Elijah had never done anything like this before, and he was calm and cool all morning, so he couldn't have run at the officer with a knife, roaring, in Cinders Lane"?' I checked.

'No,' Nielssen replied.

'Is there any evidence that mentally ill people are more dangerous than others when they're in crisis?' I asked.

Nielssen didn't hesitate.

'You can't deny it; 8.8 per cent of homicides are committed by people with psychotic illness, who comprise about 0.5 per cent of the population. They're grossly over-represented in other serious violence that includes violence to yourself, they have a very high rate of suicide, especially suicide using violent methods and that can include suicide by cop, of course. So yes, the mentally ill obviously are more dangerous because they're irrational, and often frightened. Rational people wouldn't disobey the cops because it's a serious offence and you get a hiding.'

Piecing together what Nielssen had told me, the psychotic elements of Elijah's illness had the potential to make him dangerous. The more frightened he was, the more irrational his thoughts and actions were likely to be. Where Jeremy and Tracey saw patterns in Elijah's behaviour, strangers who came across him in crisis were more likely to see him as unpredictable. Their fear and his when Elijah was in crisis made everyone more vulnerable — including Rich. Elijah's natural tendency to non-violence — flight rather than fight under duress — could be overturned if circumstances changed in a way that fed into his delusions; and all of this could happen very quickly.

'Tell me about Antony Waterlow,' I said, changing the subject to Nielssen's recent court appearance. I wanted to know what the catalyst had been for this psychotic man to kill members of his family.

'Basically, it was a medical bungle,' Nielssen said matter-of-factly. 'A classic example of missed opportunities to intervene and treat a person who had left lots of hints that violence might occur. He had been unwell for seven or eight years. There'd been lots of warnings of him being angry, frightened, holding grievances against his family and making threats involving weapons. There were clear signals as to what his diagnosis was and the treatment he required all the way along.'

Antony did not accept he was ill, and refused to take medication. His delusions were about his parents and siblings ruining his life, Nielssen explained. They were chronic and persecutory in nature so every time he confronted his family, Antony would end up in a violent rage. His family had asked numerous times over the years that he be scheduled and forcibly treated, but for one reason or another it never happened.

Nielssen had been consulted by one of Antony's doctors eighteen months before the final crisis, and on the information provided to him, he had recommended that Antony be admitted to hospital involuntarily for treatment. The admission didn't happen.

When I read the coronial findings into the death of Antony's father and sister, mention was made of Antony's ability to mask his illness and deceive people with his charm.

The reason Antony's doctors gave for not admitting him to hospital against his will was that whenever they saw him, the threat he presented was not grave enough to justify the move. These judgements were necessarily subjective, Coroner Paul MacMahon said in his findings. He took care not to criticise the decision not to schedule Antony, but he recommended changes to the *Mental Health Act*.

> So that it expressly states that in determining whether to schedule a mentally ill patient ... the term 'for the person's own protection from serious harm,' should be understood to include the harm caused by the mental illness itself.

MacMahon also wanted to see emotional harm included in the equation with physical damage when someone was assessed for their ability to inflict 'serious harm' on themselves or others.

'Is there any way to predict whether someone like Elijah would end up doing what Antony Waterlow did?' I asked Olav Nielssen.

The two men's delusions were quite different, Nielssen said. Elijah appeared to have acted out of fear; Antony was tormented by rage based in a belief that his family was ruining his life.

'With fear, it's fight or flight. So Elijah's cornered, so he picks up a bread knife. But it's possible if he was allowed to run, he'd have been OK. The same might have applied to Roni Levi on Bondi Beach or some of the other people who've been shot by the police over the years — if they'd been given some room,' Nielssen theorised.

We were back to nebulous immeasurable circumstance.

Were there key constructive things police could do when they were faced with someone who was highly psychotic and frightened? I asked.

'From my experience, dealing with the mentally ill brings out the best in the police, and they're really quite good at it,' he replied mildly. 'I mean, they're frontline mental health workers.'

I asked if he thought the police approached people with mental illnesses differently. The police force was not a homogenous group, Nielssen pointed out.

'You've got everything from the school bully to the bleeding-heart social workers, so it depends who turns up on the day. Do you get these Bondi Beach shooters who are out on the town the night before or do you get someone who has a schizophrenic sibling and really understands it? This is the luck of the draw. From what I understand, they are trained to get command of the situation, when perhaps being able to negotiate from a distance would be the safer option.'

I brought up a complaint police had raised in their criticism of *Four Corners* — that when they went to the trouble of taking a mentally ill person to hospital, the same person was often allowed to go home or leave because medical staff would not admit them.

'Is that a fair complaint?' I asked.

'I reckon our mental health system is very inefficient and they've got a good case,' he replied.

Australia's mental health system was in crisis, Nielssen stated calmly.

'I think one of the main reasons is that it just hasn't grown with the population of Australia. Australia's gone up by 50 per cent in population without a relative increase in mental health beds since the mid-1980s.'

His reflections sent me down another rabbit hole. After ten minutes of googling at home that night, I could have filled a suitcase with reports on the crisis he had pointed to.

A senate committee report from 2006 said Australia had gone from having 30,000 acute-care psychiatric beds in the 1960s to 6,000 in

2006.[7] Australia's population had doubled in that time. Much of the reduction in bed numbers was due to the closure of asylums in the 1980s and 90s, which were replaced with services based in the community.[8] More than a decade after asylums began to close, a national inquiry by the Human Rights Commission found government money saved by shutting institutions had not been transferred at sufficient levels into community mental health care. Clinicians and consumers had been crying foul for years about shocking levels of under-funding and the tragic impact it was having on people's lives.[9]

By the early 2000s, despite some systemic change, the story was still the same.

> The dream of closing psychiatric institutions and moving towards community based care has turned into a nightmare. Community care is under resourced and integrated services are lacking. Too many people are denied treatment and slip through the gaps.
>
> *Advocacy group for carers,*
> *2005 report by the Australian Medical Association (AMA).*

The explanation every report gave for the gap in services and quality of community care was a lack of funding to meet the volume of need.

'The public housing estates that are real no-go areas for police are full of people with mental illnesses that aren't being treated,' Nielssen told me.

The reasons why were myriad, but one was that community facilities and mainstream hospitals didn't have room for everyone who needed care. Accounts of people being discharged too early were scattered through the reports.

---

7 A National Approach to Mental Health 2006

8 2005 AMA report

9 2005 AMA report

Psychiatrists have said to me that they are constantly in this ethical dilemma where they have somebody who is really sick and needs admission to hospital and they have somebody in hospital who is still sick but not as sick as the one who needs to come in. They have to juggle and take these risks ... They send them out into the community where there are no supports for them. [10]

Some people who knew they were heading for a crisis asked for help, but there was none to be had, the 2006 senate report expounded:

Some of the most devastating evidence presented ... told the stories of those who knew they had become unwell, had tried to seek hospital admission, been denied and subsequently sought to harm themselves or others. There were many instances of death or injury that were easily attributed to not being admitted.

Many of the deaths referred to were suicide, but others involved police. Nielssen explained that in 1990, legislators raised the threshold for admitting someone to a mental health facility involuntarily. The change was designed to protect the patient's human rights, including the right to refuse treatment, but it also resulted in people entering the mental health system at a more advanced stage in their illness, Nielssen explained. By the time they reached the new threshold of being at risk of 'serious harm to themselves or others'[11], they were dangerous, including to the police.

The reports piling up on my screen described Australia's mental health system as 'dysfunctional.'[12] There was a nationwide shortage of psychiatric nurses, and the supply of psychiatrists was also under

---

10 A National Approach to Mental Health 2006

11 *Mental Health Act 2007* (NSW)

12 A National Approach to Mental Health 2006

threat. A representative of the AMA described how potential trainee psychiatrists were being put off:

> They go into these emergency rooms and they see how dysfunctional they are. If you have a patient who is psychotic, what do you do? You spend a lot of time on telephones trying to find a bed somewhere. You cannot get them in. The treatment they need is in-patient facilities. They are not available. The emergency rooms get clogged up … Many doctors who have said: 'Look, I wanted to be a psychiatrist,' said once they started to see how the system was not working, [they] decided they would go elsewhere.

The federal government had responded to the committee's report with a commitment of $1.8 billion over five years 'to improve mental health services in Australia'. The pledge included a new program of twelve free appointments a year with a psychologist or other professional trained in mental health care. The appointments were available for anyone diagnosed with a mental health disorder, and they were fully rebateable through Medicare.[13]

Scrolling through the horror stories that prompted such a move by government, Liz Holcombe's words at Tracey's funeral came back to me.

'This whole thing of talking about it, telling everyone. We thought we would de-stigmatise the victims … but we had no idea how many people would come out … We're fucking it up, and you have to ask — since we decided disclosure was the way to go, have outcomes improved? If you look at Elijah's story, you'd have to say no.'

She was right in principle, but Elijah had been lucky. His care in the mental health system was exemplary. He was admitted voluntarily, on the spot, to a specialised mental health unit; he stayed a month and was

---

13 Department of Health | Evaluation of the Better Access to Psychiatrists, Psychologists and General Practitioners through the Medicare Benefits Schedule initiative: questions and answers

encouraged to stay longer. When he decided to leave, his medical records showed Elijah was linked up with a community mental health team and had regular appointments with a psychiatrist. He made the decision to stop taking his medication and disengage with services that were open to him. When he asked Armidale police to take him to hospital, he was taking the first step to re-engage. Elijah's only trouble with the mental health system had surfaced when staff at the hospital drew police into the loop. Elijah's experience of the health system had been far ahead of that of other people.

2012

16.

I opened my husband's card on Christmas morning and a gift voucher tumbled out for a writing workshop in Melbourne with a famous author.

'Take a few extra days. Stay at a fancy hotel, see some friends,' he said with a smile. 'You need a break.'

Stella had just turned two. We had talked about having another child; we even mapped a timeline out on paper. The fortnight before the writing workshop, I weaned myself off my medication. I couldn't continue on what I was on if I wanted to get pregnant. I breathed gingerly for the first week, waiting to topple, but nothing happened. The more I reduced my medication, though, the more a dreamy vagueness washed through me.

Two days before I left for Melbourne, I started new anti-depressants. The first dose hit so hard I slept for fourteen hours. I could barely move or think for another ten. There was no way I could take it and hope to function. With no time to see the doctor before I left, I boarded the flight to Melbourne unmedicated.

My search for someone to explain Elijah's schizophreniform diagnosis had turned up another expert, with a different set of skills to Olav Nielssen.

Associate Professor Stuart Thomas had a PhD in forensic mental health from King's College, London, and was central to a project between a prominent Australian university, a state-wide forensic mental health service, and Victoria Police. The project, PRIMeD (Police Responses to the Interface with Mental Disorder), was based in Melbourne. It had funding to investigate current police procedures and practice in dealing with mentally ill people.

When I emailed Stuart Thomas, he responded with a promise to send me relevant papers and an offer to meet if I ever came to Melbourne.

I stepped off the plane into whipping wind and caught a cab straight to his office. The Community Forensic Mental Health Service crouched between an overpass and railway lines in Clifton Hill. The building was shiny plastic white; its windows were tinted black. Stuart Thomas's workplace looked like a drug dealer in a sports car, cruising to score.

The receptionist sat behind a glass partition in a tiny waiting room full of patients. She tapped a code into a security pad and led me upstairs to Thomas's office.

He was taller and younger than I'd expected, with short dark hair and a straight-line mouth. His smile was wary. Dark eyes in a pale face and shadowed scars of teenage acne. In the street, I'd have picked him as a detective. English Soccer League stress balls filled a fruit bowl on his desk. When he reached out a hand, the contact was direct.

The notebook under my arm was full of facts from the papers he had sent — Victorian police transported someone to hospital, a psychiatric facility, or a police station for mental health-related issues once every two hours. Almost all of those people had a diagnosed mental illness, and half had a criminal record. What I wanted to know from Thomas was whether police used greater force on people they knew or suspected had a mental illness; and if they did, was it justified?

'Would you like a cup of tea?' he offered with British politeness.

We walked past offices to a modest kitchen. Thomas busied himself finding clean cups, and I asked about his move to Australia: finding a house, settling children into schools, de-coding Victoria's football culture.

'How did you convince the police to get involved in your research? Why did they take the risk?' I asked.

Thomas quirked an eyebrow.

'Actually, they came to us.'

The then Chief Commissioner of Victoria Police, Christine Nixon, had approached the Service directly, he said. Senior police recognised that dealing with mentally ill people was a growing part of the job. Nixon wanted to partner her police force with academic and clinical experts to develop evidence-based policy and practices across different areas of policing.

'We came to the table with a blank slate and designed a five-year program of research around core questions Victoria Police and the researchers agreed on,' he said.

The questions were in the papers he had sent: How often and in what circumstances were police and mentally ill people coming into contact with each other? How much of a burden was this on police, and what challenges did they face with mentally ill people? What factors drove police use of force against this cohort?

They started with an evidence base of close to zero, Thomas says. He was surprised to learn that changes to policy around training had been based on generalised hunches in the past, not evidence. It proved what a radical shift Chief Commissioner Nixon and her supporters were attempting to make.

I asked him what I had asked Olav Nielssen — were people with a mental illness in crisis more dangerous than other people police dealt with generally?

'Statistically speaking, yes. But the base rate of offending is low. Take schizophrenia, for example — nine out of ten people with schizophrenia don't offend,' he said, and launched into the carefully qualified language of an academic talking statistics.

Research showed that when a person with a diagnosis of schizophrenia did offend, they were significantly more likely to be guilty of violent offences, including family violence, than a group of otherwise similar people who did not have a schizophrenia diagnosis. The risks needed to be seen as relative, he stressed.

We walked back to Thomas's office with our tea.

Of the PRIMeD reports I'd read before our meeting, the one that had shocked me most was an analysis of people fatally shot by Victorian police between 1980 and 2008. Of the forty-eight people in that group all but six, a doctoral student discovered, had a history of contact with the mental health or criminal justice systems, or both, before they were shot.

The rate of psychosis and schizophrenia in the group was respectively eleven and seventeen times higher than in the general population.

Substance abuse was twenty-three times higher, and 80 per cent of the group was known to police as offenders. This breakdown made by the doctoral student was more informative than the singular fact that 87 per cent of people shot by police in Victoria over twenty years had a mental illness.

'What's the evidence on police use of force against mentally ill people?' I asked once we were seated.

'Police are no more likely to use severe force on people with a mental disorder than [on] the rest of the sample group we studied.'

What *was* significant, he added, was that mentally disturbed people used or threatened to use weapons against police more often than people in the sample group.

'I don't understand how that works,' I said. 'If most of the people Victorian police shot were mentally ill, how can it be that police are no more likely to shoot a mentally ill person than anyone else?'

'It's about escalation and what triggers crisis,' Stuart Thomas said, leaning forward across the table.

The standard police approach to resolving an encounter was based on asserting an authoritarian presence, using short clear commands to quickly assert control, he explained. While the approach worked well in the majority of situations, it was problematic when police were faced with a person in mental crisis.

For someone who was mentally disturbed, brief commands and the assertion of authority tended to escalate their crisis, Thomas said.

He was giving me the research that backed up Olav Niesslen's first-hand observations.

When the mentally ill person's behaviour deteriorated the police response would also escalate.

'This means that the police response increases from verbal commands to more coercive and therefore physical means, because the person does not comply with their commands or may become or appear aggravated, upset, or angered. So, relative to people who do not have a mental illness, police are more likely to resort to more coercive force (including fatal force) when the person has a mental illness.'

Understanding and accepting that these crisis jobs would take time to resolve was the core challenge in training police to deal with people who were mentally ill, Thomas said.

'The evidence tells us police need to allow the person time and space for the crisis to reduce. That way, the person who's unwell remains involved in the decision-making, and, in a sense, maintains some sense of control over the resolution of the situation.'

'So, what triggers crisis?'

Thomas grinned. That was the next ten years of research, but he had a hunch it was a mental or emotional spark for the officer or mentally ill person that set the snowball rolling. Once researchers figured out what it was, police could be trained to avoid those triggers and prevent situations reaching crisis point.

Police wanted help in this part of their role, Stuart Thomas told me. Most officers would rather call in mental health professionals than deal with a psychiatric crisis on their own, but if access to medical support wasn't reliable — and police said that was often the case — officers had to make do on their own.

The service that police were encouraged to call for help was a Crisis Assessment and Treatment Team (CATT): a mobile unit of psychologists, psychiatric nurses, social, and support workers.

The senate report I read after speaking to Olav Nielssen had been scathing about CATT's record.

> The essential characteristics of these services [are] their 24 hour, 7 day per week availability and focus on short-term intervention. However, several submissions commented that the poor response record of the Crisis Assessment and Treatment teams (CATT) had earned them the nicknames 'Can't Attend Today' teams or 'Call Again Tomorrow' teams. If the CAT teams are to be effective and supported by consumers and carers there is a need for better resources and training.
>
> *A National Approach to Mental Health 2006*

One advocacy group held up CATTs as 'probably the best example of what happens when governments fail to adequately fund services. From the consumer perspective CATT would be the most disliked and criticised service in mental health', because they were famous for being unavailable in a crisis.

Carers and advocates for mentally ill people recognised it was the police who were picking up the pieces.

'If the police service is to continue to be left to deal with the results of an inadequate health service, they need to be given whatever training is needed to help them to deal appropriately with people with mental illness,' wrote a woman whose son had been shot dead by police.[14]

'Do you think someone's mental state *should* influence the way police respond to them?' I asked Thomas.

'Given half of us will experience some sort of mental illness over the course of our lives, and one in five of us will in a year, there's arguably a systemic shift needed in the way police respond.'

I could tell he was treading carefully.

The cultural shift towards accepting that their role included social support was ongoing among police, he ventured.

'I've been amazed by the level of compassion shown by some police

---

14 A National Approach to Mental Health 2006

towards people who are on the fringes and aren't officially "police business",' Thomas said.

A percentage of officers PRIMeD had engaged with checked on the welfare of an unofficial 'caseload' of mentally ill people who lived in their command.

Not everyone embraced the shift towards more welfare-based policing, he admitted. Some were frustrated at having to 'babysit' people in hospital waiting rooms, especially when at the end of a long wait, the hospital allowed the person back on the streets. *Four Corners* had received complaints like these after Elijah's story aired.

'The local hospital in my area has a "secure" mental health ward,' one officer had written. 'I have on countless occasions taken a mentally ill patient in desperate need of care to this facility and been told that they do not have any beds available or that the patient is not ill enough to be admitted. Sure enough the patient is released and within days and in some cases hours, we are called to a job with that person involved.'

Melbourne was still asleep when I arrived at the writing workshop on Sunday morning.

I was met at the door of a converted warehouse by a man in thick-rimmed glasses. He led me to a fishbowl conference room, where six other women were seated at a table.

When our teacher arrived, we swooned and twittered. She was detached and famous in pale-blue cashmere.

She talked about what drove her own work — the desire to make contact, and the shame that rushed in whenever she exposed herself. We had to learn to stare that feeling down if we wanted to be writers, she warned.

We had each sent samples of our writing ahead of time for the teacher and other students to appraise. Every woman took her turn to talk about her work and receive feedback.

I told Elijah's story haltingly, defensive and fearful in turn.

'I'm waiting to find out if the policeman will be charged, so the story isn't over yet.'

I searched for a focal point outside the glass room.

'What I'm really struggling with is whether or not to include my own mental illness in the story.'

The woman writing about anorexia crossed her arms. The crime writer snorted openly. The famous author's face was unreadable. I sweated with shame, but I couldn't stop.

'My experience doesn't compare to Elijah's; it's never been as serious as his. But I feel like it's dishonest to leave it out.' My voice was shaking.

'Why don't you write it in and then decide? You can always take it out later,' suggested the woman who was writing about Jewish migration.

The art therapist touched me gently on the arm, 'I think you have to let people know you.'

'I didn't realise when I read your piece that the story wasn't finished,' our teacher said. 'Your problem is you don't know where you stand.'

'What do you mean?' I asked.

'You can't know why you're really telling a story until it's over; that's why you're struggling. You have to wait until the story is finished before you know what you need to say.'

At the end of the day, there was a flurry of number swapping. The art therapist gave me her card.

'Let's stay in touch.'

The crime writer and biographer were talking loudly about publishers. I left to find a cab. The Jewish migration writer was on the footpath.

'Want to get a drink?' she asked.

We raced across the road to a bar like schoolgirls and settled into a smoky couch.

'So — what did you think?' She raised her eyebrows.

I breathed out hard, and she burst out laughing.

'What do you think you'll do about your personal story?'

I concentrated on my glass.

'People don't want to know about it, do they?' I asked rhetorically. 'I imagine I'll write it in then cut it all out.'

Tears rose in my chest. She reached across and squeezed my arm.

'Sorry,' I said. 'I hate being such a basket case. It's embarrassing.'

'I've got to get to the airport — want to share a cab?' she asked.

I shook my head and tried to smile.

'Darwin's a retail desert. I need to see some shops before I leave Melbourne.'

She pulled me into a perfumed hug.

'Good luck with it.'

The faces of women in the workshop dogged me the whole way home to Darwin. Their alarm and pity reinforced what I knew about the risk of public admission. If I told my story with Elijah's, I would be labelled. The phrase 'mental illness' in conversation was the verbal equivalent of Elijah's bread knife — an ordinary object, able to strike fear. If I owned it, I risked being defined as damaged goods.

I went to the GP for new medication as soon as I got home. As the chemicals in my body rebalanced, peace returned to my mind and movements. My shoulders unwound, my throat relaxed; a fortnight later, I was able to look at people's faces without flinching.

'It's nice to have you back. I missed you,' my husband said in March.

The sadness in the truth of those words is impossible to convey. The toil of keeping our life afloat had fallen entirely on his shoulders while I drifted somewhere unreachable. I had been 'gone' for almost two years. I could not erase the bruises I had left or say that I was better for good.

We let go of our thoughts of another child. There were some things I knew I could not do.

The decision brought a lightness I didn't expect to feel — relief. I could protect one child from my pain when I was sick, but more than that was beyond my resources. It was too much to expect of myself or to ask of my husband when I went 'missing'.

I began the slow task of repair with a notebook for my husband, filled with all the reasons I loved him. We threw a party in Sydney for his fortieth birthday, and when the weekend was over, he flew home with Stella.

I rented a car and drove to Wee Waa.

17.

Nothing at the Cottonfields Motel had changed. The sheets were still soft from work-worn bodies, and the string of lights was still in place. There was no special reason for my visit; just a wish to see the Holcombes outside crisis, in the normal wash of life.

It was Monday night, and Quentin had a story on *Four Corners* about Adam Salter's shooting. I thought I might watch the show with Jeremy and Fiona, but when I called he didn't mention it, so I walked out under the blue-washed sky to catch the last of the evening's light.

Down the main street, past the pub to the bowling club where Tracey's wake was held. Half a block further, at the swimming pool, the road faded out where the streetlights stopped. Footsteps crunched behind me, and I picked up pace. A woman stepped up the gutter beside me.

'Sorry, I didn't mean to scare you. I'm in a hurry to get to the hospital.'

She waved a thin dark arm at a building ahead of us, sweeping my fear away, then pulled out a mobile and strode ahead. The bones of her spine made a path down her T-shirt.

'It's bad, he's in hospital. We had to get the police to bring him. I'm there now,' I heard her say.

We reached the hospital. She stopped to sit on a low brick wall and cried into the phone in rasping breaths. Over her shoulder I saw a paddy wagon pulled up in the ambulance bay. I dropped my head and kept on walking.

It was everywhere. Pain and fear and the police being called.

Help me. Protect me. Take away this person I don't recognise. Bring me back the one I love.

I watched *Four Corners* alone in bed that night with a beer and toasted sandwich.

Quentin chronicled the day of Adam's death in November 2009. Adam stabbing himself with a knife in the kitchen, his father pleading with him to stop; the call to the ambulance and police; the blood-smeared kitchen; the moment of quiet before Adam lunged and police ran; 'taser, taser, taser', *bang.*

Sergeant Sheree Bissett and her colleagues told their superiors she called on Adam several times to 'drop the knife', but when he lunged at Constable Abela with the knife, she fired.

'I think it was a terrible mistake,' Adrian Salter said from the small screen at the foot of my bed. 'I really believe that she had … I don't know, a rush of blood to the head and didn't know what she was doing … And I don't know why the police can't just say so and say "Look, we are sorry we killed your son." What's so difficult about that?

'[Adam] was an upstanding, fine member of the community by anyone's estimation … He had a good job, he was well respected, he got on well with everyone, he was friendly, he had a great sense of humour, he was active and adventurous. He paid his taxes. He paid his debts. So he was looking forward to a productive life and a productive career.'

'How do you remember him?' Quentin asked.

'… a great mate, a friend, and a son to be proud of.'

It was almost identical to the answer Jeremy gave when Quentin had asked him the same question about Elijah.

Two sons, both eldest children; shot within five months of each other by NSW police. Bright, athletic men with charm and talent who married young — perhaps unwisely. Both with delusional psychoses that came on quickly and who, in the last months of their lives, against advice, stopped taking their medication. Both from families who refused to bow to the stigma around mental illness. What were the chances?

Jeremy called mid-morning and offered to book a table at the pub for Wednesday night.

'I'm going to be tied up for the next few days — I'm renovating some flats. You've got other people to see in the meantime, haven't you?' he asked.

'I do,' I said.

'I've got something I want to give you. Call me after lunch and I'll come and find you. It'll only take a minute,' he said.

I spent the morning with Elijah's sisters at the Little Crooked House.

Jordan was nineteen now. She looked a lot like Tracey; big blue eyes in a heart-shaped face and a cloud of henna-reddened hair. A German beer-hall dream.

Her older sister was still a study in darkness: black clothes, black hair and eyes. Laura was short like Jeremy's mother, but more inclined to scowl than smile.

A queen-size mattress and pile of pillows crowded the floor of the living room. A TV sat jammed in the corner against the couch.

'It doesn't work,' Laura said when I asked if they'd watched *Four Corners* last night.

I wanted the girls to broaden my vision of their brother with memories only siblings can share.

'Was Elijah very different when he was sick?' I asked.

No one in Wee Waa knew Elijah was sick until the day he died, his sisters agreed.

'For them it was straight out of the blue. Elijah's illness was so irrelevant to the personality that everyone else saw,' Laura said.

'What about you?' I asked.

'We really didn't have much idea about it,' she admitted. 'I have maybe one memory of Elijah being odd.'

She described him walking her home from a friend's one night and staring at the house they grew up in next-door 'for what seemed like an hour'. Laura had thought it was a bit weird but not frightening.

Jordan remembered Elijah rambling on the phone from Sydney when he was catching a train home after work one night.

'It was like he was just going on with random things, telling me everything he saw,' Jordan said.

'The last time he was home, we didn't see him,' Laura explained. 'He was in Narrabri and we were told we weren't …' She stopped. 'He just needed a bit of time.'

'Were you worried when he went missing?'

'I was just like "Oh, it's just Mum being worried". Mum and I went into the police station in Narrabri and made a statement. She told them "He isn't a threat to anyone but himself, do not approach him, do not go near him. He's terrified of you." They said, 'We totally understand, if we see the car, if we see him, we'll call you,"' Laura said.

Tracey was anxious after they left that she hadn't given the police her number.

Jordan bounced on the mattress, bursting to add a detail to the story.

'I remember when both of you got home she did ring them back, because I was standing next to her in the kitchen next to the phone, and she was telling them her mobile number but she forgot the last nine on the end,' Jordan said. 'And I was like, "Mum, nine!" She kind of said it to me, but I don't know if they would have heard.'

At Elijah's inquest, Chris Hoy had pinned Tracey's wrong number in police records on Senior Constable Brett Allison. But Jordan was saying the mistake could have been Tracey's. Why had counsel assisting not thought of that? Why had Hoy assumed the mistake was Brett's?

'Did you think, "Elijah is OK, he'll turn up" when he went missing?' I asked Jordan.

'I remember Laura making a joke about it — "Well, he's not dead!" — to keep Mum calm,' she said.

'I looked at it as Elijah just running away from the pressure of the city and his relationship with Allison,' said Laura. 'We thought he was just panicking a bit about—'

'Commitment.' Jordan broke in and rolled her eyes.

The girls moved back and forth through the aftermath of Elijah's death.

'Elijah's funeral was bigger than Mum's. I remember hating the songs at EJ's funeral, thinking who the fuck picked these?' said Laura drily.

Jordan cracked up. 'They were pretty bad. That was Dad. I remember not crying until we walked out. Then out at the cemetery I was kneeling; crying and singing.'

Later, at the wake, people crowded around a fire in the backyard of the Little Crooked House, drinking and playing music.

'There were so many people here, but it wasn't overwhelming. It was like, "Thank God" because I don't have to think about it,' Laura said.

'After that the roles changed entirely. I remember Aunty Nira telling me, "You have to be the mum now — she's broken",' Jordan remembered.

The feeling I'd had in Cinders Lane returned. This room was too small for the enormity it held.

Tracey stayed in bed for weeks after Elijah's funeral, the sisters said.

'It was either a pile of papers on the bed or a canvas — just the blanket changed,' Laura recalled.

'If you met Mum in her thirties or forties, you'd think nothing could take her down — she was helium,' Jordan said with a giant smile. 'Not only that, if you were being beaten by stuff she would take you up, too. She would come right down to where you were, scoop you up, and take you to the heavens with rainbows and butterflies.'

She lifted her arm in an arc, and I saw balloons like birds above the Wee Waa cemetery.

'Mum went from being larger than life, cuddly big paint-all-over-everything, to this frail little old cold woman scared of everything.'

'What do you want to come out of Elijah's inquest? What will make it feel like it's finished for you?' I asked them.

'I don't want it to be finished, I want it to be *complete*,' Laura said emphatically. 'I want both sides to be told and a decision to be made, and

I want it to be accurate. I still don't know what happened.'

The legal process was a distant abstract.

'Every now and then I think, "Oh, what's happening with that?" It's not "I wish they'd just hurry up and get that bastard" or even "I wish they'd hurry up and tell everyone that Elijah was innocent." I think it will be much easier to just know "This is what happened". Someone can't keep changing the story after that,' Jordan added.

They were haunted by images from news reports.

'We couldn't really picture it, but as the images came out we could. He must have been so scared.'

Jordan's doe-eyes turned hard.

'It was his final moments and he was terrified, and that's how it ended. It's like, the whole scary movie thing watching it for us; that's all it was for him.'

I stopped on the verandah to talk to Tarney on my way out.

He put down his guitar and motioned me to a chair.

He was a silent mountain of a man with thick dreadlocks and meaty hands. A Viking Buddhist in a metal T-shirt. We'd met before on one of my Sydney trips to see Tracey.

'It's good the girls got to speak to you,' he said.

I nodded.

'I'm glad I got to come back. How are you doing?'

'Well, thank you.'

Tarney was taking the first half of the year off uni. Time to heal.

'Your family has dealt with more in the last two years than the average person faces in a lifetime. I can't imagine what it's like to lose a brother and then your mother so soon afterwards.'

'Losing a mother is awful and sad, but it's not unnatural. Losing a brother is like losing part of yourself. It was almost the opposite of Mum dying, because with her, there was this massive relief that the pain she had been in was gone and finished. It tempered the grief of her dying.'

There was no relief in Elijah's death, he said.

He talked about the trip home from Sydney after he learned his older brother was dead. When they arrived at Jeremy and Fiona's house, everyone collapsed. Fiona listened to the messages from police; David Phelps and his father were distraught.

There was nothing Tarney could do to ease their suffering.

'I remember going up to Elijah's room and getting all his stuff and putting it in a bag. Dad walked into the bathroom and saw EJ's toothbrush and lost it. He was vomiting. We put all of EJ's stuff out of sight.'

But there was nowhere to put the pain.

I waited for Jeremy on the dried-out oval near his mother's house, where a journalist had stopped Jordan and a friend on the way home from school in the days after her brother's shooting and asked if they knew Elijah Holcombe.

Jeremy pulled up in a battered truck, his forearm on the window ledge. He leaned out and passed me a DVD.

'I found this at Mary's the other day. You asked for it ages ago. It's the video of Elijah's funeral.'

We squinted at each other in the midday sun.

'You still right for Wednesday night?' he asked.

'Definitely.'

'Seven o'clock alright? We eat early.'

I nodded.

'Thanks for the video.'

He eased the old truck into gear. 'Alright. See you then,' and drove away.

Tracey Holcombe's best friend lived out of town. Over the bridge, right at the roundabout, four kilometres past the railway bridge.

A pair of golden retrievers raced around the corner when they heard my car. Sue Duncan followed a minute later in gardening clothes and gloves. The dogs turned circles through her legs and she put out a hand to calm them. I followed her trim frame to a gauzed-in verandah. Clumps of mown lawn fell from her boots onto the floor.

I'd spent the morning with the kids at the Little Crooked House, I said.

'I'm trying to get a rounded picture of Elijah. Parents have a different view of their children to everyone else—'

Sue cut across my diplomacy. 'I never saw a mean bone in his body, ever. Always the most loving, beautiful child. Even when he did start to have his problems, I only knew about it because Tracey would confide in me. I never saw any of that other stuff at all, and I was at the house a lot. Milk with your tea?'

'No, thank you.'

''Cause it's something — being a small country town — people don't want to know about, or it's frightening,' Sue said, leaving out the words a small town didn't like to say.

Sue and Tracey had known each other since they were kids. When Elijah went missing, she was the first person Tracey had called.

'She said, "I'm here with the girls, I don't know what to do." I said "Just give me half an hour to pull some things together." So I grabbed everything to make pumpkin soup; I'm a great believer that in a tragedy, you have to have something to do. I grabbed a roast out of the fridge and potatoes and pumpkin. I thought "Well, at least we can cook".'

I leaned back in my chair and listened. Her words came rapidly, charged with conviction.

'When Jeremy told Tracey Elijah was dead, she couldn't breathe properly. She was shaking uncontrollably — she was in a trance, "They've shot my boy, why, why?" It was like the movie scenes.'

Sue called her husband and asked him to bring her a bag of clothes.

'I slept with Tracey that night. I slept with her every night for the five nights I stayed there because she didn't want to be alone. She was in this ball, and I just had to cuddle her. I was her best friend; it was what I had to do for her. And it was hard, I have to admit it was really hard, the emotional drain of it,' Sue confided.

She brushed crumbs off the table and tipped them into her empty mug. I followed her to the kitchen.

'The saddest thing I remember at Elijah's funeral was that Jeremy insisted they all go up and stand at the front.'

Sue put the mugs into the sink. Water spurted from the tap and sprayed her shirt.

'She never told any of us she was doing it. When she went up in church we said, "Where are you going?"' Sue pursed her lips at the memory.

Tracey, Jeremy and Fiona, Tarney, Jordan, Laura, and Fiona's children stood across the altar in front of the congregation.

'It was the saddest — you ask anyone in that church. Jeremy wanted a scene of unity because it was all after the breakup. I reckon forty-five minutes, an hour, they're all standing there with their arms around one another. Tracey's legs almost collapsed on her a couple of times — you could see her. She was holding it together; it was the saddest thing I've ever seen. I've never seen that at a funeral and I never hope to see it again.'

Sue scrubbed the mugs with vigour. Tracey's other burden on the day of Elijah's funeral was looking after Allison's parents.

'They came out from the States — they knew no one. The only person they knew was their daughter. So Tracey had to spend 90 per cent of her time at her son's funeral looking after these strangers that she didn't know. I mean, how do you do that?'

Sue's fridge was covered in positive-motto magnets. She had survived her own health scare; she knew the dangers of bitterness, but she couldn't stem her anger at the hand Tracey was dealt.

She watched her childhood friend retreat and shrink in the months that followed. When Elijah's inquest started, the only way Tracey would leave the cottage was if they went to the nursery on the edge of town.

'I would try and get her out of the house because it was depressing.

She had a shrine to EJ — the big table was just a shrine — photos of him, his watch, trinkety things, the flowers that people had sent. There was a native bunch that dried — it stayed there for — well, they cleared it before Tracey died,' she said.

'We'd always gone to the bakery every morning together, but Tracey didn't want to see people. The woman at the nursery knew us. She'd put chairs out and bring us a cup of tea. It was quiet there.'

I'd been to the Wee Waa nursery. It was just like the one in my parents' town — same climate, same plants, same garden ornaments. I looked around Sue's kitchen. The bone china mugs and floral oven-mitt; the buffalo-grass lawn out the window. I was back in another childhood place, but the surroundings hadn't shrunk this time. I saw my reflection in the oven door. I was an adult in the landscape of my childhood.

I showered the day from my skin back at the hotel, and pushed Jeremy's DVD into my laptop.

By some freak glitch of the recording, the altar flowers and Elijah's casket appeared in black-and-white, but everything else was colour.

I watched as Jeremy, Tracey, and Fiona walked to the altar, followed by a string of children, just as Sue had described. They stood shoulder to shoulder in front of the congregation, a mass of black pins waiting to fall. I wondered why Allison wasn't in the line-up? Neither Jordan nor Laura had mentioned Allison being at the funeral, and Sue, Tracey's friend, had only spoken about her parents. Even in recollections of her husband's funeral, Allison was elusive.

Jeremy walked to the pulpit to give the eulogy.

A long time later, Tracey led the group off stage. Tarney stayed behind, perched on a stool. He laid a black guitar across his lap and picked a lament from its pool of darkness. The tune warmed mid-section, remembering a life in motion, before returning to its loss. The black-and-white coffin jarred against the surrounding colours, and

Jeremy motioned Tarney off stage.

I closed the lid of the laptop as a voice called from outside,

'Hello. You home?'

I opened the door to a round olive face lit by a 60-watt smile.

'Adam?'

'Bags is fine. You're Kate? How ya doin'?'

Jeremy and the girls had told me to track down Elijah's high school mates, Bags and Dorey. Bags was Adam Baguley.

He bounced inside like a super ball, moving in all directions. Between my exhaustion and the pace Bags talked, it was hard to catch a lot of what he said. I asked him for normal stories about Elijah, not hero tales — I'd heard enough of those. It was a pointless request.

'He just had a presence — it was unbelievable. When he came to Narrabri high school, first thing I thought was "He doesn't fit in here". He just stood out majorly. Tracey said she loves all her children equally, but Elijah was a bit special,' Adam giggled. 'The whole family is just ridiculously wonderful.'

'Did you know in high school that he was depressed? Did you talk about it?' I asked.

'We'd always go to the gym. 'Lije and me were big on the endorphin factor. He never spoke too in depth about his own personal problems; he was always just helping other people. If you were sitting in the lunch area and in the distance you saw him talking to someone, you could just tell he's helping them out with some ridiculous issue.'

Adam sat on the room's only chair and fiddled with my notebook.

'Later on, like when it happened at uni, I heard about that pretty much as soon as it happened, from another friend. I went around and seen Jeremy, and he said, "Yeah". That was September 2008. Eric and I flew to Sydney for a weekend just to chill out and hang with EJ and stuff. And it was awesome; we all played a lot of guitar. That party — you heard about that?'

I nodded.

'It was just before we visited him. He drank a bottle of vodka, thought he kissed a girl,' Adam scoffed.

'How was he when you saw him in Sydney?'

'He didn't look good — he looked beaten down, blackened eyes sort of thing. We went downstairs and sat near the water because he lived on the water. I said, "Alright, what's going on? Tell me about these delusions", and it was completely like talking to him as he normally would be.

'I said, well, these things aren't true, Elijah, and he said, "I know they're ridiculous, it just feels like this is what's happening. I swear there's people trying to kill me." I remember actually saying to him, later on, "Well, Elijah, if people do kill you, then we'll believe you".' Adam moved from side to side, laughing like a hyena.

'It's just fucking unbelievable what's happened. I don't know if it's just that I know him, but it seems so unjust it's not funny, because he just wouldn't hurt anyone ever. All he would have had to say was "Elijah, put the knife down" —'

'The cop who shot him did say that quite a few times,' I said.

Adam looked away and around the room.

'He would think that Elijah was unpredictable, but it wouldn't matter how messed up Elijah was — he wouldn't hurt anyone. He was scared, he was just simply scared, that's why he was running from him,' Adam said more quietly.

'Do you think Elijah was scared all the time when he was sick?'

'I'm only guessing, but I think it was something that lingered and had peaks. You get adrenalin; start running for no reason. It's quite a common delusion — figures of authority. He was so easily fixed, that's the thing as well, get the medication right, get the stress right.'

Adam spoke with confidence about Elijah's state and medication because he'd had to learn to manage his own anxiety and depression, he said. Elijah's shooting came soon after the death of another close friend from cancer, he explained. Combined, the two deaths pushed him into a depression that lasted two years.

'But I got the good medication now — it's ridiculous when you find the right one. Just amazing,' he said.

I smiled.

'What, you too?' He whooped and raised his hand for a high-five.

'Old Dorey's good on this stuff. He thinks about it a lot,' Adam said on the way out. I passed him my notebook, and he scrawled out Eric Nielsen's number.

In my dream that night, the three friends cruised the main street of Narrabri in Jeremy's beat-up Fairmont. Elijah was in the driver's seat; Bags and Dorey hung their arms out the windows. They laughed and joked and the wind blew their hair, and the heart of every girl they passed was breaking.

The silverside and cutlets were pushed aside; the drinks were nearly empty.

Fiona was in the ladies.

'You need to talk to Fiona, too,' Jeremy said. 'She's suffered as much as anyone through all of this.'

I thought of the pictures of Elijah's funeral: his family stage-managed into papering the cracks, strung like clothes on a washing line. I nodded.

'Sure. If she wants to.'

Fiona crossed the dining room, and Jeremy turned the conversation to *Four Corners*.

'We didn't miss the parallels that the Salter boy's parents had broken up, and his own relationship. Wonder where his wife was the other night?' Jeremy snorted. 'And the personality — kind, smart. Spooky, isn't it?'

There was a sharpness to Jeremy tonight that I hadn't felt since we first made contact.

'We were talking before you came about why you want to tell Elijah's story. Why do you care about it so much?' His eyes were unreadable.

I swirled the dregs of my beer and drained the glass. This was why I had come to Wee Waa.

'My Dad grew up on a property like you, and Mum's a townie, like Tracey. They got married really young. I'm one of four like your kids, and there's mental illness on both sides of our family. I've never been as sick as Elijah, but the first time I had problems, I was about fifteen, like him. I wasn't diagnosed until I had a proper breakdown after a relationship broke up when I was twenty-eight,' I said.

'So you get it,' Jeremy said.

'I think I get some of it. I'm not the only one in my family …' But the sense of betrayal was too strong to continue. 'My family don't talk about it,' I apologised.

Fiona nodded. 'My mum and her twin sister are schizophrenic.' She smiled.

'You can tell when people understand on a different level. You've always approached it kind of differently,' Jeremy said.

'In the right circumstances, what happened to Elijah — it could have been my family.' My voice trembled. 'Sometimes I think it could have been me.'

The waitress came to clear the table, and the three of us stood to leave.

The air outside was cool. Jeremy stepped off the kerb to cross the street.

'See you at home,' he said to Fiona.

'You'll drop in at the flats on your way out tomorrow?' he said to me.

'Of course. Thanks for dinner.'

He planned this before they came.

Fiona and I found a table in the beer garden. We were like teenagers thrust together by our parents, awkward and defensive — *this wasn't my idea.*

She lit a cigarette and crossed an arm beneath her breasts in the same pose the papers had captured in Cinders Lane. Her most vivid memories were of the inquest. Her cigarette darted across her face as she recalled how vulnerable they felt on the first day.

'Obviously, we were looking through the crowd to see if we could see the person who shot Elijah — not that we had any idea what he looked like, but we thought maybe we would see him and just know.'

'And did you?'

She shook her head and tilted her face to blow out smoke.

'We were sort of astounded when we saw who it was. He was a lot shorter than we both thought. From the little bit that police had told us, we just pictured this really big, wide, muscular body-building looking person, and he just looked like a typical average person on the street. He had a baby-face look about him. Not in a youthful way but a vulnerable way.'

Five or six supporters accompanied Rich to court every day. There were always police in uniform amongst them.

'Sometimes when I caught him looking our way I got the feeling that it was — how do you put it?' She sighed heavily. 'That he was guilty and he knew he was guilty, and it was like he was looking at us not coyly, but trying to hide that guilt, and then sometimes it was like deep sympathy and regret on his face.'

Fiona had restless hands and long, loose hair; she didn't seem comfortable sitting still. She used her whole body when she smiled, but now her shoulders curled towards her chest.

I asked her what she made of the witnesses who said Elijah ran at Rich. She listed possible explanations — they were too far away to see what happened; their view was obstructed; they watched too much TV; maybe they'd been drinking. But her most truthful answer was the simplest one.

'I just didn't believe them.'

A guard dog launched itself against the tin behind us as someone walked past the fence. We swore and jumped out of our seats then subsided with nervous giggles. With our hearts thumping, Fiona described the tension in the courtroom.

Each day was more raw and painful than the last, she said.

'A lot of the witnesses were really hurting.'

By the end of the second week, the air crackled. Part way through Joan Whitburn's evidence, the woman who watched from her office window, Jeremy had to leave the room.

'He broke down, and the Coroner asked if he wanted to go. I remember him saying, "For fuck's sake, if that's not enough for you, what is?" I remember there was one more witness and then there was the long wait.'

The Coroner called the head of the investigation team and lawyers for the police out of the room.

'That was the toughest.' Fiona breathed out hard.

'Because you knew something was happening?'

'Absolutely. We knew this wasn't something she just did — leave the room. Then Philip Stewart turned around from the bar table and looked at us and nodded. Then I just remember the Coroner asking everybody to rise—'

Fiona wiped away tears with trembling fingers.

'We went down and thanked Philip and the opposing legal team, and then Jeremy turned to me and said, "I have to shake Andrew's hand. I don't know why but I just have to shake his hand and thank him".'

The dog rattled its chain against the fence and whined.

'Jeremy just very quietly and gently stuck his hand out, and I'm sure he said thank you — but he may not have said anything at all. I remember Andrew gripping Jeremy's hand almost like he didn't want to let it go. There were tears from both of them. Andrew didn't say anything.'

David Phelps remembered the handshake differently. Perched on the edge of my bed at the Cottonfields Motel the next morning, he eyed my dictaphone like it was a snake. David was Jeremy's cousin and closest friend.

'Our families had farms side by side, and when we were kids we used to have correspondence school on the farm, and Jeremy was next door. So we went to school together. We've known each other from year dot,' he said.

David was in his fifties now, with sun-mottled skin and hands he didn't know where to put.

'Were you there when Jeremy shook hands with Rich?' I asked.

He nodded.

'Jeremy said "I should go over and shake his hand", but he was feeling uncertain whether to approach him or not. So I went over to Stier.'

Detective Inspector Greig Stier was Rich's boss, and the senior officer from Armidale who'd spoken to Jeremy after Elijah's shooting.

"I was just saying goodbye; Stiery and Rich were talking to each other and that was the closest I'd been to Rich the whole process. Rich, when he realised I was there he went "Oh!" and stepped right back. I said goodbye to Stiery, and I shook Rich's hand and that allowed Jeremy to come into it. Jeremy sort of thanked him for bringing an end to it all. I think he wished him well, and Rich was a bit choked up and just nodded in acknowledgement and was a bit overwhelmed,' Phelps said.

'How do you know Greig Stier?' I asked, intrigued.

'We played football as young blokes. He's a very good friend,' David explained. 'I spoke to Stiery about how Rich was handling it. He was doing it tough.'

David shifted on the bed, physically provoked by his ambivalence towards Rich. He didn't share Jeremy's determination to forgive, but his friendship with Greig Stier was an unexpected bridge between the Holcombes and police.

David cleared his throat, and I turned off the dictaphone. We talked about crops and rainfall before he shared a final memory.

'I promised Tracey before I went up to Armidale that I'd let her know what was happening. I used to phone her every day.' He rubbed his hands and the dry skin rasped. 'When I called her from the foyer on the last day, all I said was "Your boy's been cleared", and then I just cried.'

All I see when I replay the moment is Jeremy's frozen face.

He met me with a paintbrush in one hand, out the front of the flats he was fixing up. We sat on paint tins in the sun and talked. The freshness of the air matched the sharp blue sky. He made a joke about getting old, and I slapped him on the thigh. It was time to go. Half way down the drive I turned back.

'I forgot one thing I wanted to check with you,' I called out.

Jeremy raised an eyebrow.

'When you picked up the car in Armidale, what was in the back that Elijah had slept under — was it a doona or clothes?'

I still can't fathom what possessed me. What was I thinking to toss such an intimate question across the space between us like it was no more than a twenty-cent piece? I was thinking how well the Holcombes were coping; how generously they had shared their feelings. I was thinking the DPP would make a decision soon, and Elijah's story would find an end before the close of winter.

Ten days after I got home from Wee Waa, the NSW police killed another young man.

18.

The Daily Telegraph summed up Roberto Laudisio Curti's death in eight words: 'Six cops, one shirtless man, three Taser shots.'

The 21-year-old Brazilian student had walked into a convenience store in Sydney's CBD at 5.30am on 18 March 2012, bare-chested, and announced that the world was about to end, the daily press reported. Curti asked for help. The staff sent him packing, but he came back, jumped over the counter, stole a packet of biscuits, and then ran away again. Police approached Curti ten minutes later, further down the street. He ran, and at least five officers chased him.

'The officers did not taser him all at the one time. They tried to apprehend him but he was still able to push them away and keep running,' a police source told the *Telegraph*, '… until the final shot ended the incident. Witnesses claimed he screamed "help me" as the officers held him down.'

Within days, the Brazilian Consulate revealed that Roberto Laudisio Curti was on a night out 'like any other young male on a Saturday', when he came to police attention.

'He was so healthy and a good student, he studied at a very good university in Brazil; he had friends here and family. So he went out just for fun', a consular official told the *Sydney Morning Herald*. The official also made it known that the Curti family was 'extremely wealthy and well connected' and would not let the matter rest.

Australia's Department of Foreign Affairs and Trade (DFAT) requested a briefing from police. The NSW Police Minister announced the state Ombudsman would oversee the Homicide Squad's investigation into Curti's death.

A coronial inquest was compulsory. It was listed for October 2012, in front of Coroner Mary Jerram.

Elijah's anniversary razed the Holcombes every year, but in 2012 it weighed more heavily than ever. Jeremy wrote to me four days after Curti's death.

From: Jeremy Holcombe
To: Kate Wild
Subject: Re some follow-up questions
Date: Thurs 22 March 2012

We are both surprised at how much we have been affected by revisiting Elijah's story in detail; very much compounded by the Adam Salter story and of course most recently, the police brutality administered to the young Roberto.
Right now I can feel my anxiety rising as the season changes.
The light changing and the chill starting to creep in as we move towards the 2nd of June. I will soon start marking off the temporal landmarks: Tracey's birthday, Easter and Fiona's birthday, then the Wee Waa Show. It starts slowly then accelerates; that first phone call from Elijah, going to pick him up, the trip home, the self harm. The panic when he disappeared. The road trip. The phone call. Then it starts to slow down as we come out the other side. The funeral. The grief. The Critical Incident discussions. The unexplainable. The world still turning. It was surreal at the time. Now each year is doubly surreal. It is also surprising how physical it is. I start compulsively pacing. Fiona gets teary and breaks out in hives.

I wrote to Rich with a new request. 'In the last twelve months I have gained a strong sense of Elijah's life and character through stories his friends and family have told about him. With your permission, your family and friends could build a portrait of you in a similar way without endangering any legal proceedings. I am certain the people close to you would like anyone reading this story to understand and care for you as much as they do. But unless I have a better understanding of who Andrew Rich is I can only give readers a cut-out of a police officer standing in your place,' I pleaded.

Autumn deepened. Jeremy worked on the flats past midnight and into the early hours — anything to keep his mind away from Elijah's third anniversary. In April, he gave up smoking. He told Fiona that giving up was 'easy'. But Jeremy wasn't easy. He pushed Fiona beyond her limits until she left Wee Waa and him.

Working at the flats alone one night, Jeremy found he couldn't breathe. He lay on the floor, convinced he was dying, but after ten minutes the pain subsided. He told no one about the repeated attacks he had in the next six days, but when the sixth attack hit, he drove to the kids' house. Tarney and Jordan identified the problem — their father was having a panic attack. They got them, too. The Holcombe children took Jeremy to Wee Waa hospital. There was no doctor on duty, so the nurses called the emergency mental health line. Jeremy was triaged at the highest level of need, then passed between two or three or more people on the phone. A doctor on call in Wee Waa was eventually called in, and Jeremy was admitted to hospital for the weekend.

The chemical shift from giving up smoking had reduced the effectiveness of his anti-depressants. On top of the stress of Elijah's anniversary, Fiona's departure, and the hours he worked, the chemical change had blown his system, a psychiatrist later explained to Jeremy. She increased the dose of his medication, and the world returned to a semblance of normality.

Meanwhile, Fiona had applied for a job on the Central Coast and was asked in for an interview. Ten minutes into the panel's questions, Fiona began to shake and cry until she couldn't speak. Days later, she called Jeremy. He took her to hospital, and she was admitted to the psychiatric ward in Tamworth for three weeks.

By the time I heard all of this, it was early August. Fiona was back in Wee Waa, living at the flats. She and Jeremy were taking it slowly, living in different units. Tarney had gone back to uni. Laura was driving a forklift, and Jordan had a job in childcare.

I hadn't heard from Rich.

That was the state of play when the NSW DPP reached a decision on charging Rich.

19.

'I can send you the press release a few minutes ahead of everyone else,' the woman from the DPP said on the phone. 'I know you've been following this case for a long time.'

'Can you tell me what it says?' I asked.

'You'll appreciate I can't pre-empt the Director's announcement.'

'When will the release go out?'

'It will be finalised today.'

I called Phil Stewart as soon as she hung up.

'If they're making it public it means they've sent Jeremy a letter. Give him a ring. I've got nothing,' he said.

I didn't have the courage to follow his suggestion.

The press release arrived at one minute to 5pm. I was sitting in the car in Darwin and saw it come through on my phone.

29 August 2012

Dear Kate,

The Director has determined not to commence proceedings against Senior Constable Rich for murder or manslaughter following the fatal shooting of Elijah Holcombe.

The Crown had to determine if a charge of murder or manslaughter could be supported on the available evidence and if so, whether the Crown could rebut a claim of self defence or partial self defence.

Mr Holcombe was shot in Armidale on June 1 2009. The Coroner suspended an inquest into his death in October 2010 and referred the matter to the ODPP in March 2011. The file was received in April 2011.

Kind regards

The Office of the DPP was so busy justifying the delay of fourteen months for the decision, they had quoted the wrong date for Elijah's death. He had died on the second of June, not the first. I emailed my phone-friend and warned her to correct it before the press release went out.

I turned the ignition and the air conditioner roared. I drove down Bagot Road through Darwin's northern suburbs, past prehistoric palms with leaves as big as windows, and stopped at the Nightcliff jetty. The shade of the casuarinas smelt of piss and pigeons. I had to talk to someone. I called Quentin, but got his message bank.

'Did you get my email? The DPP response is in, they won't charge Rich,' I mumbled. 'Talk to you later.'

I dialled like a drunk person. David Sweeney was scathing. He wanted to challenge the decision immediately.

An ibis scavenged through leaf litter, scattering rubbish in a search for scraps. I ripped a thumbnail off between my teeth. A water bird dived into the ocean like a spear. I shut my eyes. My phone vibrated. It was Jeremy, asking me to call.

'It's what I was expecting,' he said.

'I wasn't. I don't understand it, not after the coronial.'

'We got a letter from the DPP that spells it all out.'

'What happens now?'

'Dunno. There might not be anything else. We're waiting to hear more from Phil Stewart; there's still the civil case.' He sounded almost accepting.

'Sure—'

I walked sightless through the park back to the car and drove home.

Jeremy sent me his letter from the DPP. It was dated 28 August 2012, addressed to Mr Jeremy Holcombe and Mrs Tracey Holcombe.

I stalked my study like a wasp caught in a jar. Tracey had been dead a year. Did these people not care about the lives they dealt with?

The Director of Public Prosecutions, Lloyd Babb, offered his condolences for the loss of Elijah then got straight to the point.

> I wish to advise that after much consideration and careful analysis of all the evidence I have determined not to commence proceedings against Senior Constable Rich for murder or manslaughter or for any other criminal offence arising from the death of Elijah. Given the tragic circumstances of this case and the conflicting evidence of the eyewitnesses, I have set out some of my reasons below.
>
> The circumstances in which Elijah came to be shot are tragic. However, once Elijah had picked up the knife, Senior Constable Rich was acting lawfully when he approached him and drew his firearm.
>
> In my view the preponderance of evidence is capable of establishing (and the Crown would have a difficulty negating) that Elijah did move forwards towards Senior Constable Rich just prior to the discharge of the firearm.

I looked up preponderance. 'Superiority in weight, force, power, number.'

Lloyd Babb had run the trial in his head, allowing the jury to weigh the evidence of witnesses from Cinders Lane.

> I have carefully considered all the evidence on this point. The combined effect of the evidence of a number of the eye witnesses would, in my view, lead to the jury accepting that Elijah moved towards Senior Constable Rich.

The rest of the DPP's decisions flowed from this assumption.

> I have formed the view that the Crown would not be able to negative the reasonable possibility that, at the critical moment when Senior Constable Rich pulled the trigger, he genuinely believed it was necessary to discharge the firearm in self-defence. This conclusion excludes any charge of murder being laid against Senior Constable Rich.

The central issue in the case, Babb said, was whether it could be proved beyond reasonable doubt that Rich's response was unreasonable 'in the circumstances as he perceived them'.

'The critical time to consider is the moment before the fatal shot was fired,' Babb stated.

The 'critical time' was the only moment missed by CCTV cameras in Cinders Lane. The moment that people saw Elijah move, stand still, step back, step forward, run. The moment in which, Lloyd Babb had decided, a jury would determine that Elijah moved.

> Whether [Rich's] response was reasonable must be assessed from the perspective of a properly trained police officer, in the circumstances as Senior Constable Rich perceived them to be.

What Rich perceived in Cinders Lane and how he responded was a legal reality. It had weight and importance. Elijah's perception that a man he didn't know was pursuing him with a gun and claimed to be a police officer didn't.

Rich gave Elijah no explanation for how or why he had the keys to Jeremy's car. Elijah was not obliged to go with him when Rich said he was wanted back at the hospital. Yes, running from Rich was an irrational thing to do, unless you knew that Elijah was convinced the police were involved in a plot to kill him on orders from his wife.

Elijah's perception of reality was distorted. But by the means used to measure Rich's culpability — 'the circumstances as he perceived them' — Elijah had a reasonable argument of self-defence when he took up a knife to ward off a man who was chasing him with a gun. Didn't he?

If the legal system's algorithm allowed for Rich's distorted judgement, why wasn't there room for Elijah's?

The DPP's letter had an answer of sorts.

> Unlike other members of the public, police act under a duty to uphold the law and to protect members of the public. Further, in my view, if a police officer is acting lawfully and in accordance with the training manuals and protocol, it could not be said as a matter of law that his response is unreasonable.

In a contest of realities, the law took the side of police. As long as an officer played by the rules learned in training, 'it could not be said as a matter of law that his or her response is unreasonable'.

Rich had not broken the rules, in Babb's judgement.

> I have determined that there are no reasonable prospects of the Crown proving beyond reasonable doubt that Senior Constable Rich's response was not a reasonable one in the circumstances as he perceived them. There is therefore no reasonable prospect of a conviction for manslaughter based on excessive self-defence.

Lloyd Babb believed the evidence supported a view that Elijah moved towards Rich before Rich fired. That gave a reasonable defence of self-defence for Rich, and made Elijah's death a legally justified homicide. The DPP did not believe a jury could reasonably be convinced otherwise.

The grief that cut short Tracey's life was not a matter for the DPP. Joan Whitburn's evidence from her office window, Andrew Strudwick and Stephen Swain's declaration that Elijah was standing still, did not hold sway. If a police officer acted in accordance with their training, their perception could not be flawed. Reality resided in a training manual somewhere, not in the mess of human frailty that collided in Cinders Lane.

PART TWO

20.

It was October 2012 in Darwin — the season of the rainless build-up. Storms threatened, but delivered no more than static shocks and shattered tempers.

I sat in a cane chair on our patio, rolling a beer bottle between my palms.

The Coroner's findings in the coronial inquest for Roberto Laudisio Curti had been handed down. A copy was spread across my lap.

The inquest had heard that Curti was under the influence of LSD the night he died. More than a dozen officers had chased him, but when they caught him no one could hold him down. Police witnesses said that the 21-year-old had a superhuman strength they were used to seeing in methamphetamine users. Was that what had driven their extreme response — a suspicion that Roberto was on ice? I wondered.

A senior sergeant involved in police training gave evidence before the Coroner that the force police had used against Curti was 'consistent with current NSW Police SOPs and training'. This was the line that had me staring into space.

Eleven officers holding Curti down, Tasers fired at him fourteen times, two while he was handcuffed on the ground; two and a half cans of capsicum spray. All for a uni student who'd stolen a packet of biscuits on a bad acid trip and run away. How could what the police had done to Curti that night be legal?

Curti was under the effect of an illicit drug, Coroner Jerram acknowledged in her findings.

But he was guilty of no serious offence. He was proffering no threat to anyone. There was no attempt by police to consider his mental state. He was, in the words of Mr. Al Shayeb, 'just crazy'. Left alone, there is not a shred of evidence that he would have caused any harm, other than to himself ... Roberto's only foes during his ordeal were the police ... No one had told him he was under arrest, or why. We now know that he was almost certainly in a psychotic state of paranoia and fear [brought on by the LSD], but this did not translate into any violence other than his need to flee.

Haunting night-vision of Roberto Curti naked on the footpath, with the knees of a police officer on his chest, had beamed across the country in the week of the inquest. The vision came from cameras mounted on officers' Taser guns. Images of the 21-year-old pushing himself against a plate-glass window with the shadow of half a dozen police around him were everywhere online. You could hear Curti's cries for help in YouTube videos.

My husband ferried a tray of meat from the BBQ to the table. I pierced a slab of kangaroo and dropped it on my plate.

'I read the Curti findings today,' I said.

'Which coroner heard it?'

'Mary Jerram.' I re-filled his glass and passed the salad. 'She's doing the Holcombe inquest, too.'

'What did she say about the cops?' he asked.

'A pack mentality like *Lord of the Flies*; she said they had no idea what the problem was or what crime they were supposed to be averting.'

'Ouch,' he said.

'It's not going to help my chances of convincing Andrew Rich to speak to me, if that's what he thinks he's in for. Got any suggestions?' I joked.

'Who's Rich's counsel?'

'Brent Haverfield. He represented some of the cops involved in Curti,' I said.

'Why don't you just call him?'

'Would you take the call if you were representing Rich?'

My husband grinned at me.

'No chance.'

Brent Haverfield sounded young and flinty through the phone. I pictured him in a dark suit, freshly shaved, gesturing to a colleague to go ahead, he'd see him back at the office.

I wanted to talk to Andrew Rich over a coffee; Brent could come if he wanted to, I pitched.

Out of the question, Haverfield replied.

'Where's the harm in Andrew seeing the whites of my eyes to make his own judgement?' I asked. 'If he decides he doesn't want to talk, I'll go away — I promise.'

'That's not in my client's interests. This coroner has a history,' Haverfield said.

'I'm not out to do a hatchet job,' I pleaded. 'I want to meet Andrew so his voice is in my head. If I can't get a sense of him as a person, he'll have no humanity in the story. I don't want that and neither do the Holcombes.'

It was my best card and my last one.

There was nothing to stop Mary Jerram referring Rich to the DPP again if he revealed something incriminating in our conversation — she'd done it before, she could do it again, Haverfield said. He would advise Andrew Rich 'in the strongest terms' against speaking to me at any time. It wasn't worth the risk of self-incrimination.

It wasn't worth staying on the phone.

Haverfield would probably use this exchange to shore up Andrew's faith in him. *She's a journalist, they twist your words. You don't want to talk to any of them, mate. I told her you wouldn't speak to her. Keep your mouth shut, and we'll see you through this.*

If Rich hadn't committed an offence, how could he incriminate himself? If he had, how was justice served by letting him avoid accountability?

I checked the records of Jerram's inquests, but found nothing to support the claim Haverfield had made. Jerram had referred other inquests to the DPP, but she'd never sent anything back for a second turn, as far as I could see.

I checked with Phil Stewart the next time we spoke, and he asked where I heard the story.

'Brent Haverfield.'

Phil laughed.

'Brent Haverfield was a cop and police prosecutor before he became a barrister. He gets briefed to represent cops in trouble all the time — he's playing hardball.'

With the question of Rich's criminal culpability settled, it was open to Mary Jerram to continue Elijah's inquest. Now that the DPP had decided the case would go no further, her inquiry into Elijah's death could not interfere with another court's work.

The remaining witnesses on Jerram's list could be called back to give evidence. Andrew Rich was on that list. Even if he wouldn't tell me his story, he would have to tell the court.

I marked off Elijah's twenty-eighth birthday in the first week of November 2012.

Three days later Stella turned three; she was full of declarations and fierce emotion. Her arm and wrist still met in a crease of fat. I loved her more now than I ever had.

But some days agony would fall like a piano from the sky, unannounced and crushing. I would lie in bed and stare at walls contaminated with my thoughts. I didn't want to die, but it felt like the only way to kill the pain that I wanted to fling out of my body or vomit on the ground. I did not want to die; I wanted to stop dying in this and so many minutes before and after this one. I wondered if I should shave my head or damage my body to make the pain visible. To make the world take notice and care.

21.

I raced through pitching rain with Sweeney's voice pressed to my ear. It was almost Christmas.

'The Coroner's listed Elijah's inquest for March. They've put it down for two days,' he said.

'What can they possibly get through in two days?' I snapped.

I started the car. Wipers thumped the windscreen. Puddles formed around my feet. I was late for a party.

'Don't know yet. There'll have to be meetings with the other side to agree on witnesses.'

'But they'll make Rich speak, won't they?' I asked.

Nothing was decided, Sweeney stressed. The courts were closing this week for Christmas; it would all be thrashed out next year.

I could barely see the road in front of me.

Half the women were in fancy dress; all the men wore short-sleeved shirts. The grown-ups danced beneath the elevated house and shouted about politics. The kids got naked and filled the pool. Everyone was going south for Christmas.

I waved at my husband across the crowd and walked past the spitted lamb up to the deck to hide. I ended up in a conversation with a couple I didn't know. We leaned on the railing, searching for a breeze, and watched electricity crack the sky. My chest and jaw were tight. I waited for the world to break along the lightning's jagged line. We made small talk about the early wet season, and one of them asked what I did for work.

'I'm writing a book.'

'What about?'

'A young mentally ill man who was shot by the police.'

'Is it that guy on Bondi Beach?' the husband asked.

No one ever asked if I was writing about Tyler Cassidy holding two carving knives on a skate ramp in suburban Melbourne. No one ever named Adam Salter or Roberto Curti, let alone Elijah. Everyone picked 'the man on the beach'.

'You're thinking of Roni Levi,' I said. 'That happened fifteen years ago. My guy was shot in Armidale in 2009. They both had knives,' I offered as compensation.

'What I don't understand is why the cops don't just shoot at people's legs — why do they have to shoot to kill?' the wife pitched in.

'Have you ever fired a gun?' I asked.

She hadn't. The last time I had was shooting rabbits as a kid, but I knew how hard it was to hit something.

'A millimetre's shift of your hand with a pistol will change your aim completely. So police have to aim for the greatest mass if they want to be sure to hit their target, especially if it's moving. It ends up being fatal, because the biggest and most reliable target on a person is the most fatal choice — the torso is where the major organs are. That's why police are taught to only take their gun out if they're prepared to kill someone. Because if they use it properly, they probably will.'

The first notes of *Silent Night* on a piano floated up the stairs, and I excused myself.

'I'm going,' I said to my husband.

'What's wrong?'

'I'll talk to you at home. I can't do this tonight.'

In the morning, I went to the library and borrowed *Shoot and Demonise*, the book on Roni Levi's case. The cover was a grainy image of a man in the crucifix position, his chest thrust forward, challenging two policemen. They both had guns trained on him.

'The central fact in the Levi case is the knife,' wrote legal academic James Miller. 'What, after twenty-six minutes, changes about the knife, causing police to shoot?'

Roni Levi was a 36-year-old photographer, with no recorded history of mental illness. The night before he died, friends took him to St Vincent's Hospital in Darlinghurst. They suspected he was having a psychotic episode. Emergency Department staff assessed Roni as calm, compliant, and of no risk to himself or others, but they asked him to stay for further observation. Hours later, Roni left the hospital undetected and returned to his flat in Bondi. He was in a heightened psychotic state, salivating, glassy-eyed, and unaware of his surroundings. He took a knife from the kitchen and walked out the door; his flatmate followed him. Roni tried to flee, and when he couldn't outpace his friend, he threatened him with the knife. His flatmate went to the police.

Roni walked to the beach, holding the knife, and wandered in and out of the surf fully clothed. Fifteen minutes later, six police officers shadowed him as he weaved from the waterline up the beach towards the high sandstone wall of the promenade. Police tried all sorts of tactics, including gentle persuasion, to convince Roni to drop the knife. Waving it towards the ground and in front of him, Roni pushed police up the sand toward the beach wall. One officer tried to knock the knife from Roni's hand with a baton, but Roni turned on him and the officer backed away.

Roni was killed by simultaneous shots from Anthony Dilorenzo and Rodney Podesta. The two men told investigators they fired because Roni lunged at them with the knife after he turned away from the officer with the baton. They said Roni forced them into a position where they had no room to retreat; they had 'no choice'.

'At the moment of shooting Levi must … become more than just a man with a knife in a public place,' Miller wrote. 'It is not enough that he may appear aggressive or out of control or suicidal. Weapons should be fired in the line of duty in this situation if, and only if, Levi posed an immediate threat of serious injury or death. This is the only legal basis upon which police officers may fire their weapons.'

The coronial inquest into Levi's death examined whether he moved towards police in the seconds before they fired. Lawyers and witnesses all agreed he did, but further evidence showed Podesta and Dilorenzo had another thirty metres to travel before they backed into the wall they claimed Roni was trying to pin them to.

Firing their guns was not their only option. They could have retreated further, Miller claimed.

The two police officers were the last two witnesses called at Roni Levi's nineteen-day inquest. Dilorenzo took the stand first. Four minutes later, Podesta replaced him. Both men declined to give evidence. They exercised the right of every citizen, including police officers, not to incriminate themselves.

Miller took care to point out that both officers took this route on their barrister's advice.

The Coroner in Levi's case found a prima facie case that Podesta and Dilorenzo had committed an indictable offence. He referred the matter to the Director of Public Prosecutions.

The then-DPP, Nicholas Cowdrey, concluded after three months deliberation that, 'the prosecution would not be able to prove beyond reasonable doubt that the officers did not act in self-defence'.

No charges were laid in Australia's most memorable case of 'mentally ill man shot by police'.

I read excerpts of the Levi book to my husband over dinner.

'They refused to give evidence. How is that possible?' I raged.

'The Coroner could have compelled them to speak if he really wanted to,' he answered.

It was helpful to have a lawyer in the house sometimes.

'Can Rich do the same thing — is he allowed to say he doesn't want to speak?' I asked.

'Yes.'

'And then there's no way to test his word about Elijah roaring and saying, "Shoot me, shoot me" and running at him — if Rich decides he doesn't want to talk?'

'Do you think he's lying?' my husband asked.

'I don't know. How can anyone know unless they test his evidence?'

'What if Rich really believes that's what happened? Imagine you're him. He's under pressure, his response and state are heightened, and in those seconds, he thinks he hears Elijah say those things. Say what he's described is some kind of post-traumatic response?' my husband challenged.

'If that's his response to the level of threat everyone else says Elijah posed, then he shouldn't be in a job where he carries a gun,' I bit back.

We finished dinner and moved to the couch with books and another drink.

'What about this …' I said a little later. '"Taken overall, the evidence before the Coroner was strongly against the proposition that a lunge was made by Levi against either of the officers who shot",' I read.

'Levi's case was referred to the DPP by the Coroner,' I told my husband. 'But the DPP said the prosecution wouldn't be able to disprove that the police acted in self-defence. Just like Elijah's case. It's like the police get to meet a different standard to everyone else.'

My husband put down his book.

'Let's suppose everything you say is true. You have questions about what Rich says Elijah did, and you think he might have fucked up majorly. What do you want the legal system to do with that? Do we make it a criminal offence? Do we put Rich in jail for making that mistake?'

Faced with the end point of my argument, my rage collapsed. I didn't want Rich to go to jail. I didn't want him punished. I wanted him not to have killed Elijah, and if I couldn't have that, I wanted Elijah's death not to be Elijah's fault.

I knew I was on dangerous ground. Whoever spoke controlled the narrative. The Holcombes were speaking, Rich wasn't, and whatever his reasons, his silence put him at a disadvantage.

I only had one side of the story. I didn't know Rich's. I didn't understand the fear that prompted him to pull his gun; I didn't know what he felt and thought in Cinders Lane, or why he made the choice to shoot. No matter how much I felt for Elijah, feelings couldn't tell me what happened in Cinders Lane; and left with that void, I was trying to fill it.

This was the power and danger of my job. Stories mattered, and if you got them wrong, they mattered even more. The human brain was designed to seek out narratives or make them up to make meaning of the world. If Rich did not fill the gap in my understanding, then conjecture, assumptions, and other people's versions would flourish in the opening. I wanted to understand more than anything what drove the most difficult decision of Rich's life. But only he could tell me.

2013

22.

'She told me acceptance is the end of suffering, so I've accepted that what happened to Elijah was fucked,' Jeremy said on the phone from Wee Waa.

He had been seeing a psychologist again.

'I finished up just before Christmas when she told me I was cured, which means this is as sane as I'm ever going to get.' He laughed grimly.

Jeremy and Fiona would be at the re-opening of Elijah's inquest in a few weeks.

'How are you feeling about it?' I asked.

'I don't know what there is to feel hopeful about. What can happen? I would think Rich is going to get on the stand and stonewall.'

'The DPP's decision is made; he can't be charged, he's got nothing to lose now. Maybe it'll be a relief for him to tell his side of the story?' I offered.

'The lawyers say he'll probably object to giving evidence. If he does that and sticks to his original statement—' Jeremy breathed out heavily.

'If he objects, is that the end of it — he just doesn't talk?' I asked Phil Stewart, who would be on the Holcombes' legal team again when the inquest re-opened.

'Not necessarily,' he said.

The Coroner could grant Rich a certificate under the *Coroners Act* so that nothing he said could be used as evidence in another court, Phil explained. The certificate was used to induce reluctant witnesses to speak. It effectively protected a witness from self-incrimination, which was Rich's lawyers' ultimate concern. Jerram had indicated at the directions hearing that she would offer one to Rich, but lawyers for the police argued against it, Phil said.

A certificate would let Rich tell his story without risk of being charged.

He would be safe, and the Holcombes would get to hear what had happened. How could the police force have a problem with that? I asked.

Phil Stewart figured it was a tactical move.

The Holcombes were suing the NSW Police, and anything Rich said at the inquest could impact on the outcome of that civil case, Phil said. The police force was jumpy about that possibility, because they were the defendants in the civil case, not Rich.

'But if his inquest evidence can't be used anywhere else, how can it affect the civil case?' I asked. Phil tried to explain, but the legal complexities were beyond me.

The inquest would happen in Sydney this time instead of Armidale, and the line-up of lawyers had changed significantly.

Patrick Saidi QC would represent the NSW Commissioner of Police in place of Ray Hood. Saidi was also defending the State of NSW in the Holcombes' civil case.

Jeremy Gormly SC replaced Chris Hoy, who had been counsel assisting the coroner in Armidale. Gormly had assisted Jerram on Roberto Laudisio Curti's inquest. Jerram would preside over Elijah's case until its end.

Phil Stewart had called in James Sheller SC to help represent the Holcombes at the inquest.

Rich's barrister was still Brent Haverfield, with the addition of Murugan Thangaraj SC.

'How many witnesses will the Coroner call?' I asked Phil.

'Rich and one or two others. It's still being worked out.'

'What about Dufty?'

'Probably not,' he said.

'What do you mean?'

'No one can find him.'

'It can't be that hard. Are they even trying?' I asked, incredulous.

'Someone said he's sick, they reckon he's left the police,' Phil said. 'Will you be at the inquest?'

'Yes. I'll fly down for the whole thing.'

23.

In the weeks leading up to the inquest's re-opening, I spoke to Jeremy on and off. He and Tarney were in mediation with police on the civil case.

Tracey had described 'a huge weight lifting' when Elijah's inquest in Armidale was suspended. In her mind, the Coroner's decision to refer the case was acknowledgement that Elijah did nothing wrong. That was all she ever wanted, Tracey told me, but six months later, she sued the police. Tarney had taken over his mother's claim as the executor of her will, which was why Tarney and Jeremy were the ones in mediation. I still struggled with the fact they were pursuing the case. It felt like a sign that their compassion had reached its limits.

Tracey's claim was against the State of New South Wales as Rich's employer, but the damages it detailed were all about Rich's actions.

The claim made an argument that Rich and other officers should have known Elijah would be afraid of them, because Jeremy had described Elijah's delusional beliefs to police in Narrabri the previous day. He'd given explicit warnings when he reported Elijah missing that his son was frightened of police and would run if they approached him. That information had been accessible to any officer in the state via a database called COPS, the statement pointed out. If police had done their job, it argued, someone at Armidale Station should have checked Elijah's record on the system. If Rich had informed himself, or been informed, about the nature of Elijah's delusions before he went to find him, lots of things might have been handled differently.

I tried to imagine Rich's feelings about the civil case and the re-opening of the inquest. He had waited two years for a decision from the DPP. What had that pressure done to him? I imagined him slumped at the kitchen table, a soft hand on his shoulder. *Close your eyes, try to get some rest.* The laneway appears, his eyes crash open. Dress for work, report for duty, but the knowledge follows him wherever he goes. *I killed a man. I had no choice.*

24.

The Glebe Coroner's Court in Sydney was a travesty of a building. It hunkered so close to the edge of Parramatta Road it looked like it might trip and fall into the traffic at any minute.

Two camera crews perched on the narrow footpath outside. A man with a homemade poster hovered near them. Roni Levi, Adam Salter, Elijah Holcombe, Roberto Curti, and Gillian Harman's names cascaded in neat handwriting below its heading, 'Justice Why Do You Hide?'

I risked a sideways glance. No sign of religious overtones. Good personal hygiene, stocky legs, suntanned arms, pressed shirt and shorts. The poster-holder looked like a bushwalker, but his close-shaved beard made me think of a shipwright.

'Do you know someone in the case?' I asked.

The shipwright shook his head.

'I thought some of my friends might come. I've never done this kind of thing before. "Why are you spending your spare time on that?" they said. "Enjoy your retirement." But I can't.'

He stuck the poster under his arm and offered me his hand.

'I'm Brian.'

'Kate. What got you interested in this case?' I asked.

Brian read a lot. Newspapers, coronial findings, Ombudsman's reports.

'Something has to change. They can't keep shooting people. Did you read the book about Roni Levi? I got so angry I had to put it down and go off for a walk.'

A taxi pulled up. The cameramen ran. Jeremy and Fiona climbed out first. Jordan and Tarney followed. They linked arms and walked together, all eyes down. The cameramen walked backwards, catching the Holcombes' sombre faces for the news. David Phelps came last, like a faithful sheepdog rounding up his flock.

A circle of men in dark suits clustered in the foyer. One figure among them wore riding boots and moleskins. I recognized him from the CCTV vision; he was shorter than I had expected. Dufty's auburn hair was thin on top. They'd found him.

Fiona wound a necklace through her fingers on the opposite side of the dingy room. Jeremy had disappeared. Tarney and Jordan watched the door.

I slipped past everyone, into the courtroom.

Sack-coloured chairs faced the Coroner's bench in rows. The only natural light came from tiny windows high on the wall. I chose the second last row from the back.

The bar table, where the lawyers sat, stretched across the room below the Coroner's bench. A barrister at the far-left end scratched his thumb against his nostril. His eyes were pouched, his eyebrows unruly. Patrick Saidi SC, Counsel for the NSW Police, reminded me of a walrus. Beside him, Murugan Thangaraj shifted papers into piles with light, swift hands. He bounced with energy, like a boy with a new bat tapping at the crease.

At the opposite end of the bar table sat Phil Stewart and James Sheller. Phil towered above his senior counsel like a giant over a choirboy.

The detectives filed in in their shiny shoes. Dufty peeled off and slipped into the back row. A glamorous journalist slipped in beside him. She clearly had no idea who Dufty was.

Counsel assisting the coroner, Jeremy Gormly, bustled in. He was a Toby jug come to life; dignity rendered cheerfully. Brent Haverfield followed. His hair was a bristling pelt above sharp eyes.

The room was full. Uniformed police joined Dufty in the back row.

Tarney, Jordan, and David Phelps were on my left. The crowns of Jeremy and Fiona's heads were visible near the lawyers.

'All rise.'

Coroner Mary Jerram entered, elegant and neat. She seated the room with a throaty order, and Gormly gave forth in rich, round tones.

'Your Honour, this is the resumption of a mandatory inquest into the death of Elijah Holcombe … What remains outstanding in practical evidence concerns the basis for the discharge of Senior Constable Rich's firearm and the chain of events that led to that discharge …'

The journalists in crayon-coloured jackets raced their pens along the page. The court would sit for two days. The Coroner would call three witnesses.

'The first of the remaining witnesses to be called is a former police officer, Mr Greg Dufty,' Gormly announced.

The second witness would be Senior Sergeant Davis, an expert in police training and the use of police force.

'Finally, there is an intention to call Senior Constable Rich,' Gormly said. 'Because I am aware that there will be an application that Senior Constable Rich not be called, some of the comments I now make need to be heard in light of the fact that there will be outstanding a determination of whether or not he does give evidence.'

Even forewarned, the words still stole my breath. I couldn't see Rich's goatee anywhere. Was he waiting in another room like a boxer preparing for a ring parade? I dared a half-turn. Dufty's long, thin nose entered my line of sight. His green eyes, deep-set, didn't shift. He leaned his torso forward in his seat and rocked slightly. Impatient.

Jeremy Gormly's baritone rolled across the room.

'Given the time that's elapsed since the initial hearing, I propose reciting a narrative of events … Let me just say that sadly Elijah's mother Tracey died after the previous hearing of this inquest.'

He paused and let the words hang in the room — part eulogy, part accusation.

Dufty clasped his hands.

'Elijah, by all accounts, was a particularly presentable, intelligent, and articulate young man,' Gormly began, and walked the courtroom through Elijah's life. Pens raced along the page; Elijah turned the corner in his father's car and drove to Armidale. Rich and Dufty joined the story.

Dufty's head fell forward when Gormly reached the camping store.

'The encounter was brief. Senior Constable Rich, who had the car keys of Elijah's father's car, seems to have held them out.'

Police scratched their chins in the back row, scritch, scritch.

'Elijah seems to have perceived, and it would seem correctly, that if he approached Senior Constable Rich he might be arrested … In any event, Elijah's response was to start running … He wasn't, of course, armed with any weapon at this stage. Elijah at that time wasn't wanted for any offence, he hadn't committed any offence which would justify restraint under the *Mental Health Act*, but it would appear that that's a matter that needs to be explored in the evidence. Certainly, he hadn't acted violently towards any person up to that time or himself at the time, and he doesn't appear to have threatened harm to anyone that day or indeed any other day. Nevertheless, Senior Constable Rich pursued Elijah Holcombe, chasing him along Armidale streets through a mall and into the Caffiends café.'

The bread knife was on the bench. The row in front of me paused to shake their writing hands.

'It has to be said that the moment Elijah picked up that knife, the situation somewhat changed,' Gormly said, and the air around him picked up charge.

My mind flashed to Roni Levi. *The central fact in the case is the knife. … At the moment of shooting Levi must become something more than just a man with a knife in a public place. He must do more than merely gesture with or brandish the knife.*

Gormly continued. 'The only basis upon which he picked it up seems to have been because he was being chased.'

I saw Roberto Laudisio Curti fleeing bare-chested through the streets of Sydney. As all the civilian witnesses and a few officers told the court, at all times Roberto was merely trying to get away. No one had told him he was under arrest, or why ... he was almost certainly in a psychotic state of paranoia and fear but this did not translate into any violence other than his need to flee ...

The skin beneath Tarney's eyes was sunken, like finger marks in dough. Jordan was an Easter Island statue.

Gormly reached Cinders Lane, 'where Elijah dropped his sloppy joe'. I could see the triangle of his jumper in the tree, and below it, Elijah's body taking the blows of CPR from strangers.

'He walked past a number of people; there was no harm or threat to those people,' Gormly reassured the courtroom. 'When I say no harm or threat, he was not endeavouring to engage with those people or threaten them in any way, he was simply walking with the knife.'

An officer behind me dragged his thumb through the pages of a notebook. The court clerk's earrings were tangled in her hair. The Coroner's mouth was a line not to be crossed.

'There's considerable difference between the eyewitness accounts about Elijah's actions and movements immediately prior to the firing of the shot,' Gormly said. 'There are persons who gave evidence that Elijah made some movement towards Senior Constable Rich just before the shot was fired. That's consistent with what Senior Constable Rich says ... His evidence is essentially that Elijah turned, roared, said various things including "shoot me", and started to run towards him. Then there are witnesses who appear to deny in fairly categorical terms that Elijah made any movement toward Senior Constable Rich ... If one weighs up the evidence by numbers and position, one would have to say that there is a body of evidence that says he did not move.'

An insect chorus of pens clicked in the back row. Dufty fiddled with his watch.

Having taken the room to the irreconcilable moment, Gormly

reduced his inquiry to four clear questions.

'Firstly, what was the basis for Senior Constables Rich and Dufty to pursue Elijah Holcombe from Rusden Street? Secondly, to what extent was the knife picked up by Elijah a change in the course of events? Thirdly, to what extent was the discharge of Senior Constable Rich's firearm a last resort and otherwise within police training and directions; and finally, what if anything might have been done to achieve a better outcome? I put that last issue particularly because of the mental health issue that emerged in this case.'

Gormly reminded the court of Rich's call for backup from the kitchen door of Caffiends. Rich came to the decision to shoot Elijah between the end of that phone call and the midpoint of Cinders Lane, Gormly said.

'A gap in time of no more than about one minute and fifty something seconds elapsed between the time Senior Constable Rich made his phone call to the police station and the time that the shot was fired. On any view … it was a very short period of time. It's for that reason that I will ultimately be making submissions that Senior Constable Rich would be required to give evidence so that there can be some explanation of the reasoning process he used when firing his gun.'

I knew from my own research that the back door of Caffiends and the place where Elijah died were both three hundred metres from the police station. Rich's decision to shoot crystallised over a distance of roughly eighty metres, thirty seconds after he stepped out the back door of Caffiends.

The story was narrowing, rushing towards its end like water down a drain.

'I call Gregory John Dufty,' Gormly intoned.

Patrick Saidi sprang to his feet and stroked his tie as if it were a cat. He bowed his head towards the Coroner.

'Your Honour, I appear on his behalf … Former Constable Dufty suffers from post-traumatic stress disorder, and I've indicated to him, Your Honour, that if he has any difficulty whilst giving evidence, to let Your Honour know.'

'Of course,' replied Jerram. 'Please do, Mr Dufty.'

Dufty had been with the police for twenty years but he didn't look more than forty. The police in the room leaned forward in their seats.

'You've obviously retired from the police?' the Coroner said lightly.

Dufty was working as a labourer for a landscape gardener.

'Is that less stressful?'

'A lot,' Dufty snorted.

The Coroner granted Dufty a Section 61 certificate, which gave him the same protection from self-incrimination she had foreshadowed giving Rich.

In jerking words, Dufty told the court that he had left the police fourteen months ago: 'I was discharged.' His contact with colleagues in Armidale had been 'very, very minor' since.

'Have you been in touch with Senior Constable Rich?' Gormly asked.

A couple of times in the street, just to say hello.

'You haven't socialised together?'

Dufty's 'no' was angry.

Gormly took Dufty to the search for Jeremy Holcombe's car.

'I think you understood that Elijah had come to the police station and more or less said he had taken his father's car from Narrabri or Wee Waa, and driven it to Armidale?' Gormly began.

'Your Honour, I object. I think the correct interpretation is "he had stolen",' Saidi interjected.

The distinction was important. A stolen car gave Rich and Dufty a reason to chase and arrest Elijah.

'What did *you* understand, Mr Dufty?' Gormly asked.

'My understanding was — through a conversation that I had with Senior Constable Rich — that we were going to look for a car that had been stolen ... I said "Is this guy in custody, or — where is he at the moment?"'

Rich didn't know where Elijah was, so Dufty called the station. The duty officer said Elijah was at the hospital.

'At some time before you arrived at the hospital, you learned that Elijah had left. What was your purpose in going to the hospital after you'd heard that he had left?' Gormly asked.

It was Rich's idea to go to the hospital, Dufty said.

The Coroner broke in. 'Who was the senior officer of the two of you?'

'Me.'

There's your PTSD, I scrawled. *Rich initiated, Dufty followed. But Dufty was supposed to be in charge. He could have stopped it.*

Rich was in the Emergency Department for 'Thirty seconds, maybe,' Dufty said. When he came back to the car, he said, 'The guy's absconded, they want to get him back.'

What did he and Rich talk about on the drive between the hospital and the camping store on Rusden Street? asked Gormly.

'We just discussed which way he might have went. I was saying, from memory, "Is this the police issue, is there a schedule, is there anything like that?"'

If staff at the hospital had scheduled Elijah under the *Mental Health Act*, Rich and Dufty had grounds to arrest him and return him to the hospital.

'Was there a schedule?' Gormly asked.

'Not that I'm aware of.'

'Was there any discussion between you and [SC Rich] as to whether or not Elijah had been scheduled?' Gormly pushed.

'I think I just asked the question, "Is he scheduled or what?" From memory, I think [the answer] was, "They just want him back".' The words were gruff.

Dufty described the moment Rich approached Elijah outside the camping store.

'He said something like "Elijah, Elijah, I've got your keys. I'll give you the keys." I think [Elijah] stopped, and Senior Constable Rich said, "It's the police; I've got your keys. I've got to give you your keys."'

Gormly wanted to know exactly how the keys were offered. Were they held out; were they jangled?

On an outstretched palm at chest height, from about three metres away, Dufty said. He didn't remember any jangling.

'Senior Constable Rich said "I've got your keys, I'll give you your keys back, come and get them and—"'

'Come and get them?' Jerram pounced on the addition.

Dufty's voice was thin. 'I've been receiving treatment for two years for post-traumatic stress. I'm taking various medications and going to different centres and that, and my memory is not that great, so I'm just going on what I basically can remember.'

Dufty was shaking. The Coroner suggested a break, but Gormly asked for one more question.

'Did you understand that Senior Constable Rich was going to try and arrest Elijah?'

'My belief was that we were going to take him back to hospital,' Dufty whispered.

The Coroner turned to Dufty and reached her hand across the bench towards him.

'I know it's horrible for you. We'll start again at twelve,' she said.

Everyone took off in search of coffee. I walked around a corner straight into Jeremy and Fiona.

'We're hiding. We didn't want them to get pictures of us smoking,' Fiona said.

'Kate, do you know you have biro all over your forehead?' Jeremy asked.

I rubbed at my forehead. I was relieved to see them. David Phelps appeared from behind me.

'I've been speaking to Rich's lawyer,' David said. He was talking about Murugan Thangaraj. 'He's friends with some Sydney relatives. Small world. Seems like a nice enough bloke.'

'What did you make of Dufty?' Jeremy asked me.

'I just want to give him a hug,' Fiona said, and we all went quiet as Haverfield and two detectives came around the corner.

When Dufty returned to the stand after the break, Gormly gave his memory a prod.

According to Dufty's statement, Elijah asked Rich to throw him the keys in Rusden Street, outside the camping store. Why didn't Rich comply? Gormly queried.

They wanted Elijah to approach so they could apprehend him, Dufty said.

'We believed he was mentally ill. We were going to have a conversation with him, see how he was travelling, and get him back to the hospital.'

'The conversation seems to have been intended to lead directly to apprehending,' Gormly observed.

'That would probably be true,' Dufty agreed.

'Was it your understanding that to apprehend Elijah in those circumstances was a valid thing to do or were you leaving that to Senior Constable Rich?' asked Gormly.

'I have faith in my partner,' Dufty snapped, 'and from the conversation that he had at the hospital, the hospital had concerns for [Elijah's] welfare and we were going to bring him back to the hospital.'

James Sheller stood to cross-examine Dufty. His hair was like a new-hatched chick's. If it weren't so short, it would have fluffed around his head.

No one said to Dufty or Rich that Elijah had been scheduled at the hospital, and no one directed them to make an arrest over the 'stolen' vehicle, did they? Sheller put to Dufty.

He agreed.

'It was your understanding, I think, that Senior Constable Rich intended to apprehend Elijah. Is that correct?'

It was.

'And as you know, the process of arresting someone requires, among a number of other things, specifying a reason for arrest, correct?'

Correct, said Dufty.

'And you know now that there was no reason for arresting Elijah in Armidale on the second of June 2009—'

'I object, Your Honour,' Patrick Saidi bellowed.

'Well, I press it,' Sheller retorted.

The cold fact was that no one at Armidale Police Station had given a single direction about Elijah to either Rich or Dufty. Aiken's request was that Rich find the car; that had come out in the Armidale inquest. From Dufty's evidence today, it seemed the idea that the car was stolen had also come from Aiken. Rich had taken it upon himself to add Elijah to the brief, and Dufty went along with it. Watching the brittle man in front of us, I suspected that decision tortured Dufty.

'*Do* you know now that there was no reason to arrest Elijah Holcombe while he was standing in Rusden Street on the second of June 2009?' asked Sheller, skirting Saidi's objection.

'I believe there was a cause to arrest him. Due to the fact that the hospital required him back,' Dufty said carefully, 'and I still did not understand what had happened about the stolen motor vehicle.' Arresting Elijah for the car was in the back of their minds, he said.

Gormly had covered this ground already, and Dufty had told him the hospital staff's concern was what prompted the search for Elijah. He hadn't mentioned the 'stolen' car to Gormly.

Sheller went for the fault lines. Did he or Rich check the status of the car before they stopped Elijah in Rusden Street? Why didn't Dufty mention the car to investigators after Elijah's shooting if it was such a significant consideration?

Patrick Saidi's objections rose in number and volume as Sheller continued. His eighth burst forth like an eruption.

'Your Honour, in order to understand this objection, one needs to understand this — there are civil proceedings on foot. I understand my learned friend is acting in those civil proceedings.' Sheller's questions were a fishing exercise designed to serve the civil case, Saidi implied.

'I object to this!' Sheller thundered. I waited for him to slam a ruler on the table.

The inquest was a testing ground for the Holcombes' civil case against police. Saidi represented the State of NSW, and Sheller the Holcombes, in each matter. Limiting Dufty's evidence here protected the State in the civil case. Drawing evidence out of him served the Holcombes.

'Your Honour is looking, with respect, at what happened between Senior Constable Rich and the deceased,' Saidi insisted; Dufty's views and actions were irrelevant. He leaned his bulk across the bar table and pushed the argument with his chest.

'We know the pursuit that followed was that of Senior Constable Rich of Elijah. It's Senior Constable Rich's state of mind that's relevant.'

But Dufty followed Rich's lead all day, so didn't they share a state of mind?

The Coroner dismissed Saidi's objections, and Sheller asked Dufty if he thought Rich's decision to chase Elijah was a good idea.

'Yes. A pursuit's a pursuit. If someone takes off running, you — you follow them,' Dufty answered.

I had read Dufty's statement to police so many times, it was like a lucid dream. Dufty took a different route to Rich and Elijah during the chase. When he turned the corner into Cinders Lane, he saw Rich crouched down holding Elijah's arm. Dufty arrived as Rich pulled Elijah's upper body, 'pale as pale' and motionless, onto the kerb. 'Oh Duff, can you help him?' his partner said, but Dufty was confused by Rich's distress. 'You're going to have to put pressure on that wound,' Rich said, and Dufty's senses focused. He saw the blood and smelt the gun smoke.

After the shooting, Dufty and Rich returned to the station separately. At some point in the evening, Rich asked Dufty to go back to the camping store and get his backpack from the car.

'Do you recall whether you were asked to go to his motor vehicle to get the backpack in relation to missing capsicum spray?' Sheller asked.

'No. It was because he had a headache.' Dufty's eyes were broken glass embedded in his face. He poured a glass of water.

'I knew that he suffered from migraines,' he rasped, and rubbed his hands against his thighs.

'And your understanding is the only purpose of getting his backpack was to get painkiller medication?' Sheller asked.

'Yes, that's correct.'

I had entertained Phil Stewart's theory that Dufty took Rich's OC spray from the bag at this point and 'lost' it to help Rich. But watching him now, drained of defiance and broken, my animosity collapsed. It didn't matter if the spray's disappearance was accidental or designed. Rich would still have shot Elijah.

Gormly's cross-examination was short and tight. It was as though he found the focus point where Dufty's answers sprang into view. Dufty went looking for Jeremy's car at Rich's request. He was Rich's passenger on the trip to the hospital. He chased Elijah to help Rich out. Dufty's information about Elijah came from Rich or Aiken back at the station. He was a follower.

Dufty stepped down from the witness box. Jeremy Holcombe met him in the aisle.

'Mr Dufty,' I heard him say.

Dufty clutched Jeremy's outstretched hand but couldn't raise his eyes. Jeremy told me later that Dufty said, 'Mr. Holcombe, I am so sorry.'

'Please look after yourself,' Jeremy replied.

'It was the closest thing to an apology I've heard yet,' he told me. 'I don't think he could believe I wished him well.'

Senior Sergeant Peter Davis was a smiling man with meaty forearms. A man upon whom the sun has always shone, I thought. His tie was held down by a police tie-pin, and a copper bangle circled his wrist.

Peter Davis was accustomed to appearances at the Coroner's Court, where his evidence was often sought as an expert in the use of police force. It had been Davis's report on Rich and Dufty's use of force against Elijah that raised my hackles when I read a summary of the brief.

Jeremy Gormly stepped Davis through the types of force available to Andrew Rich on the day he chased Elijah, from the least to most fatal options, beginning with capsicum spray.

Would capsicum spray have been useful to Rich in dealing with Elijah, if he had it? Gormly asked.

Possibly, said Davis. The spray was effective within three and a half metres; it wasn't an option he would recommend in Rich's situation. Three and a half metres was too close to get to someone 'approaching with a knife'.

I paused in my scribbling. Was his fast-forward to the view that Elijah 'approached' Rich with the knife deliberate? The truth had not been settled either way.

From what distance was it safe for Rich to use his gun? Gormly asked.

The closest was seven metres. It could be safely used at a greater distance depending on how accurate the shooter was, Davis replied.

Police in Armidale weren't using Tasers in June 2009, Gormly told the court. But if they had — 'I take it that you as an expert in force would have preferred to see an officer use a Taser rather than a gun in that situation?'

'Certainly not something recommended, no,' Davis replied in friendly tones.

Gormly's surprise was genuine. 'I'm sorry, I don't understand.'

At the distance Rich fired from in Cinders Lane, he only had time for one shot, Davis explained. With a Taser, there wouldn't have been time to reload if the first shot missed.

Implicit in his answer was an acceptance that Rich's life was under threat, and therefore shooting Elijah, more than once if necessary, was justified.

'You're saying that by reason of the presence of the knife, it's the individual officer's decision whether he would use a Taser or a gun?' Gormly asked.

'Yes.'

Davis had put on steel-rimmed glasses. He now looked like a librarian.

Gormly turned to Davis's report for Critical Incident investigators on Elijah's shooting.

'You say, "to avoid excessive application of force, police officers should use the minimum amount of force that's necessary",' Gormly read.

Davis nodded.

'Officers confronting a situation must firstly gain control. Secondly, must endeavour to —'

'Maintain control,' said Davis, his instructor's instincts taking over.

'Control and de-escalate,' Gormly corrected. 'Do you agree the mere holding of a weapon such as a knife is not sufficient reason for an officer to discharge his firearm?'

'If it's not a threat, no.'

'Would you agree, too, that an aggressive, angry, or mentally disturbed manner in itself is not sufficient for an officer to discharge his firearm?'

Gormly pushed his glasses to the end of his nose and peered over them at Davis.

'No, at that stage, no.'

Rich controlled the distance between himself and Elijah in Cinders Lane, Gormly posited. Elijah was fleeing, Rich was in pursuit. If Elijah turned and moved towards him, Rich could control the distance by backing away, provided he hadn't hemmed himself in. Correct?

'To a point,' Davis conceded.

Gormly pointed out that the exception to the statement was that

Elijah could turn and run at Rich.

'Yes,' Davis acknowledged with a smile.

Whether Rich was entitled to shoot at this point depended on how far away he was from Elijah, didn't it?

'Yes,' Davis agreed, and then turned ninety degrees. 'It would depend on the reaction of Elijah, yes.'

Wouldn't it also depend on the reaction of Senior Constable Rich? Gormly asked. 'I mean, he could back off if he were far enough to do so?'

If he were far enough away, yes, said Davis.

Gormly's voice hardened. Rich yelled directions and commands at Elijah but failed to establish any real communication, didn't he? The outcome of Rich's failure was that Elijah refused to comply and Rich shot him — wasn't that right?

'Well, I don't necessarily agree with that, no.' Davis was unruffled.

'Is that because you have accepted the evidence that Elijah started to run aggressively and threateningly towards Senior Constable Rich?'

'That's correct ... based on that assumption from what I've read of all the witnesses involved, yes.'

A new quietness filled the room. The police in the back row were especially still.

'If it was based on the assumption from all of the witnesses involved, you would agree wouldn't you, that a majority of the witnesses said Elijah *didn't* do what Senior Constable Rich said he did?' Gormly queried.

Davis conceded there were several witnesses who disagreed with Rich's story.

'Not several, the majority.' Gormly's voice rose. 'Why did you accept the version that was co-ordinate with Senior Constable Rich's —'

'Your Honour, I object—' Patrick Saidi began.

The Coroner batted him away, and Brent Haverfield rose to his feet.

'Well, Your Honour, will you hear me on that? There were three camps of witnesses — a camp that says "can't say one way or the other". There's a camp that says there was movement and a camp that says there was no movement. To lump those that can't say one way or the other with those that say there was no movement is just unfair.'

Haverfield's words were weighted with frustration. He had a point. The numbers were more malleable than Gormly made them out to be.

Counsel assisting moderated his tone. Was the correct conclusion to draw from the evidence of the three groups of witnesses, in Davis's view, that Elijah ran aggressively with the knife out, threatening Rich?

Davis confirmed it was.

'Would you consider that a better way to analyse what occurred ... was that Senior Constable Rich did not de-escalate and brought himself far too close to Elijah ever to be able to engage in communication?'

Gormly thrust the question at Davis, but Saidi cut across him.

'Your Honour, I object ... what is emerging and has emerged clearly during the course of this inquest is that counsel assisting appears to be taking a particular point of view of the evidence ... i.e., that there was something wrong in terms of the police officers pursuing or what happened in Cinders Lane.'

We were watching a brawl in a gentlemen's club. Whiskey on the velvet chairs, books knocked off the shelves. Jerram leaned back in her chair. Let the boys sort out their own scrapes.

'Mr Gormly?' she said when Saidi had finished.

Jeremy Gormly's face was a mask. He bit out his words with fists clenched on the lectern.

'A fundamental issue to work out is exactly what happened between Senior Constable Rich and Elijah Holcombe in those final few seconds, the final two minutes. We have various versions of the event, and here we have an opinion from an acknowledged expert in the use of police force, and he has given a clear and unequivocal view that Senior Constable Rich did no wrong and that everything he did was justified ... I am testing him on what another interpretation of the events might be. I will test all evidence.'

Gormly cloaked his rage in perfect enunciation.

'The fact that it's a police officer does not stop me from doing so. Your Honour, I defend the questions I am asking. Senior Sergeant Davis with his considerable experience both in the witness box and force appears to be handling them perfectly well ... The line of questions seems appropriate ...'

The boys had had their scuffle.

'I agree with you, Mr Gormly, please keep going.'

Gormly returned to the critical juncture.

'We were trying to work out what it was that Senior Constable Rich could have done to avoid discharging his firearm,' he reminded Davis.

Asking Elijah questions rather than yelling commands might have drawn Elijah into conversation, Gormly offered.

Possibly, but it was a dangerous gamble getting that close to someone with a knife, Davis replied.

'That's my point, Senior Sergeant Davis,' Gormly was beaming. 'What I put to you is that in the space of two minutes, and with the closeness that Senior Constable Rich got to Elijah, he excluded himself from the opportunity of engaging in de-escalation and conversation.'

Davis had a different take. The lack of communication was Elijah's choice. Rich gave him verbal commands and afforded him an opportunity to respond. Maybe Elijah didn't understand the orders or maybe he refused to comply, but from an operational perspective, Rich did the right thing — he told Elijah what he wanted him to do.

'You're looking at it in black and white,' Davis said, 'and there's clearly greys in amongst it there, where police have to look at everything. Not just simply to communicate and get a conversation back. That just may not occur, and frankly it rarely does.'

From a police perspective, when Elijah refused to follow Rich's orders, the unpredictability of the situation heightened. Elijah had the opportunity to respond and didn't, Davis said. His refusal was a warning sign. It signalled risk.

'Let's for a moment assume there were no witnesses who said that

Elijah turned and ran at Senior Constable Rich,' the Coroner said to Davis during Sheller's cross-examination of the senior sergeant. 'What would you say then about what Senior Constable Rich could or should have done, or whether it was appropriate?'

Davis recalibrated.

'OK, so are you asking whether he should have discharged his firearm at that stage? Because he certainly wouldn't have been justified in that circumstance, no,' Davis said unblinkingly.

'Even if Elijah had turned towards him?'

'Correct.'

'And even if the knife was still in his hand?'

'Correct.'

'But if he stood still — no justification for using the gun?'

'No.'

James Sheller took his witness back and zoomed in on the final seconds of the scenario Jerram painted.

'If Elijah had taken one step forward as it were, does that represent a tipping point between the decision to shoot or not?' he asked Senior Sergeant Davis.

'Not from a teaching perspective, we don't — that's something that only Senior Constable Rich could talk — Certainly an officer at the time must assume that the individual is certainly a threat to them — and then that may well be the catalyst for what could cause them to discharge their firearm.'

It was the first time Davis had struggled to shape an answer.

Official estimates of the distance between Rich and Elijah when Rich fired his gun was eight to nine metres. Davis told the court a person of average fitness could run six and a half metres in two to three seconds. It was clear that if Elijah had run at Rich, intending to stab him, he would have reached his target in under four seconds. If Rich's life was in danger that day, he had correctly judged the need to defend himself. What damage Elijah could inflict with a bread knife was not addressed by any of the lawyers.

Davis stepped down after two hours of questioning as sunny and calm as a man could be.

'That brings us now to Senior Constable Rich,' said Gormly.

25.

Fiona was right: he had a baby face. His head was close-to-shaved; his suit packed to the seams. Rich was heavier now than in the photo taken hours after Elijah's shooting, which I'd seen in Jeremy's copy of the brief. In fact, he looked completely different. He had sat directly behind me for the last five hours.

Mary Jerram leaned from the bench down to Rich in the witness box.

'Senior Constable, there's just one thing I want to say to you before you begin. I am really, really sorry that you have had to wait so long for this.'

Rich looked at her without expression.

'I tried to stir up the Director [of Public Prosecutions] to make a decision, and it was bad for the family, too, but just appalling to have that hanging over you for such a terrible length of time, and I am very sorry.'

Jerram settled back into her seat. Everyone else leaned forward.

Gormly's voice came like a thunderclap.

'Senior Constable Rich, is your full name Andrew Rich?'

'Yes, it is.'

'Where are you stationed at the moment?'

'Armidale Police Station.'

'Do you object to giving evidence?'

'I do, sir.'

'Upon what basis do you object?'

Rich retrieved a statement from the inside pocket of his suit.

'Your Honour, if I may. I object to giving evidence on the grounds that the evidence may tend to prove that I have committed an offence against or arising under an Australian law, or I am liable to civil penalty.'

Would he speak willingly if she granted a certificate preventing his evidence being used against him in other proceedings? the Coroner asked.

'No, Your Honour.'

'Alright. If you step down then and have a seat wherever you're comfortable, I'll hear from the lawyers.'

The Coroner had expected nothing else.

Murugan Thangaraj handed a document up to Jerram on the bench, and she called a fifteen-minute break to read it.

The row of journalists kept their seats; although it was a tantalising piece of news, the *Coroners Act* prohibited them reporting that Rich had objected to giving evidence.

Fiona walked past with Jeremy. He smiled at me as if to say, 'I told you, didn't I?' I left the courtroom. Jordan was slumped on a couch in the foyer, the cheer of her geranium lipstick wilting.

I eyeballed the huddle of detectives. David Phelps walked over and clapped a hand on a dark padded shoulder. A head turned sharply, and smiles broke out; it had to be Greig Stier, his football mate. Rich was next to him. I waited until the bell rang, calling everyone back in to court, then crossed the foyer.

'Andrew, hi. I'm the Kate who has been writing you letters.'

He smiled the smallest smile and flicked his eyes across me. He nodded but didn't speak.

'I appreciate this isn't a good time, I just wanted you to know who I am.' There was no expression on his face of either recognition or displeasure. The detectives were waiting to take him back inside.

'I'll keep writing to you if that's alright. Maybe when this is over …' I raised my hand in a small wave and slipped past the huddle into the courtroom, my heart thumping.

Rich returned to his seat behind me, and his senior counsel, Murugan Thangaraj, spoke for him for twenty minutes straight.

'It's all in section 61(7) ... I'm going to paragraph 19 of Grove J's first decision of Borland [2006] NSWSC 982 ... The use of "therefore" by my friend in par 19 we take to mean—' *Blah blah blah.*

Phrases appeared above the fog like flashes from a lighthouse. I scribbled them down, willing the act of writing to reveal their meaning. Eventually, an argument emerged.

If Rich was forced to give evidence, the DPP may become aware that Rich lacked a defence of, for example, self-defence, said Thangaraj. The Holcombes or the Office of the DPP could renew their efforts to mount a criminal case against Rich if it became apparent he could not defend himself. The Coroner had a legal duty to consider the implications. Her Honour could not place Andrew Rich in a position where he would incriminate himself, Thangaraj warned.

It was the same argument that Brent Haverfield had made to me months ago. What if, in telling me his story over coffee, Andrew said something that exposed him to further criticism? The risk that the Coroner or someone else might instigate legal action was too high.

The Section 61 certificate the Coroner had offered Rich would not protect his client from being sacked, Thangaraj contended. There were bodies outside the courts not bound by the Coroner's certificate; one was the NSW Police Force. If it became apparent through Rich's testimony that he'd acted contrary to police regulations, the Commissioner of Police could dismiss or discipline him. Alternatively, the Commissioner might record an adverse finding that affected his salary, his prospects of promotion, and the type of police work he could do. His client may be transferred to another town, Thangaraj argued.

To protest against giving evidence because it might lead to consequences Rich didn't care for seemed a farce. No consequences could fall on him unless someone proved his actions were unlawful. If Rich's own evidence decided that, wasn't it just that he should pay a price?

Further, argued Thangaraj, why should his client be made to take that risk when the court had access to his version of events in the statements Rich had already made to police investigators?

'The fact is, our client gave a directed interview that was contemporaneous. He then participated in a walk-through, also contemporaneous, and then a second directed interview some months later ... He said that Mr Holcombe had a knife. He said that he heard a roar and [saw] him coming towards him and he said he thought he was going to be stabbed,' Thangaraj declaimed.

The Coroner might not agree with the evidence in Rich's statements; she may, in fact, reject it. That was not the point, Rich's counsel said.

'The starting point is not "Why should he give evidence?" This is a person who is entitled to exercise a right of silence unless circumstances dictate that that very important right ought to be removed.'

No matter how compelling the facts, it was not mandatory for Rich to talk about them, the court was told.

I couldn't comprehend how Thangaraj could state the point so blithely. How did the legal system do its job if people were allowed to say, 'You can't make me speak'? Every witness to date had been cross-examined on their version of events. Their statements were given within days of Elijah's shooting, just like Rich's, and their memories were considered sufficient for the law to rest on. Why should Rich be any different? Did his lawyers fear his story would crumble under scrutiny?

Heads wilted like thirsty flowers. David Phelps sneaked a look at his watch. How much longer could this go on? The Coroner ran a time check. The lawyers had thirty minutes left. James Sheller wished to speak 'for about thirty seconds, Your Honour'. Patrick Saidi would need five minutes.

Sheller requested Rich be compelled to give evidence for the Holcombes' sake.

Patrick Saidi argued that 'serious matters' would be triggered if that happened; the Coroner must remember her obligation to the interests of justice, he warned.

It was months before I understood that 'the interests of justice' was a legal term, not a rhetorical flourish pulled out of Saidi's sleeve.

Their purpose in this instance was to help the Coroner decide whether calling Rich's evidence served the greatest good. One question was balancing the need for Rich to explain his actions against the impact that evidence might have on his career and life. Another question the Coroner was bound to ask 'in the interests of justice' was whether criminal or civil proceedings relating to the witness and the subject matter of the inquest were 'live' in other courts.

Saidi argued that if Rich gave evidence, it would affect the civil case the Holcombes had brought against police.

'There are the interests not merely of Constable Rich but the interests of the parties [in the civil matter] ... and in this case, an interested person is, in fact, the Commissioner of Police and the State of NSW,' Saidi solemnised.

The certificate that protected Rich from self-incrimination in the Coroner's Court would not protect the Police Commissioner or the State of NSW if Rich's evidence played badly for his employers, Saidi said. The principle of vicarious liability meant Rich's employer may bear legal responsibility for his decision to chase and shoot Elijah. If Jerram forced Rich to speak and his evidence showed he had acted beyond his powers, the State might have to bear the cost.

Cry me a river. Where was the injustice in that? But Saidi hadn't finished.

'Your Honour, it is my client that has the option of extending acceptance of vicarious liability or denying it ...'

Patrick Saidi went on to explain that his client, the NSW Commissioner of Police, would consider denying vicarious liability for Rich in the civil case if the senior constable's evidence before the inquest showed he acted outside his training. With a metaphorical arm across Rich's throat, Saidi implied that the police hierarchy was prepared to throw Rich under the bus if the Coroner forced him to give evidence.

Without the legal protection of his employer, Rich would be left to face the civil case on his own, which meant bearing the cost of his own defence and damages if the Holcombes won.

'He's at risk at the hands of my client. Once you take that into account, Your Honour may determine the interests of justice should not dictate his giving evidence,' Saidi finished.

Someone on the police side of the ledger — a lawyer or executive — was gambling on Jerram not wanting to expose Rich so brutally. But there was reason to believe the threat was a bluff.

Jeremy Holcombe had told me weeks before the inquest that the police would never hang Rich out to dry. That assurance had come from a barrister involved in negotiations on the civil case. The barrister worked for the police. If it turned out Elijah's shooting was unlawful, the State would not be able to fund its vicarious liability for Rich through its insurer, the barrister had said. But they would cover Rich no matter what, and they would never admit liability — ever.

He may have been bluffing, like Saidi was, but the knowledge left an ugly question in the air. Was Rich's silence forced on him in return for his employer's legal protection? Or had he struck a deal that protected him and the police force in a single move?

'He didn't look very sorry, did he?'

David Phelps took a draught of his beer and looked at me over the rim of his glass.

We had walked out of court to the nearest pub.

'He didn't look at all the way I'd imagined him,' I said.

We were talking about Rich.

Tarney played with a coaster on the table. Jordan fed coins into the jukebox.

'I didn't see Rich and Dufty talk to each other, did you?' I asked.

Jeremy shook his head.

'I asked Stiery if Dufty's stress condition was related to this case,' said David.

'What did he say?' Jeremy asked.

'Yep, directly to this.'

Jeremy changed the subject.

'So the kids are selling the Little Crooked House, Kate.'

'What! Why?' I turned to Jordan. 'Where are you going to live?'

'What do you mean you're selling it? You didn't tell me; what if I wanted to buy it!' Phelps protested.

'Because you would have dozered it, Dangles,' Jordan said drily.

'And sub-divided,' he added with a grin. ''Nother beer anyone?'

The girls were moving into one of the flats Jeremy was renovating. Tarney had a share house in Sydney; he was rarely back in Wee Waa now. Jeremy and Fiona were looking to buy a place on the coast. Life was moving on.

ABC television covered the inquest's re-opening that night. They played a clip of Tracey from our *Four Corners* story. 'He went for help and they shot him like an animal in the street,' she said. Today was her fifty-first birthday.

26.

No one was pretending Rich would speak on the second day of Elijah's inquest. Voices were louder; knots in the foyer had unwound.

Rich was dressed in a black suit and blue-striped tie. Police in uniform stood on either side of him, an inch of air between their bodies and his shoulders.

Phil Stewart beckoned me with a crooked finger.

'Sweeney tells me you think the DPP got it right, that a jury couldn't convict Rich on the evidence from the laneway,' he said when I crossed the room to him.

Sweeney and I had had a sharp discussion. I squirmed, searching for a half-lie, but I couldn't find one.

'I can't see how a jury could find beyond reasonable doubt when the evidence on whether or not Elijah moved is so all over the place. I think legally the DPP is right, even though I want it to be different.'

'No, the DPP is wrong. His whole assumption is based on Elijah having moved, and the evidence doesn't back him up. There isn't a "preponderance of evidence" that Elijah moved. You've seen the letter, haven't you?' Phil asked.

He was unperturbed by my disagreement but determined to show me my position was wrong. It was almost 10am; people in the foyer started moving in to court. Minutes before the Coroner appeared, Phil beckoned me down towards the bar table and flourished a piece of paper.

'Here,' he said, and read aloud from the DPP's letter, stabbing the offending sentence with his finger: '... "the preponderance of the evidence is capable of establishing that Elijah did move forwards towards Senior Constable Rich just prior to the discharge of the firearm." Now that is blatantly wrong. The numbers don't back that conclusion. It's wrong,' and on he went, arguing the point in front of everyone.

I found my seat, crimson and branded. Rich would never trust me after that display.

Jerram entered, her silver earrings twisting on their stems.

A roll of lollies passed from officer to officer behind me, followed by the cautious crinkle of waxy paper.

Jeremy Gormly stood to argue why Rich should be compelled to speak. He scoffed at any risk the Police Commissioner might sack Rich. The Industrial Commission would be onto the police in a flash for unlawful dismissal, and rightly so, if Rich lost his job in such circumstances, he said. As for the idea of transferring Rich or bringing adverse findings against him, the likelihood of that could be inferred from the views of Senior Sergeant Davis, who told the court that in his professional view, Rich had done nothing wrong.

Rich sat with Greig Stier two rows in front of me. He sighed.

Gormly's vowels reached spherical roundness at the thought the court might rely on Rich's statements rather than hear him speak. Rich's interviews and walk-through were available to the Coroner, but the Coroner retained the power to test Rich's accounts in the same way every other witness had been tested, Gormly said. His tone made it clear he intended the power to be used. To Thangaraj's suggestion that Rich's statements from four years ago were more valuable and accurate than anything he might add now, Gormly retorted that two directed interviews, a walk-through, and the experience of sitting through ten days of evidence in Armidale would no doubt have kept events 'actively on [Senior Constable Rich's] mind for a very long time'.

Rich could not get comfortable. One minute, his foot rested on his knee; the next, it was on the ground. He slumped in his chair then pulled himself straight. He flattened his hands against his thighs.

The Coroner's certificate could not stop Rich's evidence being used against his employers in the civil case, Gormly conceded. But the police and the State of NSW could not throw off responsibility for Rich that lightly either.

If it were proved Rich shot Elijah in the course of his duties, the NSW Police remained vicariously liable for those actions, Gormly claimed. There had been ample time for the Commissioner of Police and State of NSW to revoke Rich's legal protection; the civil claim had begun in 2011, he pointed out. The prospect of police cutting Rich loose in the civil case was 'so remote as to be not a matter that Your Honour need take into account other than to the most minimal degree. It simply isn't going to happen,' Gormly declared.

Counsel assisting had placed his own wager on the bar table. The NSW Police wouldn't dare hang Andrew Rich out to dry by denying him the legal protection they owed him, and if they tried, their threat would fail.

I stumbled into the foyer at the next recess, drunk with lawyers' arguments.

'Ma'am, may I speak to you a moment?'

A tall police officer in uniform loomed above me.

I nodded, and he led me to an alcove near the front door. I prepared myself to be reprimanded over Phil Stewart's letter-waving that morning. I would no doubt be reminded of some confidentiality clause. Phil would get a piece of my mind when this was over.

The officer's eyes were paler than pale blue.

'You are the lady who has been writing to Andrew, is that right?'

Grasping for connection, I saw the name badge on his pocket — Matt Lynch.

'Yes, Matt, that's right.' I gave him what I hoped was a measured smile.

'Don't call me Matt,' he said quickly, and I waited for the upbraid to begin — *It's Inspector Lynch, and furthermore ...*

'I'm not Matt Lynch. My name is Roger Best; I'm Andrew's

supervisor. I left my badge at the hotel so I borrowed this one — I didn't want to come without a name badge.' It was his turn to blush. 'Sorry, we had Lebanese for dinner last night; I've probably got garlic breath …'

'That's OK, it's fine.' I grinned like a cadaver, completely lost.

'Andrew is very keen to talk to you. It's just his barrister pulling him back.'

I swallowed a wave of nausea.

'I'm really glad to hear that. That's great news—'

Roger Best smiled and straightened back to his full height.

'We'll be in touch once this is over. How can I contact you?' he asked.

I passed him my card, and in five long strides he was back at Rich's side. I looked across for confirmation, but Rich only skimmed his eyes across my face. Even his desire to speak was voiced by someone else.

Murugan Thangaraj walked out of a side room. *Please God, don't let him have seen that exchange.*

He perched on the arm of a couch in the foyer, writing notes. I crossed the room.

'Can I ask you something about the arguments in there?' I nodded towards the courtroom. 'I don't understand how the police can deny Rich vicarious liability.'

Thangaraj put his notebook down and grinned.

'Even though he was working for them, if he did the wrong thing by their rules they don't owe him protection. It's called wilful conduct. If that happens, Rich is on his own. He's defending charges personally, not as an officer doing his job. The certificate won't protect him. That's why we don't want him to talk. What else didn't you understand?'

'I can't see how Rich is allowed to just say "I don't want to talk about it" when he's killed someone. That makes no sense to me at all.'

'But the right to silence is a fundamental principle of common law — it's been around for centuries. You're saying you think it's wrong?' Thangaraj was astonished.

'I do when you've killed someone. Whether you meant to or not, even if you were completely justified, if you kill someone you have a responsibility to explain why you did it. Rich is a police officer; it's his job to enforce the law. How is it moral for him not to talk?'

'This isn't about morality. It's about his legal rights, and they're the same rights as everyone else. It's up to the prosecution — I know this isn't a criminal case, but it's up to the State to prove a person is guilty without any help from the accused. That's what the right to silence is about — the State has to be able to prove what you've done without your help,' Thangaraj explained.

'But Rich isn't going to be charged, the DPP has already decided that. So what has he got to lose? The Holcombes need to hear him say why he made the decision he did; and Rich might have a good explanation but we need to hear it,' I argued.

'So you think the Coroner should make him talk?' Thangaraj asked, bemused.

'Yes.'

'Even if it means the DPP re-opens his case, and Rich gets charged and goes to jail because he didn't avail himself of the right to silence everyone is entitled to?'

'He killed someone. That's too big to be allowed to choose not to talk about, and I don't think he will go to jail. I don't see how it would happen.'

Thangaraj shook his head. 'You're married to a lawyer?'

I nodded.

'And you don't believe in the right to silence? Does your husband know?' he teased.

I wondered if, under his barrister's mask, he believed in his heart the legal arguments he was making.

The afternoon ran like a silent film in front of me while the tall police officer's words looped in my head. *Andrew is very keen to talk to you. It's just his barrister pulling him back.*

Why would Rich talk to me but not the Coroner? He'd ignored my requests for the last four years — why change tack now? Beneath my confusion, I felt a thrill; then something clicked.

If Thangaraj won the fight to keep Rich silent, mine might be the only story told about Cinders Lane. Phil Stewart's piece of theatre with the letter, Thangaraj's right to silence speech, and Roger Best's message from Rich made sense. I was being lobbied. But what was Rich's reason for wanting to talk to me?

Life had been out of control for him ever since Cinders Lane.

Officers confronting a situation must firstly gain control, Senior Sergeant Davis taught his recruits. Then they must maintain it.

Did Rich believe he could get it back by telling me what happened for him, so I could tell his story? Was I an insurance policy in case his lawyers succeeded in shutting down his chance to speak? I swung between certainty he wanted to speak to me and a nagging fear I was being played.

The room fell quiet. The lawyers had finished.

'This is a terrible thing to say, but I don't think I can give you a decision today,' the Coroner said.

Mary Jerram would tell us in ten days whether or not she would force Rich to speak.

27.

I walked outside and caught a taxi to the eastern suburbs. A friend had invited me to Passover celebrations.

'Traditional, not religious,' she assured me on the phone.

'It will go all night, so pace yourself,' her husband whispered when I hugged him at the door.

It was a relief to exchange the sombre courtroom for the colour and warmth of a family gathering. In a crowded living room, three generations rapped a version of the exodus from Egypt. Plagues of lolly frogs and paper lice rained down, sparklers made a burning bush out of a pot plant, and kids ripped crepe paper to part the sea. The Jews reached freedom, and, catastrophes dispensed with, we filed in uproar to the dining room. At a table set for thirty, I ate bitter herbs and matzo balls, and tried to hide my own bitterness. As the adrenalin drained away, there was only anger. Nothing about Elijah's death was resolved.

The elderly woman beside me drew me in with a ropey hand.

'I'm Melanie's Hebrew teacher, Esther.'

Her hair was a white cloud. She nodded to me and joined in a hymn in Hebrew, her nods converting to the rhythm of the foreign words. I sat back in my chair and let the music and conversation form a vacuum around me.

The name 'Elijah' had special meaning in this room. Elijah was revered as a prophet in Judaism, Christianity, and Islam. But Judaism held him in the highest esteem. When Jews gave thanks at Passover, a place was set at the table for Elijah, and the front door was left open. He would appear unannounced one day, the stories said. He hadn't for the last two thousand years, but the religious never give up hope.

Perhaps the job that waited for him was what kept him away, I thought that night. For millennia, rabbis had put aside unanswerable legal and moral questions 'until Elijah comes'. Like a parent's promise of 'later' to nagging children, Jewish leaders had found a way to put aside questions they had no answer for.

My friends had set a place for Elijah at their table and, even in this affluent suburb, the front door was open so he could slip in quietly. What question would I put in Elijah's hand if he appeared tonight?

Esther had me in her bony grip again. She fought her way through the wall of noise to tell me she was a Holocaust survivor. For some questions, there are no answers.

I woke the next morning with the feeling of a hangover and walked down to the beach. The air was soft, and the ocean threw off beads of light. I ordered coffee. The wind picked up the docket from my table and blew the curling scrap along the footpath.

I walked back to my friend's apartment. I sat in the gently dappled light, waiting for my taxi to the airport, and watched the fluttering world outside the window. The pink hibiscus, frilled and plump against the fence; the cubby house in unkempt grass.

The courtroom and its questions sat in notebooks in my suitcase.

I flew back to Darwin with Rich's message tucked inside my mind. I told no one, not even the Holcombes.

28.

Jerram's judgement arrived in an email from David Sweeney ten days later, on 5 April 2013.

'The interests of justice require that Senior Constable Rich give evidence in these proceedings and I exercise my discretion under Section 61 to require him to do so,' she decreed.

Jerram framed her decision as a matter of police accountability.

'The right of a police officer to carry and use a firearm is an entitlement allowed to few others. To give the Court and the family of Elijah his explanation of why he shot Elijah may fairly be expected as a counterpart in public accountability of that entitlement,' Jerram wrote.

Rich's interviews and walk-through were not sufficient to exempt him from bearing witness, despite Mr Thangaraj's argument to the contrary, she said. For the necessary standard of scrutiny to be reached, Rich's version of events must be tested. The NSW police force had questions to answer, too, on how it prepared its officers to deal with mentally ill people in crisis.

'Elijah had, and was known by at least some police with whom he was involved on the day of his death, to have a mental illness. This shooting of a mentally ill young man is not, sadly, an isolated incident. Questions arise inevitably of whether the police are being sufficiently trained in and made aware of the discrete needs of mentally ill persons and methods of dealing with them ... These are significant issues, which require further exploration.'

She swept aside Patrick Saidi's argument that the Police Commissioner's position in the civil case could be adversely affected by Rich's evidence, and his threat that the Commissioner might be forced to retract vicarious liability for Rich in the civil case.

'No one receives full immunity for their actions by reason of a certificate, and a Section 61 [certificate] ... is not designed to protect individuals, even police officers, from any form of adverse consequence of giving evidence other than self-incrimination for a criminal act and a degree of civil penalty,' wrote Jerram in a swingeing slap-down to counsel for the police.

Rich's legal team were quick to respond. Within weeks, they had filed a request in the Supreme Court for orders to have Jerram's decision overturned.

29.

Murugan Thangaraj and Brent Haverfield were determined to keep their fight against Jerram's decision out of the media. When the hearing in the Supreme Court of NSW opened in June 2013, Thangaraj secured an interim non-publication order — no journalist was to report the proceedings.

The public was unaware that Rich had already avoided being cross-examined in the Coroner's Court, because the NSW *Coroners Act* prohibited the publication of 'any objection made by a witness to giving evidence on the grounds that the evidence may tend to prove the witness had committed an offence'. The fact that Rich had recited those exact words to Coroner Jerram could not be reported.

The legal teams representing Rich and Coroner Jerram made their arguments under a cone of legal silence, and the judge retired to consider his decision.

Justice AJ Barr returned two weeks later and dismissed the application on every ground. He upheld the Coroner's right to decide that Rich must give evidence at Elijah's inquest.

Murugan Thangaraj asked that the interim non-publication order on proceedings be made permanent and extend to include Justice Barr's decision. He wanted the case and its outcome suppressed indefinitely.

He was out of luck. The work of the Supreme Court was performed in public; the community had a right to know, Justice Barr decreed.

A couple of hours later, they did.

The *Sydney Morning Herald* reported that Rich had refused to give evidence at Elijah's inquest 'on the grounds that it might "tend to prove" that he had committed an offence or that he was liable to a civil penalty'.

The Coroner had offered an exemption, the paper explained, 'which meant [Rich] would have effectively been protected from prosecution or civil action for any evidence he gave', but he was still not prepared to take the stand.

Justice Barr's findings gave the clearest account I had read or heard of Thangaraj and Haverfield's argument against Rich speaking. Their proposition weighed on two main points: that the Holcombes wanted to see Rich cross-examined in order to prove he had no reason to shoot Elijah, and that the Coroner's certificate could not protect Rich if he self-incriminated in the course of giving evidence.

Since one of the interests of justice that Jerram must weigh in determining whether to compel Rich's evidence was 'the likelihood of any prosecution or other action flowing from the evidence', Thangaraj and Haverfield argued that if she made Rich speak, Jerram would be impinging on his right to silence: a right Rich wished to exercise.

The outcome the barristers were determined to avoid was the possibility that if Rich spoke, he might contradict the version of events that was in his statement, and thereby put an end to the current claim that he'd fired on Elijah in self-defence.

If Rich made an admission of this sort, the DPP might re-consider the case for criminal charges, and the Police Commissioner could deny vicarious liability in the civil case, Rich's barristers put to the Supreme Court.

Justice Barr's response to these arguments was as clear as his portrayal of them.

Any evidence Rich gave under a certificate issued by the Coroner could not be used as evidence against him, directly or indirectly, Barr said. Neither the DPP or counsel in the civil case could make use of Rich's testimony in the way his barristers had argued before the Coroner.

Thangaraj and Haverfield had failed on two counts. Their client still had to give evidence as the Coroner had ordered, and the fact they had fought to prevent that and to conceal their efforts was now public knowledge.

Rich would appear before Mary Jerram in August 2013 — two months away.

New South Wales Police announced mental health training for all frontline officers four weeks after Rich's failed appeal. I was assured by one senior officer that the timing was a coincidence.

The training was the work of the Mental Health Intervention Team (MHIT), a unit run by Inspector Joel Murchie. Tall and taciturn, Murchie was uniquely qualified. He had survived the 2002 terrorist bombing of the Sari Club in Bali. In 2007, Murchie was approached to head up the MHIT as a pilot program. The unit became a permanent fixture in 2009, a month before Elijah was shot.

'Police are required to respond to a whole gamut of mental health-related incidents, ranging from someone having a bad day and arguing with their neighbour, right through to someone who is acutely psychotic and threatening to harm themselves or someone else, up to the siege-type incidents,' Murchie said at a press conference to announce the training.

Interactions between police and the mentally ill had doubled in six years to 36,500 contacts in 2011, the *Sydney Morning Herald* reported. The MHIT would deliver a daylong course to all police officers that included specialised instruction in detaining mentally ill people, as well as lessons from coronial findings on Critical Incident Investigations.

The course was the first of its kind in Australia, and the result of three years' work by Murchie's team. Ninety per cent of NSW police had never had formal mental health training until now.

I sent the *Herald* article to Jeremy. Good things could come of bad; institutions were capable of change, and Rich would give his evidence soon — there was hope on the horizon.

Jeremy's reply was cheerful. He enjoyed the article, he said. Had I heard Rich was running a second appeal against Coroner Jerram's decision to make him speak?

What?!

'I was kind of expecting it,' he said when I called.

'But how can he do this? On what grounds?'

The passage of time, fatigue, a tweak to his medication — something had changed for Jeremy. It was four years since Elijah's death.

'To tell you the truth, Kate, we don't spend much time thinking about it anymore. At the end of the first inquest, Rich was in tears when I shook his hand — I don't know if for himself or for what happened. But at the second inquest, he was cocky. He had the DPP result behind him. Dufty was a mess, any decent human being would be.'

I had buried myself in court cases for so long I had missed Jeremy's change of heart. He sounded like he had given up on Rich.

Since receiving the message that Rich wanted to talk to me, I'd reasoned his refusal to speak at Elijah's inquest was an act of loyalty. He was taking one for the team, protecting a long history of silence by police before the coroner. If he broke and talked, other officers might be made to give evidence against their will in future.

But a second appeal? Rich had played and lost that game already. Now he had the legal cover and excuse to do what Best said he wanted to do — tell his side of the story. But instead of using it, he was fighting on. It was impossible to know if the impetus was his lawyers' advice or Rich's own conviction.

I longed to give up and be rid of the agony of trying to understand him. Was I acting out some pathology, determined to believe he 'had his reasons' or wasn't in control of the choices he was making? Maybe his refusal to give evidence spoke for itself — he had played me for a fool. But then what did Best's message in the foyer hope to achieve? Why bother if it wasn't genuine?

Rich's second appeal changed a lot of things. It forced his scheduled appearance in the Coroner's Court to be postponed. His version of what happened in Cinders Lane would not be heard now until the civil case was over. It was a victory for Patrick Saidi's client, the State of NSW.

The risk of Rich incriminating himself in the Coroner's Court was no longer an issue, which meant the Police Commissioner's putative threat to cut Rich loose in the civil case was moot. It was a win for Murugan Thangaraj and Brent Haverfield as well. Their client would go into the civil case with the legal protection of his employer intact.

The Holcombes responded to the second appeal by raising the stakes in the civil case. Instead of restricting scrutiny of Rich's actions to Cinders Lane, they would now argue that his crucial mistake was approaching Elijah at the camping store. Rich's words and actions there had an impact that was vital to what unfolded, they would argue. Rich's behaviour amounted to an assault on Elijah, the Holcombes' legal team would allege.

It took a long conversation with David Sweeney and time with a legal dictionary before I fully understood the new proposition.

The legal definition of assault is different to its common meaning of a physical attack. The essential legal element is that an aggressor wants their victim to believe that they are going to be harmed in some way, and that the aggressor succeeds in creating this fear. The legal proof of assault lies in whether the threat would cause a reasonable person to expect they would be harmed.

No reasonable person would believe a police officer trying to hand them car keys and offering to take them to hospital intended to hurt them. What was crucial, Sweeney explained to me, was 'the status of the victim'. The example the legal dictionary gave was that an adult threatening to pull a child's hair was more of an assault than if they threatened to pull the hair of another adult.

A threat to detain a mentally ill man who believed the police wanted to kill him carried a different weight to the same threat made to a mentally stable person.

Rich should have known about Elijah's delusional beliefs, the Holcombes' civil claim argued. He should have checked Elijah's backstory, or the colleagues Rich spoke to throughout the day should have told him Elijah was terrified of police. It would be argued Rich was negligent in his duties for pursuing Elijah without knowledge of his condition, because any reasonable person with that knowledge would not have chased him from Rusden Street. Rich's attempt to detain Elijah created an expectation in Elijah's mind that Rich was going to harm him. It was an assault, the Holcombes' barristers would claim. The change in tactics was the work of a second senior barrister, Anthony Black, whom James Sheller had brought on to the case.

The logic of assault addressed something I had been grappling with since the DPP's decision.

The Director of Public Prosecutions, Lloyd Babb, believed that 'Rich's actions, based on his perception of events at the time, were reasonable in the perceived circumstances'.

Babb did not address whether fleeing from a man with a gun who claimed he was a police officer, and picking up a bread knife in self-defence, was reasonable in the circumstances Elijah perceived. Both men acted from the assumption that the other was an aggressor. They were wrong for different reasons. So why did the law honour one's state of mind over the other?

The legal concept of assault put Elijah's state of mind on equal footing with Rich's. It was willing to interpret the world from more than one perspective.

The second appeal was six weeks away. The civil case opened seven days later. The intersecting wheels of the Holcombes' legal mill ground on.

David Sweeney was busy gathering witnesses for the civil case.

He had found Joan Whitburn, the office manager who watched Rich shoot Elijah from the window of her office. Sweeney was in the middle of writing subpoenas for her and a dozen others.

'You know I have to pay for all these witnesses,' he told me on the phone.

'What is there to pay for?' I asked.

'Getting about a dozen people to Armidale, plus their accommodation.'

'Jesus. How are you going to do that?'

'I don't know. I have a credit card ...'

We laughed at the craziness of it all. Nothing in this case seemed real anymore. Whenever I tried to pull the last four years together in my mind, gravity disappeared. Meaning, reason, even simple chronology evaded me. Shock and disbelief took over. Shock at how hard the police were fighting to prevent Rich taking the stand. Disbelief that Roger Best had approached me to say Rich wanted to talk.

And where was Allison in all of this? A picture of her floated in my mind, tucked under Elijah's arm in the photo I guessed was from their wedding day. She wasn't suing police, she wasn't talking to the media, and she hadn't been to any of Elijah's inquest.

'I can't figure out if she's incredibly immature or incredibly mature. She's just completely moved on,' Jeremy had said to me.

I had written to her a second time but neither of my messages had been answered. What did her silence hold? Grief, pain, guilt, anger? Or was her story simpler than that? Was I making the typical assumption of a journalist that everyone wanted to tell their story, when some just wanted to be left alone to grieve in private?

30.

Serious men and women in billowing black robes and wigs like wood shavings walked with their heads down against the wind. I sheltered behind them and crossed the square below the NSW Supreme Court building, under-dressed in sandals and a cotton frock.

I had come to Sydney reluctantly. The civil case was opening in Armidale in a week. I was far more interested in that than Rich's second appeal, but Sweeney had insisted I come. Things might happen that I didn't expect, he hinted.

I rode the lift to the thirteenth floor and entered a courtroom of cavernous proportions. Painted portraits of red-robed judges peered down from the walls. Murugan Thangaraj and Brent Haverfield were already at the bar table.

David Sweeney hurried in. James Sheller strolled behind him.

Three heavy thuds fell on a door behind the judges' bench. A woman and two men appeared in the same red robes and wigs as the old men on the walls.

'All persons having any business before this Honourable Court now draw nigh and give your attendance and you shall be heard. God Save the Queen,' the court officer bellowed.

We were a long way from Cinders Lane.

'Andrew Rich and the Attorney General of NSW,' the officer trumpeted.

Thangaraj spoke first. It was all so quiet. Gentle voices, eisteddfod-like attention from the judges. Much fetching of books and whispered conferences on the bench above.

Thangaraj was asking the judges to decide if Rich was in real risk of removal from the police force for his actions. If he was, 'other matters follow'. I let the whispered arguments wash over me — a mix of indecipherable references to other cases threaded onto arguments I had heard in the Coroner's Court already. 'The interests of justice' chorused back and forth in baritones between the bar table and bench.

Brent Haverfield rested his face in his palm like a bored kid. Words settled over the room like thick layers of dust.

The evidence to date supported that Rich acted in self-defence in Cinders Lane; if his client gave further evidence that could change, Thangaraj insisted.

'Our whole submissions are about what might happen,' he informed the bench.

The Coroner or the Holcombe family might refer Rich to the DPP again if his evidence in the stand differed from his statement.

'That outcome can't be ruled out,' he warned.

But the DPP has dismissed that possibility, I thought. Lloyd Babb's judgement was that no jury could be convinced beyond reasonable doubt of what Elijah did once he turned around. Even if Rich admitted to something criminal, if he did it under the protection of a certificate from the Coroner, the DPP couldn't use it to stand up charges.

The judges put this issue to Mary Jerram's barrister, Natalie Adams SC, a woman with a thick dark bob from the NSW Attorney General's office.

'Assume the applicant says, oh, how to put it — "I just wanted to put a stop to it so I shot him." Why wouldn't the DPP in those circumstances, reconsider?' the older of the male judges asked.

The DPP could only use admissible evidence to reach that decision, Adams replied. Rich's evidence was not admissible if it was given under a certificate. It was out of reach of the DPP — end of argument.

Couldn't the Coroner refer Rich to the DPP again, the judges queried? Alternatively, what if Rich made an admission that influenced the DPP to change his mind about the criminality of Rich's actions?

Surely the answer was the same, I reasoned. Evidence given under the protection of a certificate was inadmissible no matter who referred it on — the certificate was pointless otherwise.

A gravelly voice piped up — 'Hasn't this coroner retired?'

It was understood Coroner Jerram intended returning to the bench to finish the Holcombe inquest, Adams told the judges.

I hadn't even heard about Jerram's retirement. Elijah's case had outlasted a coroner like the prophet had the rabbis.

At 3.10pm, it was over.

Sheller swept out of court on the far side of the room, frowning. Thangaraj and Haverfield talked loudly as they packed away their files.

The energy of the room was with Rich's legal team.

It was close to eleven when my phone rang that night.

'We've settled the civil case with police,' Sweeney said.

The words ricocheted inside my skull.

'What?'

'The police agreed to settle. We just came out.'

Thangaraj was triumphant when I confirmed the outcome with him the next day.

'They can have all the money they want,' he said. 'They've lost a son. As long as my bloke doesn't go on the stand; that was all we wanted.'

But why would the Holcombes decide to settle now, I asked? The civil case was up next week.

Thangaraj guessed that Sheller and Sweeney were spooked when the Court of Appeal hearing didn't point to an obvious conclusion. They judged the decision might not go their way, and encouraged the Holcombes to re-open talks with police to reach a settlement.

'Maybe they decided it wasn't worth the gamble,' Thangaraj speculated.

Jeremy wouldn't let the police extinguish Rich's voice for money,

I was sure. He had been prepared to run the civil case a week ago; his decision had to be based on something else. I wrote a list of questions before I called him.

For the first time since we had known each other, Jeremy answered my questions in thoughts that ran full sentences. His voice was light and strong. He didn't need to ask me to repeat a thing.

They were stunned, he said. They hadn't expected the police to accept their offer.

'But why did you make an offer in the first place if you didn't really want to settle?' I asked.

It was a legal tactic — an offer of compromise, Jeremy explained. Either side could make one at any time during negotiations. If you could show the judge you had offered to settle the case before you came to court, and the other side had turned you down, you could argue you shouldn't have to pay their costs if you lost. The Holcombes had deliberately made an offer of compromise twice as high as one the police had knocked back months before.

'We gazumped ourselves between Rich and the police lawyers. We didn't expect them to accept our offer. My health and Tarney's was suffering more the closer we got. Our big thing was always to get Rich on the stand. Four or five weeks ago, Rich's lawyers told the cops he wouldn't give evidence in the civil case even if they subpoenaed him, so we weren't going to get what we wanted out of it. It was going to cost Sweeney forty thousand dollars to get the witnesses to Armidale. It made settlement a good option,' Jeremy said.

'Did you talk to Elijah before you decided?'

'Matter of fact I did, just last week,' he replied. 'I thanked him for his help. Fiona and the kids and me all openly discussed what Elijah and Tracey would want us to do with the civil case. We always thought of it as their settlement.'

So the idea of settling was at least a week old. It wasn't about the appeal hearing yesterday.

'Have your feelings about Rich changed at all?' I asked.

'You know, right from the start I had in my head, "They've made a mistake. They've fucked up, and any minute now the Premier or Commissioner of Police will turn up on the doorstep and apologise" and my reaction was to meet them halfway on that. Well, I'm still waiting.'

The hardness returned to Jeremy's voice. Even if the Holcombes had run the civil case and won, the police would have appealed that, too, he said. They'd already applied to have the civil case adjourned; the application was due to be heard in the District Court this morning. The police wouldn't need it now, Jeremy snorted.

'For Rich himself, I just feel sorry for the poor dumb bastard. Everything he's done in the last four years has been imposed on him. I can't blame him for not being capable of the internal conflict I want. I can't imagine he's the sort of guy with the strength to stand up against what he's being told to do. I don't hate him or anything but I'm determined for my own sake that I have to take every opportunity to pin it on him.'

I held back tears. 'Are you giving up?'

'Letting go of the civil case isn't giving up. I think it will be over one way or the other by the middle of next year.'

The Court of Appeal would decide whether Rich had to face the Coroner. He would follow the inquest to its end, whatever the end happened to be, Jeremy said.

'After that I can walk away knowing Elijah and Tracey know I did my best. I don't feel the outcome of the coronial as an emotional burden. I'm just a spectator like everyone else, should it ever happen.'

I raced through the city in search of the District Court. The wind raced after me, ripping at my clothes.

I rode the lift to a dingy foyer far above the city. The application to have the civil case postponed was moot, but I wanted to read the reaction of the lawyers to last night's decision to settle the case.

A second lift pinged and three lawyers emerged seconds after me, chatting cheerily. Patrick Saidi; a woman I recognised from the Court of Appeal; and a third man, taller and more elegant than his companions. They paused at the sight of me alone in the foyer before sweeping into a glass-walled meeting room.

Minutes later Brent Haverfield, Ken Madden, and Andrew Rich arrived. Andrew's eyes slid across me. His face froze. Madden and Haverfield hustled him into the meeting room and pulled the blinds closed.

Saidi sauntered out a moment later and sat beside me.

'What are you interested in today?' he asked genially.

'I'm interested in everything.'

'No, I mean what matter?'

'Your matter, Mr Saidi.'

'What's interesting about that?' he asked with a wolfish grin.

'I think it's very interesting.'

'No, it's not, it's boring.'

'I'm sorry you feel that way about your work, Mr Saidi.'

'We're settling apparently,' said the next body out of the lift, breaking across Saidi's patter.

'What makes you interested in my matter?' Saidi asked, pretending ignorance. Haverfield and Rich knew exactly what I was doing. Everyone in that meeting room did.

'I'm writing a book about the positions we put police in and the things we expect them to handle.'

His geniality slipped a notch. 'Well, I hope it reflects reality.'

'It's my intention that it will, Mr Saidi. That's why I'm here.'

I smiled politely, and Saidi left. My blood surged with adrenalin. Sweeney rushed from the lift as Rich's phalanx of lawyers walked into court. Like his mind, his legs were always working overtime. James Sheller and Anthony Black followed more sedately.

We filed into a room with three rows of seats. It was impossible not to sit close to Rich.

The power in the room sat with the Holcombes' lawyers now. The only reason to be here was to tell the magistrate the matter had settled.

'Events have overtaken us, Your Honour,' someone began, and the magistrate dispensed with the paperwork in fifteen minutes.

Saidi came up to me in the courtroom when the judge had left.

'Will you be speaking to police for this book of yours?'

I told him I wanted to and asked if he could help me — he represented the Commissioner of Police, after all. Saidi bumbled through an answer. Yes, of course, no promises, yes, as long as the story reflected reality. I took his number and left.

Rich sat in the foyer alone and unguarded. I took my chance.

'Hi, Andrew. I don't want to make your life difficult …'

He smiled. 'That's alright.'

'How does it feel to know the civil case is finished?'

'The sooner it's over the better for everyone, especially for the family. I can't talk to them, but I hope they're OK.'

I hugged my notebook to my chest.

'But how are you going?'

'It's been a long time …'

I would count to three and sit beside him. Brent Haverfield materialised.

'Coffee, Andrew?' he muttered darkly.

'Sure.' Rich smiled at me and followed Haverfield to the lift.

'Take care, Andrew,' I said.

The sooner it's over the better for everyone, especially for the family.

My anger uncoiled. He could have shortened the wait by giving evidence instead of stringing everyone out like this.

31.

I took my anger home to Darwin and trembled in the heavy air. I could not make sense of anything.

Rich wanted to talk, but his lawyers wouldn't let him. That was the story Rich was telling. But how could he bear not to defend himself if he thought what he did in Cinders Lane was right? How did a good man live with the question that festered around why he refused to speak? Where in his body did the agony reside of knowing the limbo he held the Holcombes in? I sat at my desk and pushed words across the page like food around a plate. Why couldn't I make this story end?

I riffled the pages of favourite books for words to pull me forward. *In the end, you have to choose a side. Justice demands it,* every author commanded.

I turned to poetry to rest my mind. *The constant wear and tear of taken breath*, wrote Philip Larkin, and I thought of Jeremy's early grief. Grey, relentless winter breath, holding him to life. Tracey could not do the same, but neither of them gave in to blame.

What claim did I have then, to decide Rich's guilt or innocence?

Police were trained to pre-empt risk. To see it coming and ward it off. Rich wanted to protect the community he served. He followed Elijah intending to contain him; he wanted to take him back to hospital. Something fired Rich into action when he chased Elijah outside the camping store. Was it instinct or training that set him running?

I wasn't trained in risk-assessment. I hadn't walked towards things most people ran from every day for years in my job. So what if I thought I would have let Elijah go; if I thought I would have talked to him more carefully or used a lighter touch? I wasn't Rich. I wasn't there. I didn't know.

By the time Elijah stepped out the back door of Caffiends, minutes after the camping store, the risk he posed had risen. Rich called the station for backup from the café, but thirty seconds later he pulled his gun. He knew how close the station was, but something he saw or heard made him believe he may have to shoot Elijah. We expected police to make these judgements. Rich judged the danger to be that real. Did Elijah do something only Andrew saw or heard that made it clear he was going to hurt someone?

Andrew's answer to this question was that Elijah gave an animal roar and ran at him with a knife, screaming, 'Fuck you, shoot me, you fucking cunt. You can go ahead, fucking shoot me, shoot me.'

Andrew said he feared he would be stabbed.

We asked a lot of people in Rich's position. Jeremy was right.

He had given me his family's blessing to tell Elijah's story on terms that were crystal clear. Andrew Rich was not the enemy.

'There's no black and white here, just a lot of grey … He's flesh and blood like the rest of us.'

Society wanted police to take the risks the rest of us felt ill equipped to face. We gave them guns so we could give them our problems, believing that armed them for every situation.

Perhaps Elijah's death was the price society paid for the licence police needed to make hard decisions — and to get them wrong sometimes?

32.

A two-word message came through from Jeremy on 9 December 2013.

'He lost.'

The judgement from the Court of Appeal was unanimous. Jerram's decision stood; Rich must speak.

We flew to NSW for the Christmas holidays, and spent them on the coast.

I bought the last weekend *Sydney Morning Herald* of the year and took it to the beach. On page four was an article on the NSW Homicide Squad. They'd had a busy year, their commander Mick Willing said.

The detectives who worked for him in homicide also investigated critical incident deaths like Elijah's for the Coroner.

I had met Mick Willing at a conference in Darwin. He was dressed from head to toe in black. I watched him from a distance. When he felt my gaze, he returned it. *If you want something, front up*, his expression said.

I remembered a conversation with a friend who'd dated a Townsville cop for years.

'Cops don't trust anyone until they get drunk with them,' she'd said.

So I made sure I had a beer in hand when I walked towards Mick Willing later that evening. I was less afraid than I had been in the daylight.

The circle of men around him watched me approach and shifted their weight to allow me in. Mick listened carefully to my spiel. I was writing about the circumstances of Elijah Holcombe's death, and I wanted a police perspective on his case and others like it. Could he help?

'The coronial jurisdiction has its challenges,' Mick said, handing me a crumpled card.

'Sorry, last one I've got. Call me when it's done. I can't promise anything, but there's a lot to say about cases like these. The whole story isn't being told.'

'I don't know how to convince you that I'm genuine about wanting the police side. I had to screw up my courage all night to come and talk to you,' I said.

He smiled briefly. We waved beer bottles at each other, and I left clutching his card.

The Mick Willing who peered out of the *Sydney Morning Herald* spread on my beach towel was a greyer, more serious version of the man I remembered meeting.

'With each [homicide] case comes enormous expectations from families, politicians, and the media,' the *Herald* told its readers.

'Sometimes the expectations are unrealistic and that's hard. The guys and girls that work here are human, too, and they go home and feel exactly the same as everyone else … they hurt and grieve like everyone,' Mick Willing said.

2014

33.

Soft rain shrouded the landscape as we circled over Darwin airport. We stepped into air ripe with frangipanis and rotting fruit. The wet had arrived while we were gone.

My husband skimmed frogspawn off the pool and piled up fallen palm fronds. I opened the house and turned on the fans. Mould had sprouted on every surface — books, door handles, tables, chairs, and shoes. We wiped it off and filled the fridge with groceries.

I returned my poetry books to the shelf.

Wait without sadness and with grave impatience, Adrienne Rich advised. I stuck her poem above my desk. It was everything I could not do.

Your silence today is a pond where drowned things live, she whispered.

I lay in the dark that night, the New Year spread in front of me, and watched shadows race across the ceiling. Elijah hovered above the bed, Rich hid beneath it. The Coroner would announce a date for Rich to speak soon.

A door slammed in the dark outside.

'Get out. He's not my son, you slut! Fuck off both of you!' The voice was ragged with rage and booze.

'Calm down!' a woman slurred.

I slipped out of bed and crept up the driveway to peer through a gap in the fence beside the mailbox. Last time, I had ventured as far as their house.

I went back inside and called the police again.

'He's not hitting her yet, but it sounds pretty aggressive. I think it's the same guy as last time.'

Ten minutes later, a paddy wagon pulled up. Its lights flashed sapphire and ruby in the cut-glass rain. Two officers — one male, one female — walked up to the door across the road. I held my breath. Fifteen minutes passed before they emerged with a woman. They helped her into the wagon's cage and left.

I crawled into bed and listened to darkness echo in the gaping mouths of frogs.

The Coroner's Court announced Rich would give evidence in mid-March — six weeks away. I took my Sydney clothes out of the cupboard, cleared my desk, and cleaned the house. I mowed the lawn and returned my library books. Six days before I flew to Sydney, I logged on to Facebook to check my messages.

A photograph of Jeremy Holcombe filled my screen. An oxygen mask covered his face. Jeremy was giving a thumbs-up from a hospital bed.

'Dad had a heart attack BUT HE'S OK!!!' Laura had posted that morning.

I dialed Jeremy's mobile. Jordan answered.

'Is he going to be OK?'

'He had tests this afternoon. The doctors think he'll need a bypass.'

Jeremy called out from the background and Jordan turned away from the phone.

'What's that? He says the bypass won't happen here in Tamworth. They'll fly him to Sydney or Newcastle.'

'When?'

'Maybe tomorrow. We're waiting to find out.'

I asked her to give Jeremy my love, and croaked out a goodbye.

Jeremy had waited five years to hear Rich speak. There was no way he could make the hearing now, unless the Coroner postponed.

I rang Phil Stewart and David Sweeney. They had spoken to the court already. The hearing would go ahead.

'It needs to have an end,' Jeremy Gormly said when I called to double-check Rich's evidence would proceed as planned. The fifth anniversary of Elijah's death loomed, Mary Jerram was coming out of retirement; it couldn't be put off. 'This has to have a resolution, for all the parties.'

It was there in his voice: everyone was tired. The Coroner, the DPP, the Supreme Court, and the Court of Appeal had all turned their minds to Elijah's story, but no one could provide an ending except Rich.

I prayed for someone to take a stand and argue for Jeremy's right to bear witness when the man who killed his son finally spoke.

Fiona soothed my jangled nerves when I called that afternoon. She and Jeremy had been flown to Newcastle.

'Jeremy's actually relieved not to have to be there. All the pressure — the lawyers wanted him to make a statement. David Phelps will be there for the three days, Tarney will go on Monday. It's out of Jeremy's hands what happens now,' she said. Her voice was strong and free of emotion. Her focus was Jeremy, not the inquest. The doctors said he needed a double bypass, maybe a triple. The surgery would happen tomorrow or the next day.

While Andrew Rich prepared to explain what happened in the last fifty seconds of Elijah's life, Jeremy Holcombe's chest would lay open on an operating table. The red, bloody heart that had kept him alive through the agony of the last five years would be lifted from his chest, and surgeons would heal what could be healed.

34.

Allison's name sat on a Post-it note on my desk. I wasn't sure if anyone else had let her know that Rich was giving evidence. I had planned to contact her a final time to make sure she knew the case was almost over. Now I had something else to tell her.

The officer who shot Elijah would give evidence in Sydney next week, I wrote. The hearings would go for three days. Jeremy Holcombe had had a heart attack and wouldn't be at the hearings, I told her. I apologised for writing with bad news.

Allison replied within twenty minutes. She 'really appreciated' me writing to let her know. Would Rich speak on all three days? she asked. She needed to know how much time to take off work to be there.

On 16 March 2014, I stepped out of Sydney's Central train station. It was close to midnight. The wheels of my suitcase beat a rhythm on the footpath. The moon hung like a spider's sac, papery and full and far away. Tracey's funeral, the Court of Appeal hearing, and the settlement of the civil case had all happened on full moons.

Crumpled in my pocket was this week's horoscope, torn out of the newspaper.

> Justice must not only be done; it must also be seen to be done. Is there, somewhere in your world now, such an imperative to ensure that justice is seen to be done, that the question of whether or not it actually is true justice, has been overlooked? I venture to

suggest that for you, of the two implied priorities in that opening statement, the former matters far more.

Jeremy Holcombe was recovering from surgery. Andrew Rich would speak tomorrow. He would step into the dock and tell us what had happened and then we would all go home. *Life would begin again,* I caught myself thinking.

I dressed in the morning as if for a funeral. Black pants, inky blouse, a swipe of makeup. Magpies caroled, their joy bounced off the air like light off glass. The sky outside was clear.

I imagined Andrew waking up as though on 2 June 2009. This time with the knowledge he would end someone's life and a courtroom of people would be watching. I wished for the hundredth time that he had let me know him. Maybe after today, I would get the chance.

I arrived at the Coroner's Court far too early, which is how I saw him waiting at the lights across the highway. The round head and dark suit were the same, but he looked older, looser, cut adrift beneath his skin. He was with two men. The traffic lights changed and we walked; Rich towards the coffee shop and I into the courthouse.

The Holcombes were early, too, their group reduced to a stump by Jeremy and Fiona's absence. David Phelps was there with Tarney and Eric Nielsen, Elijah's friend from high school. Eric was 'Dorey' in EJ, Bags, and Dorey. Bags had prompted me to call him, but I'd never followed through.

'I've been tuned out of the legal stuff for years,' Dorey confessed on the phone when I finally rang him, the same day I contacted Allison.

Eric had stayed in contact with Jeremy and Tarney after Elijah died, but when Tracey died, 'it all got too much', and he had drifted out of touch, he said.

He was dressed in black jeans and black suede boots. Blonde surfer's hair swept forward on his face. He looked like he had just risen from a shore dump. Tarney introduced us, and Eric shook my hand.

The automatic doors onto the street peeled back and we stopped mid-sentence, open-mouthed.

Andrew Rich, Roger Best, and Greig Stier walked towards us. Stier reached out a hand to David Phelps.

'Good to see you.'

'Glad to see you here,' David replied.

The flush of adrenalin was on everyone's skin. David and Stier affected ease. Everyone else stood mute and embarrassed like children at a grown-ups' party. Roger Best was in dress uniform. I searched his face, but his eyes stayed low and guarded. I sneaked a look at Rich across Stier's shoulder. He raised his hand in a tiny wave and mouthed hello, and then they left.

35.

Jeremy Gormly exhaled and entered the rhythm of a now-familiar narrative.

Phil Stewart and James Sheller were in their places; so were Murugan Thangaraj and Brent Haverfield. Ray Hood — who had appeared for the police commissioner at Elijah's inquest in Armidale — was back in Patrick Saidi's seat.

Rich sat in the front row of the gallery with Stier and Best on either side. Inspector Joel Murchie from the Mental Health Intervention Team (MHIT) sat further along the row.

Gormly suggested proceedings open with a statement from the Holcombe family. David Phelps would deliver the statement on Jeremy's behalf, but he had to return to Narrabri tonight, Gormly explained. Traditionally, the family's statement was the last act of an inquest.

'There are no timing issues for me at all, Your Honour,' David Phelps piped up. Gormly had been misinformed.

Jerram nodded her satisfaction. The statement would wait until the end.

'It's a form of eulogy, isn't it?' she said, and Elijah's death dawned freshly with the word.

Gormly announced the day's first piece of evidence would be a viewing of a video filmed two days after Elijah's shooting.

Rich ran a finger inside his collar. Thirty-six hours after he shot Elijah, Rich had retraced the route from Rusden Street to Cinders Lane with detectives, to explain what happened in the minutes he chased Elijah.

I moved to a seat with a better view. The monitor blinked and Rich appeared, unshaven, outside the camping store, with a windcheater zipped up to his neck and hands pushed deep into his pockets. He objected to the walk-through in stilted formal language, and a detective holding a golf umbrella ordered him to speak. Rich lifted his shoulders against the cold. The dome of the umbrella popped with rain as the detective opened it above his head. Rich was asked where he first saw Elijah. He pointed to a sandstone wall smeared with moss. Here, walking towards the camping store, he said in a nasal voice. Elijah was about ten metres away when he offered him the car keys.

'"Throw me the keys," Elijah said, and I said — "I can't do that",' recounted Rich.

The Coroner asked to pause the tape. 'Is it possible to run it back?'

Rich sat composed before the frozen picture. The Coroner listened to the exchange again.

The group on the screen moved under an awning, and the pop of rain on the umbrella stopped. Rich pointed out Elijah's flight path — across the road, around the corner, and into the mall on Beardy Street. The picture went black, and the party reappeared in the mall in front of Caffiends café. Rich motioned with an open hand and the automatic doors slid back. The lights were off; chairs were stacked on tables pushed against the walls.

He followed Elijah into the café; they were walking by now, he said. Elijah walked to the top of the passage, turned right into the kitchen.

'Then I've heard the sound of metal on metal.'

The camera followed Rich to a dingy kitchen, identical to every café I had ever worked in. Stacks of white crockery, knife-scarred bench tops, a grubby microwave on a chipboard shelf.

The next time he saw Elijah, 'he was here like this', Rich said.

He held an imaginary knife in his right hand in line with the frame of the café's screen door.

There were three people working at the island bench, Rich said.

'They were a bit shocked. I took the most notice of the lady here.' He motioned to one side.

'I just wanted to get them out … I was happy for him to go out the door, I just wanted to get people out, away from the knife.'

Rich pointed to the bench.

'I went for my OC spray back here. Realised I didn't have it.'

The camera operator stepped out the back door and followed Rich to the edge of Cinders Lane. Rich wrapped an imaginary jumper around his arm then dropped it, repeating Elijah's movements. His arm swung freely as he pointed out the position of different bystanders.

'[Elijah] was starting to jog towards them,' he explained.

Rich stretched his arms into a crucifix.

'This was where I challenged Elijah.' His voice was clear, but its volume dropped as he went on.

'He said, "Shoot me, fucking shoot me", and he started to run at me. I thought I was going to get stabbed.'

'The time is now 7.21am. This is the end of the interview,' the detective with the umbrella said.

The monitor on the wall blinked off. Greig Stier's stubby fingers rubbed his forehead. Roger Best and Rich leaned back. Eric Nielsen slowly shook his head.

Gormly stood up. Senior Constable Rich would normally be called to give evidence now, but his lawyers wished to make an application first, he announced and motioned along the bar table.

Murugan Thangaraj buttoned his jacket and peered at the Coroner through gleaming spectacles. He wished to 'ventilate some issues' about the Court of Appeal's decision, he said.

Heads in the public gallery swivelled in confusion. The Court of Appeal had decided unanimously that the Coroner could make Rich speak.

'What's this all about?' mouthed a woman beside me.

Shenanigans, I scribbled on her notepad.

He would discuss the Court of Appeal's decision later, Thangaraj continued. First, he wanted to bring the court's attention to a previously unknown obstacle to Rich's ability to give evidence.

A document passed ceremoniously through the hands of each of Rich's lawyers and up to the heights of the Coroner's bench. Thangaraj said when the time came to discuss its contents, he would ask the Coroner to close the court.

Gormly's sanguine features hardened. Closing the court meant ordering everyone but the Coroner, lawyers, and Rich to leave the room.

Gormly pushed himself out of his seat.

'May I signal an issue between Mr Thangaraj and myself about this report?'

If the Coroner closed the court, the public would not learn what condition affected Senior Constable Rich's ability to answer questions, he said tersely.

The single other journalist in the room raised an eyebrow at me. Closing a court was no small matter. I sent a flurry of text messages to journalists at different outlets. They needed to get down here.

The Coroner was keen to get on with business; she made a temporary order to suppress publication of anything in the document. People had waited long enough. Jerram would decide if the suppression order stood after the document was discussed.

'In that event, Your Honour,' Gormly said, 'I call Senior Constable Rich.'

Rich walked to the witness stand and turned to face the room. He wore a wheat-yellow tie and bright-blue shirt; the colours of the Wee Waa landscape. He folded his hands on the bench in front of him.

Gormly established in rapid back and forth that Rich was still a senior constable based in Armidale. He worked normal duties with no restrictions and carried his full appointments.

I studied him for details, but Rich was a work of minimalism. His facial expression, his body language, the information he gave out.

I struggled to place his broad vowels in a geography. A small town on the coast somewhere?

Gormly extracted his personal history crumb by crumb.

Andrew Rich joined the police force at thirty-two. He was thirty-eight at the time of the shooting; he was forty-four now.

'Where did you grow up?' asked Gormly.

'All over the place. My dad was in the RAAF.'

Rich was in the army for ten years from the age of sixteen to twenty-six. When he left the army, he worked as a security guard at a hospital for six years. After that he joined the police. The snippets of backstory, like his body language, revealed nothing of Rich's internal life. Why did he leave the army? How much contact did he have at the hospital with people who were mentally ill? Was he ever called upon to restrain psychotic patients? These were the things I wanted to know, but Gormly didn't ask.

'I want to take you to the second of June and the start of that day,' he said instead.

Rich described walking behind the reception desk at Armidale Station, heading for his office. Acting Sergeant Aiken stopped him and pointed to a man in the waiting room. He had confessed that morning to stealing a car, Aiken said.

'Basically, he asked me to recover the vehicle for him.'

Aiken didn't mention the young man's name or that the car belonged to his father. Rich didn't know he had a mental health issue or that Aiken had arranged for him to be taken to the hospital. Rich scribbled the rego for the stolen car on his hand and went out to recover it.

'So you weren't part of the Elijah Holcombe problem, you were part of the finding the stolen car problem,' Gormly stated.

'That's correct.'

Rich's voice was strong.

Rich pulled Dufty in on the search, and when they couldn't find the car, Rich called the station to ask the young man where it was. Aiken told him Elijah was at the hospital, 'for scheduling or psychological assessment', Rich recalled. Rich hung up, but a minute later, Aiken called him back to say Elijah had 'absconded' from the hospital.

Rich and Dufty drove to Emergency. Rich went inside while Dufty stayed in the car. The nurses said they were worried for Elijah's safety. They asked Rich to bring him back if he found him.

'You were told that he hadn't actually been scheduled, correct?' Gormly checked.

'I was told he left before he saw a psychiatric registrar.'

'So he had not been scheduled?'

'Correct.'

If Elijah had been scheduled at Armidale Hospital under the *Mental Health Act*, Rich had grounds to apprehend him. But a doctor had to declare Elijah was a threat to his own or others' safety first. That hadn't happened. Robyn O'Brien, in her statement to police, had been explicit on this point: 'I told the Policeman that no scheduled (sic) had been issued, and I gave him a description of Elijah.'

Gormly summed up the situation as Rich understood it when he left the hospital

'Elijah has handed himself in in some way to the police. So far as you know, he hasn't been arrested or charged with anything, and there appears to be a mental health issue. Nevertheless, you've got a message from the nurses that they are concerned about his health and they would prefer to have him back?'

Rich agreed.

'So you got in the car and drove off starting to look for Mr Holcombe. I'm going to get you to tell us what you did and said [when you found him].'

Rich made his hands into Elijah and himself and walked them along an imaginary footpath.

'... I said, "Elijah, it's the police" and I showed him my badge and warrant card ... I was aware that he would've had mental issues at that stage, so I didn't hold it out in front of me aggressively. I held it down to my side and I said, "Elijah, it's the police" as I was walking towards him.'

'What else did you say to him?'

'I said "Elijah, I've got your keys." ... I believed he would recognise those keys. Sometimes in plainclothes it's difficult — a lot of people aren't aware that we're police officers — and in my experience, when you're dealing with persons with mental health issues it can be, can be confronting to be fronted by someone in the street saying they're police ... So I wanted to take a low-profile approach and I wanted him to interact with me. I knew he'd know those keys because he handed them in to the station. So I said, "I've got your keys" and hopefully, I wanted that to start rapport building.'

'Didn't you jangle them out and laugh at him?' asked Gormly.

'I held them out.'

'But didn't you jangle them at him and say, "I've got your keys" and laugh?'

'No.'

'You've heard a witness say that you chuckled as you were holding the keys out and dangling them at him?'

'Yes.'

Gormly jabbed at Rich repeatedly.

'Isn't that what you did?'

'No.'

'Was that other witness wrong?'

'Yes.'

'Did you laugh at all?'

'No.'

The keys were bait, Gormly suggested in a dozen different ways; used to lure Elijah close enough to seize him and take him back to hospital.

Rich denied it — he was trying to connect.

If the keys were a token of trust, why not hand them over, why not throw them when Elijah asked? Gormly challenged.

Rich was resolute. 'There's more to it than just the keys.'

'Why did you chase him?' Gormly boomed.

The courtroom door creaked open and three journalists snuck in.

Rich took a deep breath. He shifted in his seat and leaned forward.

'So my, my assessment of him was — his behaviour was stand-offish. He appeared agitated. His, his speech was clipped. Terse. So he wasn't engaging with me. I had that information in the back of my mind from the nurse that they wanted him back. I also had the information that he'd recently stolen a vehicle, which to me would show that there's some disturbance of thought patterns. If he's stolen a vehicle and handed himself in; that to me is not normal behaviour. I hadn't at that stage decided I would detain him for the purposes of, of a psychiatric assessment, until he ran across the road. That to me was the, the, the top layer. So I went, I took the advice of the nurse on board. I made my assessment of him just from his bodily — his behaviours, his speech and that he wasn't, wasn't responding.'

Did he think Elijah was trying to harm himself by running into the traffic? Gormly asked.

'That would be part of it, yes. I would say that he didn't take into consideration the traffic.'

Gormly's mouth hardened. 'He didn't run in front of a car to be hit by the car, did he?'

'I can't speak for Elijah,' Rich replied.

'I'm not asking you to speak for Elijah. I'm asking about your assessment of his behaviour. Do you understand that?' There was no warmth in Gormly's voice.

'Isn't it the case, Mr Rich, that he avoided the traffic rather than ran into it, and didn't get harmed in any way? He wasn't running into the traffic because he wanted to harm himself. He was trying to escape you, wasn't he?' Gormly threw the words across the room like javelins.

'I don't agree, sir.'

'You didn't have any basis at that stage for forming the view that he could be arrested for some criminal behaviour — correct?' counsel assisting thundered.

Thangaraj leapt up.

'Objection! Your Honour, I think it's time for our application to be made.'

It was an opportune moment to discuss a document that could limit his client's cross-examination. If Rich could not convince the court he had a legal reason to apprehend Elijah, he was in trouble.

Thangaraj reminded the Coroner of his application to close the court.

Gormly returned fire. Unless Mr Rich's counsel could establish a reason in the public interest, there were no grounds to close the court, he advised the Coroner.

'We're dealing with a few people being asked to leave the court,' Rich's lawyer argued. 'I'm happy for the family and friends to remain if that has any relevance [but] we don't see why the media needs to hear that material—'

The Coroner cut across him.

'They're not the enemy, Mr Thangaraj. They do represent the public. Why should they be excluded?'

'The reason they should be excluded, Your Honour, is because of the sensitive nature of the material in the report.'

Every journalist's warning system switched to red alert.

'If it's only a few members, as you say, who are obliged not to report what they hear, I'm still not convinced they should be excluded,' Jerram parried.

Thangaraj was becoming desperate.

'Well, it's because it's about people that have got nothing to do with the proceedings per se. It's not the family; it's not the witness. It's not the—'

'We've all got an interest in justice surely, Mr Thangaraj.'

Jerram's words were flinty.

I glanced at Rich. He was looking directly at me.

What is going on? I asked him with my eyes. His gaze didn't shift from my face.

'I think perhaps we should have the lunch break,' Gormly suggested, and everyone filed out.

Jordan had emailed me days ago to say Allison was worried about the media. Did I have any advice about how to slip under the radar if she came to court?

Tell her to dress like a law student on assignment, I wrote back. No make-up, no fancy clothes. Carry a notebook. Don't talk to anyone in the family; don't look like you're connected. Bring a friend for support, but make it a woman; a couple will attract attention.

I scanned the foyer for Allison in the break. Perhaps the idea of seeing Rich was too much in the end; it was easier to stay away. I stood in earshot of the small pack of journalists huddled in the corner. Those who were new to Elijah's case were scrambling to catch up.

'Holy fuck!' said one when he learned the inquest had been running for five years.

'Why do they want to close the court? What's in this report?' asked another.

A seasoned journalist from a commercial network smiled and gave his prediction.

'You watch. The report will say he has PTSD and he can't remember a thing.'

Jerram took the bench and the room fell silent.

Counsel for Senior Constable Rich wished to close the court to discuss a report of a medical nature, Gormly announced.

'I understand the argument to be something like it's unseemly or inappropriate for police officers as a species to have to have some aspect of their medical health dealt with in public. I oppose this argument, Your Honour … in courts all over the country, people's medical situation is being discussed in public and it's always awkward and always difficult. But what we're dealing with here is the shooting of a man by a police officer. It is a matter of such weight and such importance that the embarrassment caused to Senior Constable Rich is not a factor that can be taken into account … It's a very skimpy report. It's two and a half pages long. It contains no detail. It recites no personal aspect of his life. Were it to be an expert report, it would be rejected out of hand for inadequacy.'

Gormly surfaced for air and then dived back in.

'Furthermore, even if one looks at that report from the institutional point of view of the New South Wales Police, one would be hard-pressed — and Mr Thangaraj has not done it — to find how admitting this report harms the institution of the police.'

The courtroom door squealed on its un-oiled hinge. I recognised the woman on the threshold straight away. Allison's chestnut hair was in a ponytail. Her makeup and nails were perfect. She wore blue patent high heels and a sleeveless dark-blue dress. The notebook in the hand of the young man with her was crisp, its price sticker clearly visible. He wore a lavender shirt and sharp grey suit. They sidled along the back row into seats beside me. Allison kept her sunglasses on. The heads that had turned to mark her arrival returned to the front of the room.

Haverfield picked which way the wind was blowing. He knelt in front of Rich and whispered. Rich walked to the witness stand, and, minutes later, Jerram announced the court would stay open.

The report was 'nothing that you wouldn't expect a good counsellor to be saying about a client who had been through a trauma,' she declared. There was nothing there to embarrass Mr Rich.

Thangaraj stood to do his duty.

The report was from a psychologist, Dr O'Loughlin.

'Dr O'Loughlin began seeing Senior Constable Rich as a result of standard police practice,' Thangaraj said.

'She has seen him every year since 2009, on sixteen separate occasions, and in addition had conversations with him over the telephone.'

'No one would be surprised that he has been diagnosed with severe post-traumatic stress disorder nor that he would be on medication for depression,' Thangaraj continued.

The commercial journalist looked at me and smirked. Dr O'Loughlin and Rich had discussed the second of June 2009 on more than one occasion.

'She has made a note that she had discussions with him about his inability to remember aspects of the incident in 2010, 2011, and 2014.' Thangaraj faltered for a moment.

What aspects did Rich not remember?

'I had discussions with my learned friend about how it is that this has come about late. It would have been more convenient to us and Your Honour if we were aware of this on the last occasion, and I will explain how it came about so late in a moment.'

Was Thangaraj saying this report was new to him?

A wave of disbelief rippled through the room.

'But the important thing to note is that all of these issues were apparent to Dr O'Loughlin from conversations she had in 2010 and 2011.'

Someone in the gallery snorted, and Jerram pursed her lips. Roger Best and Greig Stier crossed their arms.

Thangaraj told the Coroner he had learned about Rich's memory loss three days ago, when he took Rich through his evidence for the first time. Thangaraj knew how incredible it sounded, and rushed to explain himself.

He reminded the court he did not represent Rich when Elijah's inquest was suspended in Armidale, but Rich's counsel at the time had not gone through his evidence with him because the matter was referred to the DPP. When the DPP dismissed the matter and the inquest re-opened, Thangaraj and Haverfield advised Rich not to speak. They knew the Coroner would either accept Rich's position or compel him, at which point Thangaraj would challenge the ruling. Either way, their client would not give evidence, so there was no need to review it with him at that point. Silence remained the status quo until Rich lost in the Court of Appeal, which created the need to go through Rich's evidence, which Thangaraj and Haverfield had first attempted to do with him the previous Thursday.

'… When it became abundantly clear that from a particular point in the chronology, his memory was non-existent, and relied entirely on just remembering what he had said in the record of interview and the walk-through,' Thangaraj told the Coroner.

When they discovered his memory was compromised, Thangaraj and Haverfield asked Rich if he had seen anyone about it.

'It emanated that we didn't even know he had been seeing a psychologist.'

Thangaraj was no longer cocky. He had received Dr O'Loughlin's notes on the weekend and her report last night. He read the report for the first time at seven o'clock this morning, he told the Coroner.

Jerram lifted her eyes from the document in her hands. It was odd that Thangaraj wasn't advised of these matters earlier than this, she said.

'I'm not criticising … I accept what you're telling me, of course.' Her voice was flat.

'There's certainly nothing convenient about it,' Thangaraj apologised. 'But the most important thing, as I said, is that the history given involves the inability to recall or the difficulties in recall existing in 2010 and 2011.'

Ignore the unbelievable nature of what you've just been told and focus on this instead. Any minute now, Thangaraj would open his briefcase and pull out a rabbit.

'So far at least I haven't heard Senior Constable Rich say he didn't remember anything. In fact, I thought his answers were very clear and he was doing his absolute best to answer factually,' Jerram observed.

'The issue of post-traumatic stress disorder doesn't mean you don't remember the whole day or the whole hour,' Rich's barrister replied.

His client's inability to recollect events began with the phone call made at the back door of Caffiends; his recall of events before then was intact, Thangaraj said.

THIS IS BULLSHIT I scrawled across an entire page.

Rich had sat in this room twelve months ago and listened while his former partner Dufty sweated his way through giving evidence. Dufty declared his post-traumatic stress, but Rich didn't let on then that he was suffering from it, too. If his recall of events in Cinders Lane had deteriorated so significantly *two years* before Dufty spoke, Rich had the perfect opportunity to say so when his partner was in the stand. Rich could have avoided two Supreme Court appeals, twelve months of stress, and hundreds of thousands of dollars in legal fees.

Jerram placed a nimble foot on the serpent's neck.

'It just seems to me that you are putting the cart before the horse if you like, in that you're … arguing he might not remember when he hasn't at any stage said he doesn't.'

Rich had left the witness box. Now he walked to the door and bowed before he stepped out of the room. I wanted to chase him and pull at the skin of his face to force an emotion out. *Where are you going? What do you want?*

The room descended into legal argument, and I slumped down in my seat.

What could more talk achieve? If Rich said he had no memory of what happened, Cinders Lane would never be explained.

I fled through the foyer and burst out of the courthouse onto the empty footpath. My face was flushed. I forced myself to breathe. I waited for the bright sound of polished shoes behind me. I waited for a hand on my shoulder to stop me at the lights.

'Andrew still wants to speak to you,' the owner of the shoes would say. 'When this is all over, he'll call you.' The messenger would squeeze my shoulder or raise a hand to wave before he left. If I was patient. If I didn't turn around.

The lights changed and I crossed. I followed Parramatta Road towards the city. The gritty wind of trucks pummelled my legs. I walked, watching out of the corner of my eye for a police car to slow and its window to roll down. *Can I talk to you for a moment, Ma'am?*

I walked past houses, shops, and universities; through Glebe, Broadway, and Ultimo. In Chinatown, I found a pub.

Fragments of the day came back. A last-minute plea of forgotten homework; the forgotten minute and a half of another man's life.

Rich was left-handed. So was I. He was a security guard at a hospital. Elijah wasn't running away from him, he was running into traffic, Rich said. Towards something dangerous, not away from what he feared. There was no public interest in Rich sharing sensitive testimony about his own mental illness, it would only distress and embarrass him. Why did the compassion I felt for Elijah not flood me for Rich in his illness, too?

Because attempting to hide his illness from the public in one breath, and using it to avoid answering questions about Elijah with the next, was insulting.

Rich had presented his decision not to speak as a conscious choice for the last three years. I had convinced myself he had his reasons. I had clung to the belief that however long it took, at some point he would explain what happened. The explanation would either be lacking or it would show why he thought it was the only choice he had. But he would *give those answers*, and we would understand. His humanity would end the story, for him and the Holcombes and everyone.

Today, he had told us that the last door to his state of mind when he shot Elijah was boarded up. Even if his decision to shoot was justified, Rich could no longer explain it to us. I should have felt sorry for the damage he had suffered, but all I felt was anger.

'He might be all the things you're thinking about him, and if you get to talk to him you'll find that out. But you don't have enough information yet. You're angry because your access is being blocked. There could be all sorts of reasons for what he's doing. Be careful about assumptions, they're dangerous.'

I had fled the pub in Chinatown for dinner with a mentor. We sat huddled in the windy corner of an Italian bistro with bowls of pasta and glasses of wine.

'But why won't he *speak*? He could finish it if he wanted to. If I'd known it would take this long … and now PTSD at the eleventh hour. Why didn't he say that two years ago? I mean, it would be weird if you *didn't* have PTSD after shooting someone, but why now? It looks so *dodgy* this late in the piece. Even his lawyers said they just found out about it. We were here a year ago for him to give evidence, why didn't he use it then?'

With the comfort of company, I was raving: unloading the day, and months of solitary doubt and fears. Was I naive to have given Rich the benefit of the doubt? A fool to believe the message from Best that Rich had a point of view to offer? I feared a smarter, harder person would have picked it from the beginning, but I was still shaking the dew from my eyes.

I tore viciously at the crust of my bread and speared salad onto my plate.

'People caught in the legal system for serious matters are like people in the medical system with a terminal illness. They're at the mercy of the expert telling them what to do. They're scared. They'll do whatever they're told if someone offers to fix it for them,' my friend cautioned.

I was tired and full of conflicting emotions. I wanted to give up. I wanted to crusade. I wanted to know what was believable and what I was right to label bullshit.

'If he doesn't talk to me all I've got left are assumptions and he's not doing anything to prove those wrong. I can't talk for him if he won't talk to me. He's not leaving me any option,' I whined.

'Write to him, tell him you feel inexorably pushed to these assumptions and you don't want to succumb to them. Invite him into the tent to tell him where you're at with it.'

She looked at me firmly over the salad bowl.

'Take all that energy you're putting in to being pissed off and find out more. You don't know enough.'

36.

Rich's time in the witness box was like a novella jammed between massive bookends. The Coroner and barristers spent hours on either side of his appearances debating what legal consequences might flow if he answered certain questions.

I didn't understand until weeks later that the unanimous Court of Appeal judgement, which found the Coroner could make Rich speak, carried a caveat.

> The applicant's ability to object is [not] necessarily at an end ... given the way in which the objection has been advanced to date, it may be that a more narrow objection may be advanced in the future.

The Court of Criminal Appeal (CCA) had accepted the Coroner could compel Rich to give evidence, but its decision also allowed Rich to continue to object to certain questions.

According to Rich's barrister, the CCA decided evidence that posed no legal threat to Rich was uncontroversial, but compelling him to speak on contentious matters was another thing altogether.

> It may be quite a different thing to determine whether, say, counsel for the family were to be permitted to cross-examine the applicant, including on his credit in relation to whether the deceased was charging at him with a drawn knife.

Thangaraj wielded this paragraph like a scythe. The decision about what evidence could be compelled required the Coroner to decide whether knowing what happened in Cinders Lane was more important than preserving the doctrine that a witness was entitled to their silence.

Thangaraj maintained he would challenge every question about Rich's thoughts, actions, and feelings from the beginning of the pursuit to the moment he shot Elijah.

Jeremy Gormly had shared with Rich's legal team fifty-seven pages of questions he wished to put to Rich.

The strident response from Thangaraj to the territory the questions ranged over forced a change in Gormly's game plan. At the start of day two, he announced that questions about Rich's foot pursuit of Elijah from Rusden Street, right through to the end of events in Cinders Lane, would be moved to the afternoon so that Rich's lawyers could object to them in one block.

The change of schedule left well-trodden subjects to fill the morning session.

Rich wore a tie the colour of an Armidale sky on a crisp winter morning on day two. His eyes followed paper in every corner of the room: his barristers' notes, the Coroner's papers, the pages of my notebook as I flipped them over. He looked tired.

Gormly dealt with Rich's training swiftly. A one-hour lecture at the police academy, seven years prior to events in Cinders Lane, on how to deal with people with a mental illness, and two online modules since then on transporting such a person. Gormly suggested, and Rich agreed, that the training was focused on the unpredictability of people with a mental illness. It included no de-escalation or rapport-development skills.

Whenever Gormly asked a question that strayed onto dangerous territory, he warned Rich not to answer until Thangaraj gave him clearance. More than once in these exchanges, Rich looked across and smiled at me.

Midway through the morning, Allison re-appeared. She wore a gold brocade shift and heels. A large, fashion-label handbag hung from her arm. Her companion's lavender shirt had been swapped for an apricot one with French cuffs. They slid into my row in the middle of Gormly's questions.

I leaned into the cloud of aftershave surrounding the young man.

'Can you please tell Allison that I'm Kate who has been writing to her?' I whispered.

He looked at me in alarm and nodded. Allison did not turn or speak when he passed the message on.

I turned back to Gormly's questioning.

'I suppose you didn't know, at that stage, anything about Elijah's personal history, as to whether he was prone to violence or not, but had you seen anything that morning which might suggest [it]?'

'No,' Rich said.

'Had it come to your knowledge from anyone else that he had any such tendency?'

The psychiatric nurse at the hospital expressed fears for Elijah's safety, Rich said. He based 90 per cent of his assessment of Elijah's mental state on her advice. The rest he took from Elijah running 'into traffic' on Rusden Street. He read that as a sign that Elijah was willing to hurt himself, he said.

When he caught up with Elijah in Caffiends, Rich reached for his OC spray as a precaution, he told Gormly.

'I thought in my mind, if it came to it that Elijah was able to come out the back door and for some reason wanted to get back in to harm the people inside, I would have the OC spray as a measure,' he said. But the spray wasn't in his pocket.

Rich saw Elijah at the back door of the kitchen.

'And he was holding a knife in his right hand.'

'In what way was he holding it?' asked Gormly.

'Blade up and the serrations to the front.'

'So you could see it was a bread knife?'

'I could see it was a knife, yes.'

'Could you see it was a serrated bread knife?'

'I could see it was serrated, yes.'

Rich's recall of his experience in the kitchen was photographic. He remembered where the café owner, the chef, and the kitchen hand were standing; what he said to them, what they did, which way the back door opened. He remembered his phone in his hand as he stepped out the back door, and what he said when Aiken answered.

'He's got a knife, he's in Cinders Lane, I need someone up here to help out.'

Whenever Gormly asked what Rich had thought or felt at a certain moment, Thangaraj intervened. Rich sipped water from a styrofoam cup while they sparred.

Gormly described Rich resting after he finished his phone call to the station, hands on his knees, bent over in Cinders Lane.

'You seem to have been there for perhaps a few seconds?'

Rich looked to the bar table for help.

'No, I don't recall, sir.'

'What happened then?' asked Gormly abruptly.

Haverfield and Thangaraj leaned their heads together and muttered.

'I object,' Thangaraj called out.

'You are not suggesting that I shouldn't hear anything about what happened in the lane, are you?' The Coroner was incredulous.

'We are. We are now talking about the events directly leading to the firing of the shot. From now on, we are at a very critical stage of the entire incident.'

This was the point, on his barristers' account, at which Rich's evidence risked self-incrimination. They continued to insist there was a risk of Rich being re-referred to the DPP if his evidence in court differed to his statement.

Rich took another sip. Everyone in the room leaned forward.

Gormly conceded that an answer 'may tend to prove' Rich had acted outside the law. He withdrew the question and re-approached.

'Can you describe for us the pathway that you took — that is, the

299

direction and places you walked — from the time you entered onto Cinders Lane?' he asked Rich.

'I don't have a recollection of it.' Rich's face was stricken.

Gormly described the CCTV vision that showed Rich following Elijah along Cinders Lane.

'I take it that you accept that film shows what happened?'

'Yes I do, sir.' Rich swallowed heavily.

'Do you have a recollection of that occurring?'

'No, sir.'

Rich's eyes found mine in the back row. Deep splotches bloomed on both his cheeks. He broke my gaze and poured more water.

'Can you tell us what it was that you said as you were moving along Cinders Lane?' asked Gormly.

Thangaraj was swift.

'Objection. We are talking about communications very shortly before the shot was fired. We are talking about different witnesses having different positions about what was said by both individuals. We are talking about a dispute over witnesses—' and on he went.

Rich found me again. I felt as if he were trying to tell me something.

'Can I ask my friend to ask a particular question?' Thangaraj suggested. 'Does [Rich] have any memory from this point onwards in Cinders Lane until after the shot is discharged?'

If Rich said no, there was no need for other questions. If he answered yes, they could continue the debate.

The Coroner nodded.

'Do you have any memory of what happened from the time you entered Cinders Lane until after the shot?' Gormly asked obligingly.

'No, sir.' Rich answered with his eyes locked on mine.

Jerram leaned down from the bench towards him.

'When did that happen?' she asked gently.

'Gradually over time since.' Rich's voice cracked.

'At what point does your memory revive?'

'That day is basically done; basically, the whole day from there on I can't remember.'

The male reporters swore to me later that Rich cried, but I didn't see it.

'If it is the case that the witness doesn't have a memory of these events, then there is, with respect, nothing he can say to incriminate himself in answering any question about events,' James Sheller said.

Why not allow counsel assisting his full suite of questions; Rich the inevitable answer that he remembered nothing; and a more rapid end to the whole charade, the Holcombes' barrister suggested.

'It is not going to work,' Gormly said edgily, and the Coroner called a fifteen-minute recess.

Allison stood with her friend in the courthouse doorway. A bunch of hair elastics criss-crossed faint lines on her wrist.

Eric Nielsen shot her a withering look.

'She had no idea about Elijah's problems or that she should have been helping *him*,' he'd told me on the phone.

It echoed Adam Baguley's comments in my hotel room in Wee Waa.

'It was all about the handbags for Allison'; Elijah was 'too good for her'. She was shallow, 'she liked Brittany Spears'.

'But Elijah loved her. He chose her,' I had challenged them.

Watching Allison in the doorway, the appeal was obvious. She was beautiful, young, and vulnerable. In need of care, just like Elijah.

'He was always just helping other people,' Bags had said in Wee Waa. 'If … in the distance you saw him talking to someone, you could just tell he's helping them out with some ridiculous issue.'

Allison and Elijah were both vulnerable. Elijah loved her and was drawn to help her, but his own need for care was bigger than them both. The fact that Allison was ill equipped to help and unsure of what to do didn't mean she had not loved him.

Eric stood watching her, biting his nails.

'How are you doing?' I asked.

He grimaced.

'I had to put my water bottle down before to stop myself throwing it at the prick.'

He pushed his fringe back to reveal his eyes.

'I wanted to say thank you for encouraging me to come. It's been good for me to get my head out of the sand.'

We walked back into court together and resumed our seats.

A man I had never seen before approached Rich and shook his hand.

'Just to let you know I'm here. The whole force is here,' he said.

He clapped Rich on the shoulder and took a seat.

Eric stared at the side of Rich's head from the far end of the row, like a child bewitched by a mystical beast caught under glass. *Did it exist? Well, there it was, it must*, his expression said.

Thangaraj chatted comfortably to Haverfield and Hood at the bar table. Counsel assisting was playing catch-up.

Gormly bustled into the room and cued Rich to take the stand.

The blue-glass beads at the Coroner's throat matched Rich's tie.

'We are entering the final stage now of the examination of Mr Rich,' Gormly began.

His list of questions had thinned considerably with the revelation of how little Rich remembered. Gormly had one subject left.

'I am going to ask about ... whether you had a sufficient basis to chase [Elijah] with the intent of bringing about his return willingly or unwillingly, to the Armidale Hospital under the provisions of the *Mental Health Act*.'

Gormly's voice was clipped and formal.

'I suggest to you that at the time you started to chase Mr Holcombe, you did not have a sufficient basis to bring about his detention, pursuant to the provisions of the *Mental Health Act* insofar as they apply to police officers.'

'Objection,' Thangaraj said loudly.

Gormly smiled wearily.

'Can we go through the formalities?'

The Coroner disallowed the question, and Gormly pushed on with limited success.

'I put it to you, and just wait for your counsel to object, that given the limited knowledge you had about the Elijah Holcombe case and your knowledge that someone else back at the station knew more about it than you, that your obligation at that point was to telephone in for further instructions about what to do concerning Elijah Holcombe.'

His underlying proposition, Gormly said, 'Is that given [Rich's] only task was to find the whereabouts of a particular motor vehicle and that he knew nothing else about the case — it was wrong of him to engage in pursuit of a person with a view to depriving them of their liberty under the *Mental Health Act* when he knew nothing about them except a few seconds' observation and some second-hand report from a mental health nurse.'

Thangaraj objected.

The Coroner offered to allow the question if Gormly introduced it with 'in hindsight'.

'I'll object to that, too,' snapped Thangaraj.

The tussle continued, and Jerram raised a brow.

'Would there be an objection if I asked this question of the witness: Have you, before then or since, ever taken someone in under Section 22 of the *Mental Health Act*?' she asked.

'Yes, Your Honour. I've done numerous police schedules when I was on uniform duties. Generally, you respond to jobs. I don't think I've ever been asked to do a favour that turns into a schedule,' Rich replied.

A cloud of defeat passed over Gormly's face.

'Your Honour, I don't think there's any other question I can usefully ask but I propose in submissions putting that … the factors required in a Section 22 were not fulfilled in this case … and that Senior Constable Rich was acting contrary to the *Act* in pursuing Elijah Holcombe from Rusden Street.'

Was the legal silence that protected Rich too serpentine to overcome? Was Thangaraj too determined a foe? Or was there simply no point in persisting, when the gaping black hole of Rich's memory loss hung over every question? Whatever the case, Gormly seemed to surrender.

The Coroner's voice when she spoke was grim.

'Mr Thangaraj, might I just add that it is disappointing — although I have upheld your objection — because at the outset I said we wanted to know why the chase began, and I haven't really had an answer to that, and more importantly, the family hasn't had an answer.'

The room contracted. Faces turned inwards.

'Anyway, I have said my piece.'

The cross-examinations by the bar table were brief.

'Do you recall whether the settings for previous occasions on which you have detained someone and taken them to a mental health facility were settings of violence?' James Sheller opened.

Rich leaned forward. His eyebrows and mouth were tight.

'They have been, yes.'

There were many settings, Rich said.

'Recent offences, delusional states, self-harm, violence. They were a long time ago but there were many.'

I tried to imagine those situations. Walking into people's fears and delusions armed with the same skills as the person on the street, but also carrying a weapon and being expected to know what to do.

'Do you accept that you would have been better served or in a better position if, at the time you arrived in Rusden Street, you had known specific information the police had about Elijah Holcombe?' Sheller asked.

Thangaraj objected. If Rich said yes, he would be admitting he had inadequate training for the situation but acted anyway, his barrister argued.

The charade was thin. Of course Rich was inadequately trained to deal with a mentally ill person; the court knew that by now. Of course he acted in Armidale; that was what we expected of police. I looked at Rich, resigned to the judgement of people who had never faced what he had. Built into our judgement was the false assumption that police were equipped for whatever came at them.

Rich thought when he left the station that Tuesday that he was going to find a car. No one expected his path to cross Elijah's, so no one told Rich that the boy who 'stole' the car was sick and terrified of police. Rich didn't know Elijah suffered paranoid delusions, that he was a smart, gentle man with a supportive family. Finding a beat-up Fairmont was his focus, until nurses asked him to find Elijah.

'Do you accept that from the point you started chasing Elijah things were getting worse all the time?' Sheller asked Rich.

'No.' Rich was tense, edging away now.

'Do you think you were making the situation more or less unpredictable by pursuing a person you knew would be likely to act unpredictably?'

'Objection,' Thangaraj cried.

Sheller proposed putting two questions to Rich about what happened in Cinders Lane. He knew they would be objected to, he said in his lowest register. He did not expect answers, but he wished to ask the questions for the Holcombes' sake.

'So even though there is very likely to be an objection to each question, you feel it would help the family for them to be put?' the Coroner offered.

The courtroom door squeaked. Allison walked out.

Sheller turned to Rich.

'What I want to suggest to you is that at the time Elijah was shot he was standing on the pavement.'

Thangaraj objected.

Sheller quoted from Rich's statement.

'"He took two, a couple more steps and then lurched forwards and fell into the gutter. He still had hold of the knife at the time." This is my question: for Mr Holcombe to have undertaken what you described indicates that at the time he was shot he was on the pavement.'

Thangaraj objected.

Sheller sat down, and the Coroner moved along the bar table.

'No cross-examination,' from Thangaraj or Hood.

'No further questions,' from Gormly.

The Coroner turned to Rich.

'Do you wish to say more?'

'No, Your Honour,' and the chance for an apology, a defence, an explanation, for anything at all passed through Rich's hands.

'This is a statement prepared by Elijah's father who, in his absence today, has asked me to read it out for him.'

David Phelps was on the witness stand. The room was almost empty. Tarney and Eric Nielsen had gone home. The Coroner, lawyers, police, and a few journalists were the only people left.

David adjusted his steel-framed glasses. He read slowly, taking care not to stumble.

'I've prepared this statement to provide the court a little bit of background about Elijah …'

Rich sat with his legs crossed and tucked under his chair. He looked directly at Phelps throughout the address, a soldier at attention.

'Elijah enjoyed reasonable success as a scholar and a sportsman. He was never particularly disciplined and seemed to achieve his success with the minimum of effort. He was popular with his schoolmates and was elected school captain in his final year of primary school.'

Ray Hood pushed his chair back from the bar table and listened with his head bent. Haverfield flicked through papers.

'Towards the end of 2000 [he] was diagnosed with and was being treated for depression. Elijah responded well to treatment and was able to successfully complete his HSC, and by the time he had finished year twelve he had mostly recovered. I believe it was this experience with his own illness that eventually led Elijah to study psychology.'

Thangaraj leaned forward, his fist pushed into the armrest of his chair.

'This came to us in the form of a card shortly after Elijah's passing,' David read. 'It says, "I was lucky enough to be a friend of EJ's while studying at Macquarie Uni. His sense of humour and intelligence will be sorely missed by us all ... There wasn't an event or gathering that he didn't attend, or host, guitar in hand, of course. He will be deeply missed by all his friends".'

And on he went, bringing Elijah into the room one last time.

'I hope I have captured some of Elijah's personality with this statement, and I never knew Elijah to be violently disposed.'

'Thank you, Mr Phelps. Any death of a young person is a tragedy, but it does sound as if Elijah was a bit special,' said the Coroner.

37.

I captured fragments of the barristers' closing arguments, but my attention was with Rich.

'The policing that occurred up to some of the decisions made by Senior Constable Rich was better than appropriate,' Jeremy Gormly said.

He singled out Sergeant Aiken.

'Sergeant Aiken asked, "Are you alright?" This triggered Elijah to say, "No, I'm not. I want to see a doctor".'

Rich's ankle rested on his knee. He picked at his shoelace, twirling the string until it looped in knotted curls. His breath was shallow. Mistaken or not, his choices were being dressed in shame.

'I can't criticise Senior Constable Rich for going to the hospital to find Elijah. It was a reasonable act.' But Rich should have called the station after the hospital or after Elijah ran across Rusden Street, Gormly judged.

Rich laced his hands around his ankle. The hairs at his wrists were blonde and thick.

'This problem started in Rusden Street. [Elijah] was being chased by a police officer without any reason and without any basis … The result was a cascading disaster.'

Gormly's voice was rising.

'It had all the makings of an event that was going to end badly. One can hardly be surprised Elijah picked up a knife.'

My eyes shot to the Coroner, then to police. Frustration had overtaken Gormly's judgement. It was a step too far, and he seemed to sense it.

'It can't be denied — even though Senior Constable Rich was the cause of these cascading events, once the knife was picked up things changed. I accept it would have been acceptable for Senior Constable

Rich to look upon the knife as a weapon. It was reasonable now for Rich to continue to chase because he had a mentally ill man with a knife.'

Rich's skull was flushed from crown to neck. Long fingers covered his mouth. If I approached him outside court after this flaying, he would shut like a flytrap and never open.

'What did he try to do to de-escalate the situation? The way he *would* do that is clear in these documents.'

Gormly held up training notes written by Joel Murchie and his team.

'The way for him to de-escalate is to *engage*.'

Gormly recited questions he would have had Rich ask, and Rich had no choice but to listen to a lecture from a man whose occupation did not put him in physical danger every day.

'I suggest there was the option for Rich of waiting, standing back,' Gormly stated.

Rich shook his head.

'He could have engaged rather than shot.'

One of the police lawyers shook his head.

'This is a difficult point to make, but Senior Constable Rich appears to have acted hastily, too quickly, when he perceived Elijah moved.'

Gormly pressed the possibility that Elijah may not have moved towards Rich.

'It seems the moment Elijah moved, Rich fired his weapon.'

Rich shook his head again.

'There was no one under immediate threat from Elijah including Senior Constable Rich … Senior Constable Rich says Elijah roared and said in abusive terms, "Shoot me, shoot me". What I draw to your attention is "roared". One witness corroborates what Senior Constable Rich says about "Shoot me". Others who were closer said there was no noise … It wouldn't be appropriate to determine whether or not it was said, and it has no bearing on whether or not the trigger would be pulled.'

Rich's back changed shape. His shoulders curved towards his face.

'It cannot be correct that Elijah roared and took aggressive steps towards Rich. He [Rich] may have perceived a threat but it seems the best visual witness, Whitburn —'

At the mention of Whitburn's name, Rich turned to Roger Best and smiled as if he had been waiting for her evidence to be raised.

'It's difficult to avoid the conclusion that a lot of what happened on that day was the result of a lack of awareness and training in how to deal with someone with a mental illness,' Gormly concluded.

James Sheller clasped his hands behind his back like a radio ham at an old-fashioned microphone. Gold cufflinks sneaked out of his suit sleeves.

The Holcombes' barrister supported the view that Elijah did not move in Cinders Lane.

'What can be gleaned from the walk-through?' he asked rhetorically. 'It powerfully supports the proposition there was no movement.'

Rich poked the hard end of his shoelace into his lace holes one by one.

Detective Inspector Chris Olen, whose brief of evidence had laid 2 June 2009 in front of the Coroner and lawyers so carefully, rubbed his eyes to ease his tiredness.

Sheller asserted Elijah was on the footpath when Rich fired. The police in front of me shook their heads. Rich pushed his lips into a pursed point with his fingers. He turned to Best beside him and mouthed, 'Nah'.

The Coroner excused herself for a moment, and the bodies in the room relaxed.

Roger Best turned in his seat and smiled at me.

'You're on your lonesome up there today.'

I was alone in the back row.

'You're welcome to join me.'

'I could do with the wall support. My back's playing up,' he bantered.

Joel Murchie switched seats to speak to Rich before the Coroner returned, and Ray Hood stood to speak for the Commissioner of Police.

Hood was a solemn figure. A tall man in a dark suit, his forehead was high and heavily lined. The hair he retained was dark around large ears. His face was kind.

Many issues around police training had been resolved since 'this tragedy', said Hood. Times had moved on substantially since June 2009.

In the last five years, training in how to deal with mentally disturbed clients had been given higher priority and more resources by the NSW police force, Hood said. He referred to the training developed by the MHIT before Elijah's death and its roll-out across the state in the last year. Steps were being taken, momentum was increasing, Hood said. The aim was to deliver the training to every police officer on the force.

Hood talked about Rich's experience at the hospital and described the nurses' plea to bring Elijah back. He was thoughtful but not ponderous. He de-personalised the exchange between police and nurses at the hospital. It helped to remove a sense of 'us and them' when he said a little later of the nurses' request that Rich find Elijah: 'The police are passed the ball.'

It was a fair description.

'The public would expect the police to make a concerted effort to find Elijah and bring him back,' Hood said.

He pointed to the mental health nurse's notes that showed she was concerned Elijah might be acutely psychotic. In her statement to police, she relayed telling colleagues that Elijah should be assessed for possible scheduling if he returned.

Rich's impression of Elijah was based on advice from a person with serious concerns, Hood insinuated. The mental health nurse, Carla Rutherford, had downplayed her concerns about Elijah at the inquest, but her original statement showed she was alarmed.

'Are you able to tell me who in fact has the credit or qualifications to schedule a person?' the Coroner asked Hood.

Joel Murchie leaned across the gap between the gallery and bar table to Hood.

'A medical practitioner or a nurse with the completed qualifications, Mr Murchie tells me.'

Hood communicated in his carriage and tone an understanding that

2 June was a tragedy for everyone. No one had wished ill upon another.

Brent Haverfield took the Coroner back to Cinders Lane to review the witnesses. He spoke like the cop he used to be, no-nonsense and direct.

Joan Whitburn's attention was too unfocused to capture a reliable picture of what happened outside her window, despite her proximity to Rich and Elijah, he suggested. Judy Tennant, who called out, 'Don't shoot!' was at best an 'eccentric' witness. The fact she made two statements and considerably changed her view of events between them should count against her, Haverfield asserted.

Mr Gormly claimed there were no witnesses to support the view that Elijah roared: well, Matthew Schaefer said there was noise from Elijah, Haverfield retorted. The young accountant who heard Elijah call out, 'Shoot me, shoot me', was a witness of good standing; his evidence supported Rich's credibility, his barrister said.

'Mr Schaefer is almost the furthest away from Mr Rich and Elijah, isn't he?' asked Jerram.

About thirty-one metres, Haverfield conceded. Ambrose Hallman was further away in his office above the street, he pointed out, and Mr Gormly and Mr Sheller discounted his evidence by saying Hallman was too far away.

'I put the opposite view, Your Honour.'

One floor up, with a direct line of sight down Cinders Lane, no sun in his eyes and removed from the chaos, Hallman was in an ideal position to observe the contact between Rich and Elijah, Haverfield said.

What distance was Hallman from Rich and Elijah? Jerram asked.

'Seventy-five metres, Your Honour.'

'That sounds quite a long way to me.'

'It isn't far from the action if you imagine yourself at the football. I'm sorry, Your Honour, do you go to the football?'

'Not if I can help it,' Jerram said sourly.

'The theatre then? It wouldn't be far in the theatre either.'

A titter swept through the police in the room.

The rough and tumble of the sports field versus the diction and art of theatre was a gross caricature of the law brokers in the room. But police and lawyers saw the world through different prisms of experiences, and it coloured the way they saw Rich and Elijah's interaction, too.

It was a relief when the Coroner called another recess.

I pushed into the foyer to search out coffee. Greig Stier approached me on his own before I reached the courthouse doors.

'David Phelps tells me you've been coming all the way from Darwin for these hearings,' he opened.

'Yes. This could be the last trip, by the look of things,' I replied, falling instinctively into the underplay of country speech. 'You and David have known each other a long time.'

'Yeah. We played in the Narrabri Blue Boars together as young blokes. They had their fifty-year reunion last month.' Stier rubbed his hand over his face and head. 'David tells me you're writing a book about this.'

I trod carefully.

'It's a shame Andrew hasn't been able to tell his side of the story. Everyone's waited so long to hear from him. I think we were all counting on it happening this time,' I replied.

Stier looked down and kicked the carpet with his toe.

'I've always thought it would have been a lot better if they'd organised some sort of arbitration between Andrew and the Holcombes before all of this.'

'Perhaps that can still happen.'

He looked at me sceptically.

'These legal cases — if you're in Andrew's position, you're just a jockey. You have to ride it out or they'll take the horse from under you.'

It was the same message Best had delivered a year ago. Andrew wanted to talk, but he had to do this first — whatever 'this' had become.

'I'd just like Andrew to be able to say whatever he wants to say — whatever he can remember. This whole thing must be hell for him if that's what he really wants to do,' I ventured.

We stood side by side like cattlemen at a yard fence, and Greig Stier told a story about a police officer he knew giving evidence at an inquest against his lawyer's advice.

'There were no repercussions. It was better for everyone, and the Coroner was glowing in what he said about him,' Stier said passionately.

Best and Stier viewed the legal web Rich was tangled in as bullshit. They were reaching out. Perhaps there was still a chance.

Stier's words gave me the courage to approach Joel Murchie in the recess.

'Excuse me, Joel?'

He bent down slightly, holding his police hat in large hands.

'Yes?' His expression was wary.

'I've been meaning to introduce myself. I'm writing a book about this case and I'd like to talk to you about the MHIT. I understand it would have to be when this is over. Would you be willing to talk to me?'

'I'd be happy to. Make sure you give me your number before you leave today.'

My heart thumped.

'I will. Thanks.'

'You going back in?'

I nodded. He held the door open and followed me in.

38.

We slid into the same row.

Thangaraj was in full flight.

'We say the "shoot me" comment is important evidence. Senior Constable Rich says that's what happened; Mr Schaefer says the same. It would be extraordinary if two separate witnesses heard the same thing, to discount it.'

'But when thirty-five other witnesses didn't?' Jerram challenged.

'The fact that other people don't hear it isn't the point, and they didn't say they didn't hear it,' Thangaraj claimed with semantic dexterity.

Elijah undoubtedly said the words, Thangaraj insisted. Witnesses described him taking a crucifix position, an aggressive stance.

Rich and Best were demonstrating versions of the crucifix to each other in their seats. Gormly watched and listened and shook his head.

Thangaraj told the Coroner the crucifix was one of ten issues relevant to Senior Constable Rich's decision to shoot.

The others were: that Elijah had mental health issues; he was holding a knife; he slowed from running to walking, and then turned and faced Rich with the knife in his hand. Rich was alone. His call for backup and his warnings to Caffiends' staff showed Rich was alert to the threat Elijah posed. Nurses at the hospital expressed their concerns; Elijah said 'Shoot me, shoot me' to Rich. The words were 'an aggressive stance'. None of Elijah's behaviour in Cinders Lane could be characterised as passive when his demeanour throughout the day was considered, Thangaraj asserted.

Joel Murchie signalled me to pass along a pen and paper. I handed him my notebook, and he wrote his name and number in it. I dropped my business card into his upturned hat.

Murchie reached over and patted Rich on the back.

'I'll speak to you on the phone,' he whispered.

He shook Stier's hand and waved to Roger Best.

Murchie turned at the door and bowed to the Coroner then swivelled his head and smiled at me before closing the un-oiled door behind him noiselessly.

Gormly stood for the last words of the day.

He saved his harshest for Rich, who sat with head bent and hands clasped.

'He did not distinguish the difference between someone who is mentally ill and someone who needs scheduling, and at the root cause of the issue with NSW police is that the distinction is not being made.'

There was a discussion alive at the bar table about the wording of the Coroner's findings, Gormly said. A suggestion had surfaced that the Coroner include 'in the course of his duties' to describe Rich's decision to shoot Elijah.

'If those words are used, it would necessarily mean an endorsement of the act,' Gormly said. 'I hold a strong and implacable, unshiftable view that those words not be used.'

I was woken by the phone at eight the next morning.

It was David Phelps.

My mind rushed through possibilities. Another heart attack, an accident involving one of the Holcombe kids? The hearings were over; it couldn't be good news.

'Is everything alright?' I asked.

Rich had approached him in the foyer yesterday after everyone had gone, David said.

'He came up to me with Stiery and that other bloke in the full uniform and asked if Jeremy would ever consider sitting down with him.

I told him probably, but it might take time. Maybe a couple of years. Knowing Jeremy, he probably will.'

David covered his disapproval with a laugh.

'I called Jeremy last night and told him. He thought you should know it might be on the cards.'

'Thanks,' I croaked.

The day had ended in anti-climax. The lawyers wound down, the Coroner thanked people for their patience and dedication, and we'd all rushed out to vie for taxis.

I had been standing on the footpath, queueing behind the lawyers, when Rich made his approach to David.

'The police will be better after this,' Jeremy Gormly was saying to me. 'It's just a persistent problem we have with the police and the mentally ill.'

He pushed his glasses up the bridge of his nose and disappeared into the back seat of a cab. He had found a nugget to take from this fight into the next.

'What do you think she'll say in her findings?' I asked Thangaraj.

He shrugged noncommittally. 'What do *you* think she'll say?'

'She'll nail Rich,' I replied.

39.

In the three-week gap between the end of Elijah's inquest and handing down her findings, Mary Jerram gave a speech at the Sydney Opera House. It was titled 'Justice and vengeance'.

Legal protocol frowned on coroners reflecting on the law in public, but Jerram had retired more than a year ago.

Police were outraged. Jerram had discussed the Holcombe case before she handed down her findings, they told me. I watched a video of the speech online.

Elijah wasn't mentioned. The case Jerram talked about was Roberto Laudisio Curti.

She stood in a spotlight on a circle of rich red carpet.

'In Western society, we accept that the State bears responsibility for investigating and punishing wrong-doing,' she said in the gravelly voice I knew from court.

Since vengeance was socially unacceptable, what constituted justice for the bereaved? the former coroner asked. After thirty years, she had come to the conclusion that many people who talked about justice were actually seeking vengeance. That urge had made sense to her, she said, when she'd lost a niece in an accident only a couple of months after she became State Coroner.

'I remember the black rage in my own gut, at the waste of her, and wanting to blame somebody. As if that might make you feel better,' Jerram confessed.

The feeling passed, but it taught her to empathise with the families of the deceased who appeared before her, she said. People like the Curti family.

During 'Berti's' — as his family called him — two-week inquest, the Curtis 'shook with anger' at the injustice of his death. The facts the Coroner was able to deliver were not enough for them.

She didn't mention it in her speech, but in her findings on Roberto Curti's death, Jerram referred five officers to the Police Integrity Commission (PIC), an independent watchdog on police conduct and ethics. The Commission recommended the DPP consider charges against the officers. Four were eventually charged with assault. Three were acquitted and one was found guilty.

The PIC concluded an investigation into Adam Salter's shooting, too. Its report on his death claimed four officers knowingly gave false evidence about Adam Salter's shooting. The Commission recommended the DPP consider criminal charges, and the police force take disciplinary action against seven officers. In Adam Salter's case, the DPP recommended charges against four officers for lying. When the case reached court, they were all acquitted. Inconsistencies between what police and paramedics recounted of events in the kitchen were not sinister, the judge decided. They were a reflection of the chaos that overtook events.

'Closure, my least favourite word, is very seldom achieved in the courts, and vengeance, never,' Jerram told her audience.

Each jurisdiction had its own measurement of justice; in the civil courts it was easy, she quipped. Money was the only outcome. In criminal cases, it was reflected in the length of the sentence meted out.

'But in the Coroner's jurisdiction, where I saw emotion at its most raw, I learned you can't always find the truth.'

That line, I thought, was about Elijah Holcombe.

40.

Five days after Jerram's appearance at the Opera House, she handed down her findings in Elijah's coronial inquest.

I stepped off the bus on 1 May 2014 and saw the silhouette of TV cameras. A pack of journalists stood outside. I nodded to the ones I knew and ducked inside.

Jeremy and Fiona, Tarney, David Phelps, and Eric Nielsen were a single knot on the couch. The regular cast of lawyers and police were scattered across the foyer. There was no sign of Rich. I didn't blame him for not being there.

Joel Murchie cut a swathe through the crowd.

'Hello, how are you?' he said as he passed, then disappeared into the courtroom.

'It is good to see you here, Mr Holcombe, looking so well,' Jerram said from the bench a few minutes later, when everyone was seated.

I began to tremble. I was suddenly freezing.

Jerram waited for the room to quieten.

'I intend to just go into reading the findings. It may take some time but I think it's too important not to read onto the record.'

I couldn't see Jeremy's face from where I sat, his family was gathered so tightly around him.

Eric Nielsen closed his eyes, and the Coroner began to speak.

She mentioned small details like Elijah dropping his jumper, and moved lightly across the hardest parts: Rich calling to Elijah to 'drop the knife', Elijah turning around to face him. She reminded us of the questions Elijah's inquest had sought to answer for five years.

'Why did Senior Constable Rich chase Elijah? Was he justified in doing so? Are police sufficiently trained in recognising and dealing with mentally ill people? Was Rich acting in self-defence or not when he fired the fatal shot?'

Detective Inspector Chris Olen scribbled in a notebook balanced against his knee.

Fiona clutched Jeremy's hand in both of hers.

The Coroner read out a list of people who'd described Elijah as being friendly or co-operative on 2 June: Sergeant Aiken at Armidale Police Station; Constable Shelton, who'd driven him to the hospital; the nurses in Emergency; and the kitchen staff in Caffiends.

Fiona was crying openly now.

'No person who witnessed the events in Cinders Lane described feeling threatened by or frightened of Elijah. Rather, most seemed to have felt compassion for him.'

We walked down Cinders Lane with Jerram, towards Rich and Elijah.

'Those witnesses who saw some movement by Elijah towards Rich immediately before the shooting' — and she named them: Schaefer, the young accountant, Hallman, who watched from one storey up, and Guthrey, another council worker — 'were all a considerable distance from the two.'

Under questioning, the three men adjusted their view of Elijah's movement to significantly less than their initial assessments, Jerram said. At least six witnesses were adamant Elijah made a very slight movement. One swore he neither moved nor ran, she said.

Jerram poured herself a glass of water.

Rich's partner, Senior Constable Dufty, and another man, Willow Grieves, broadly corroborated parking inspector Bernard Maurer about events on Rusden Street, she continued. Maurer said he saw Rich jiggle keys at Elijah, offer them out, and chuckle. Senior Constable Rich denied both actions, Jerram said. He testified he held his police badge out and told Elijah they wanted him back at the hospital.

'His version is not corroborated by any other witness,' Jerram said.

'Rich described his actions when he first confronted Elijah as trying to build a rapport with no intention then of arresting him. He said he only formed that intention when Elijah suddenly ran across the road through busy traffic.'

Maurer, Grieves, and Dufty said Elijah ran down the footpath before he crossed. By their account, he did not have to dodge traffic, Jerram said.

Jeremy Holcombe turned his head and I saw his face. He looked young and vulnerable.

'I have already noted the discrepancy between Rich's evidence as to his first interaction with Elijah in Rusden Street and that of other witnesses. On balance, I prefer the evidence of Maurer, Grieves, and Dufty.'

My teeth began to chatter.

'Rich's evidence then became confused and to an extent, contradictory …'

Jeremy looked neither right or left now, only at the Coroner. I shoved my hands beneath my thighs for warmth.

'During his evidence on 18 March 2014, Rich said that he now had no memory whatsoever of what happened in Cinders Lane … A report from his treating psychiatrist indicated that … Rich was exhibiting clear signs and behaviours of post-traumatic stress disorder which can have a clinical effect on memory.'

Jerram's emphasis on 'can' underlined her scepticism. When she quoted Rich's words to his psychologist, 'there are *certain parts* [of the day] I don't remember', she made the point again.

She seemed to be saying that Rich had lied, so why hadn't she confronted him while she had him on the stand at the inquest?

Next, she nailed Senior Sergeant Davis, whose opinion that the shooting was justified was based entirely on Rich's evidence and that of witnesses who agreed with Rich. Davis did not take into account the evidence that contradicted Rich. For that reason, his opinion was flawed, said Jerram. Further, Davis's concept of police control and communication was 'inherently flawed' as an approach for dealing with people with a mental illness.

She dismissed Thangaraj's attempts to justify Rich's actions just as brutally.

Three points Rich's barrister said were relevant in judging his client's decision — that Elijah had mental health issues; that Rich knew expert nurses were concerned; and that Elijah's demeanour did not indicate he was passive — 'ought to have influenced a police officer to adopt an approach that might have avoided the shooting,' Jerram said. She was not convinced on the evidence of 'the truth or accuracy' of claims that: Rich was concerned for the safety of civilians; that Elijah turned and faced Rich holding a knife; or that Rich viewed Elijah's 'crucifix position', and the alleged calling out of 'shoot me', as aggressive acts.

Jeremy Holcombe was leaning forward now. He smiled the tiniest of smiles.

Mary Jerram had stepped as close as she could to calling Rich a liar.

'It seems, overall, that the reasons Rich gave chase to Elijah were spurious and spontaneous. He has given a number of different reasons for doing so, not one of which is persuasive in justifying the chase … Elijah's perceived demeanour was not a basis for depriving him of his liberty. Nor is it credible that Rich saw Elijah as putting himself in danger from the traffic. That is corroborated by no one. Rich had no basis for arresting, stopping, or chasing Elijah.'

Detective Inspector Chris Olen stopped taking notes.

There was nowhere for Rich to hide or shelter.

The Coroner acknowledged, 'Circumstances became very fraught' when Elijah picked up the bread knife in Caffiends. On balance, it seemed Elijah made some movement when he finally turned and faced Rich in the lane, but it was 'no more than a step or two', and possibly only a stumble on the gutter, she said. There was a distance of about ten metres between the two men when Elijah turned around.

'And the moment Elijah turned, Rich, who had control of that space, fired. It was overly hasty and precipitous. Only Rich and one other witness claim that Elijah roared and said, "Shoot me." That is not credible. Even if he did, that should have no bearing on Rich's decision to shoot. It was not an invitation or a lawful one. Rich, in the tension of the moment may have believed Elijah was being, or about to be, aggressive. That may have been what Rich perceived. I don't accept that it was in fact so.

'I find that Elijah Jay Holcombe died on the second of June 2009, at Cinders Lane Armidale in the State of New South Wales, as a result of a gunshot wound to the chest inflicted by Senior Constable Rich, while Elijah Holcombe was suffering the effects of a mental illness.'

Jerram disappeared through the door behind her bench. Journalists rushed outside to form a wall across the courthouse steps.

The Holcombe party filed into the foyer and looked at each other, blank-faced. No one approached them.

'You couldn't really have hoped for more, could you?' Eric Nielsen said, testing his reaction.

He fidgeted under the rush of energy the Coroner's words had delivered.

Tarney expanded in front of my eyes. A line of electricity pulsed between him and Eric.

'That was pretty amazing,' Tarney said quietly.

The faces in the circle shifted shape as the realisation broke in waves. Elijah was free. He'd done nothing wrong. The fight to clear his name was over.

Phil Stewart strode towards the group and touched Jeremy on the elbow.

'Are you ready?'

Phil nodded at the cameras outside the glass doors.

'Yep.'

Jeremy took a deep breath, and they walked out, side by side.

I slipped out to the back of the pack. Jeremy planted his feet on the courthouse steps and turned to face the crowd.

'In the absence of any other explanation, when we hear of profoundly tragic stories such as Elijah's, we sometimes attribute blame to the victim. By doing so, we hope to convince ourselves that "this can't happen to us" or to *our* loved ones. However, the truth is, through no fault of their own, very bad things can happen to very good people.

'It has been almost five years since we lost our beautiful son, brother, and friend. At the midpoint of that period, we also lost Elijah's mother. Tracey made some recovery from the loss of her son. However, she could not recover from the injustice of the manner by which Elijah was taken from her.

'The allegation that Elijah had to be destroyed in order to protect the safety of another person has never been accepted by those who knew him best.

'We note that Senior Constable Rich has consistently refused to repeat his allegations under oath and with the potential for cross-examination. Furthermore, I have seen nothing through this coronial process that I believe goes anywhere towards proving Constable Rich's allegations.

'We have always maintained that Senior Constable Rich is entitled to the presumption of innocence. But we ask: "What about Elijah's right to the presumption of innocence?"

'It should be obvious to us all that NSW Police have a very difficult job to do. It is simply an unrealistic expectation to believe that they will always get it "right".

'As a family, we were unable to protect Elijah's life. We do, however, remain committed to protecting his reputation. As such, we must once again respectfully ask the DPP to reconsider this matter for criminal proceedings.'

I stood behind the crush of journalists clamouring with questions, and recoiled from Jeremy's surrender to the instinct for revenge.

41.

'To Elijah,' said Jeremy.

'To Elijah,' came the chorus, and everyone raised their glass.

I was with the Holcombes at a pub in Glebe, not far from the Coroner's Court.

We commandeered couches below a large TV, convinced the barmaid to relinquish the remote control, and switched channels to the news.

I plonked my dictaphone on the table.

'It's on,' I warned, and everybody laughed.

A young man came over to collect our empty glasses.

'How's your day?' he asked.

We laughed again.

'Interesting,' said Fiona.

He smiled, confused. She touched his arm and pointed at Jeremy.

'In a nutshell, this man's son was shot by the police in Armidale. It's been five years, and the Coroner brought down findings this afternoon. So today has been a long time in the making.'

He nodded sombrely. 'I remember that shooting.' He picked up the last glass and hurried away.

David Phelps ordered another round of drinks, and everyone talked at once. The day spilt out across the table.

James Sheller was 'fantastic', Phil Stewart 'a deeply good man'. 'Sweeney pulled that whole team together,' Jeremy reminded us. There was warmth for Ray Hood and respect for Chris Olen, who didn't miss a day of Elijah's case, someone said.

'Thangaraj is obviously a good operator, but he was flogging a dead horse, wasn't he?' David Phelps observed.

Fiona grimaced. She wasn't prepared to compliment Rich's barrister.

'How do you think he's doing tonight? Will someone have called to tell him what she said?' Jeremy asked. He was talking about Andrew Rich.

No one could guess how the news would be delivered. None of us wanted to think about it. David retold the story of Rich and Stier approaching him to ask if Jeremy would speak to Rich one day.

'You wonder what sort of delusions he's still under,' David snorted.

Jeremy looked thoughtful.

'Well, it's a matter of "which way is he going to go"? Is he going to try and convince me that Elijah did move and yell? Will he say "I don't know why none of the witnesses heard it"? Or is he going to go completely the other way? I dunno.'

'Either way, it's wrong. If he wants to convince you Elijah was in the wrong then it's shit to expect you to talk to him. If it's the other way, then why hasn't he said it in court? I mean, he's had his opportunity.' Fiona was unequivocal.

A KISS song blared from the jukebox, and a waitress deposited three pizzas on our table. David Phelps reached for a slice.

'He might be trying to get his own life back on track. He might say, "Look, I stuffed up". I can't imagine why he would want to talk to you unless he was going to say something like that.'

I waited for Jeremy's reaction.

'I'm quite happy to accept that Rich is …' he swirled the ice in his glass, searching for the words. 'Well, genuinely remorseful and apologetic about what happened and what he did. On the other hand, he was in tears when it got referred and when we went and shook hands with him …'

'Yeahhh?' David prodded.

'I always wondered was he crying for himself or for Elijah?' Jeremy asked.

'Because we haven't seen it since.' Fiona was angry.

'I can't get a reading on him,' Jeremy confessed.

'He might need to admit to you that he absolutely did the wrong thing, so he can get on with his own life,' David suggested.

'If he does that one-on-one, with no witnesses, he can tell me "Elijah didn't run at me with a knife" or "The gun went off too early, I panicked" or whatever, and there's nothing I can do.'

Jeremy's voice quavered with emotion.

'If he apologised and asked to be forgiven, I'd be prepared to forgive him for my own sake, but he's got to ask for it. He's got to admit he's done something wrong, to forgive him.'

'Is that what's been missing in the whole process?' I asked.

'Absolutely. They would have us believe if the same set of circumstances happened again they would do exactly the same thing. They have never admitted they had any other option.'

'Why did you ask the DPP to reconsider charges? What do you want out of that?' I asked.

Jeremy leaned back into the couch.

'I don't care. I really don't care. I sort of think I've got a duty to do it. There's nothing in it for us.' His voice was tired, but it wasn't an answer.

'If they came back and said, "Alright, we'll charge him", what would you do?' I pushed.

Jeremy let out a pained laugh.

'Ahhh. I'd say, "Fuck, please don't!" I really would.'

He sighed.

'I always got the impression from that first interaction in the street — "Here's the keys mate, come and get 'em" — I thought Rich's attitude from there was, *I'm the town bully and you're the village idiot, you're my sport for the afternoon.* Injustice anywhere threatens justice anywhere. We have this responsibility to keep the bastards honest.'

The KISS song finished and a single acoustic guitar took over. Eric and Tarney sat scanning news reports on their phones. Every outlet was running the findings. Elijah was everywhere.

Eric's phone rang. It was Adam Baguley. 'Bags' was over the moon, Eric relayed.

As the night wore on, the alcohol took over.

'I still haven't heard the proper story of your heart attack,' I said to Jeremy. 'What happened?'

'I was grouting tiles in the bathroom at one of the flats when it happened. And when I got back four weeks later, all the grout had gone hard in the bucket.'

David roared with laughter. Fiona rolled her eyes.

'There's probably a couple of months work left, then we'll list the flats. If we get a quick sale, wonderful, otherwise we'll put tenants in them before we move,' said Jeremy.

'Where are you going?'

'The coast.'

'So move to the coast and stay there permanently?' I asked.

Fiona explained they'd bought land near Port Macquarie with money from the civil settlement.

'We'll put a shed up and live in that 'til we decide what's next,' she said.

'We've sort of been thinking avocado trees. There's an avocado industry up there,' Jeremy ventured.

'Or truffles,' said Tarney.

'Are you going to build a music studio?' Eric asked, and for the first time in the years I had known them, the Holcombes began to talk about the future.

'This guy was talking about herbs for the restaurants in Port Macquarie.'

'I'd like to open a garden nursery.'

'Jordan says she's going to get a flat in Port. She wants to have electricity.'

It was almost midnight when I said farewell with hugs and wobbled my way towards the stairs.

'Come to the coast and visit us Kate!' Jeremy called out.

David Phelps offered to walk me down the stairs. He ushered me to the footpath and hailed a cab. We hugged.

'Thank you for all you've done for them,' he said, and I realised he felt I had shared his load.

42.

'What hoops will we have to jump through before Andrew is allowed to speak to me?' I asked.

'No hoops,' said Roger Best.

He was back in Armidale. Permission for Rich to talk to me was his decision.

'It's not like there's been a cover-up; everyone knows what happened. Getting another perspective out is more important than the trouble I might get into.'

Fuck the hoops, his tone implied.

'I'd like to come to Armidale and speak to him in person.'

'Things may have changed since the findings,' Best said carefully.

'How's Andrew doing?'

'I gather he knows that in the final moment, he did what he had to do. That must give him strength deep down.'

Best's voice was even. He would let Andrew know I still wanted to talk to him.

'I sent out an email after the findings. Only my personal views, of course, not the official police position,' he added.

'Would you send me a copy?' There had to be a reason he was raising it.

'I wrote it at 5am after the findings; you'll have to excuse any grammatical errors. I don't recall having the most revitalising night's sleep.'

He was still the man who had apologised for his garlic breath in the courthouse foyer. He wanted to connect.

Best's missive arrived in my inbox a few days later.

The following are some personal thoughts on the matter involving Andrew Rich and the inquest into the shooting of Elijah Holcombe ... Although I am an Inspector of police (and will hopefully stay one) they are in no way a reflection of the NSW Police Force's opinions on the matter. I have not been involved in any discussions with senior members of our organisation ... and I do not know what their views are on the events ... I believe it is imperative a different perspective is put forward to perhaps balance the discussion and inform those of you who work with Andrew of some points you may not be aware of.

Best acknowledged his own possible bias, but the Coroner's findings were so 'far from a fair and balanced portrayal of the events' that he felt compelled to speak 'in the interest of fairness and balance'.

Best wrote from the heart. He was outraged for Andrew.

Time and again the Coroner and her counsel assisting seemed to declare they were not interested in anything that suggested Elijah's actions justified the use of deadly force.

Jerram's finding that it 'was not credible' Elijah called out 'Shoot me, shoot me', as Rich and another witness claimed, was unsubstantiated, Best said.

The Coroner says she doubts the truth of those words being uttered ... the gentleman who corroborated Andrew ... was never cross examined about the fact he must have been making this up ... No investigation by the Court took place as to how or why this fellow came to be saying he heard Elijah say 'shoot me, shoot me'. The Coroner simply found it unlikely the words were said — how she arrived at this piece of analysis remains unclear to me.

The court's reading of the 'crucifix' position was dismissive of police experience. Counsel assisting refused to acknowledge the stance could be seen as an aggressive 'come and get me' gesture.

> Counsel assisting demonstrated it by doing a wonderful impersonation of the French Army as the Germans came over the hill in WWII, all the while suggesting it was not [a] threatening position.

A crucial witness in Armidale was poorly cross-examined, Best said. Joan Whitburn, who watched from a ground floor window, claimed Elijah was standing still with his hands at his sides when he was shot. Counsel for police established that Whitburn's attention moved between the scene outside and the phone she was using to call Triple-0. How could the Coroner present Whitburn in her findings as 'an excellent witness who gave clear evidence that Elijah was standing still with his hands beside him when he was shot', if Whitburn's level of distraction wasn't properly examined? Best asked.

> It seems perfectly clear to me that when Elijah ran at Andrew, who was pointing his gun at him, Elijah didn't believe he was ever going to actually make it to Andrew to stab him. Everything I've heard of Elijah tells me stabbing Andrew would never have been his real intent. So why did he do it?

Chris Olen, the investigating officer presented evidence to the Coroner of Elijah's belief he would be killed by police, along with literature about 'suicide by cop', Best said.

> This concept was never mention [sic], ever, during the hearings … I'm not in any way suggesting the Court had to accept … this was a potential 'suicide by cop' event. I find it extraordinary, almost beyond belief, however that the issue wasn't tested in any way during the inquest.

Jerram's findings fell short of justice in Best's eyes.

I know in my heart, without any shadow of a doubt, that the version portrayed in the findings of the Coroner are far from a fair and balanced portrayal of the events relating to the tragic shooting of Elijah Holcombe.

I attached a letter for Andrew to my reply, and asked Best to deliver it. The letter had nothing new to offer. Rich's perspective had been absent for so long; the Coroner's findings left crucial things unsaid; would he meet me and tell his story?

In June, the fifth anniversary of Elijah's death passed, and the ABC aired a documentary series about police shootings in Australia.

The presenter of the documentaries, John Silvester, was a long-time crime reporter from Victoria. After forty years reporting crime, he had the trust of police, and access to them most journalists only dreamed of. John knew the world police inhabited, not least of all because his father was once an Assistant Commissioner in the Victorian police. The series Silvester made with the ABC examined the context of different shootings, and how the decision to use fatal force affected the officers who made it.

Most of the cases Silvester examined were acts of self-defence against violent criminals, but that made no difference to the psychological effect the shootings had on the police involved. He also covered the rising incidence of fatal police contact with people who were mentally ill.

'Every sixty-seven minutes [in Victoria], police are dealing with people sufficiently mentally disturbed they need immediate medical treatment,' Silvester said.

He interviewed two of the officers involved in Tyler Cassidy's shooting. Unlike Rich, Leading Sergeant Colin Dods and Senior Constable Richard Blundell and their colleagues chose to give evidence at a coronial inquest.

Tyler was described at his inquest as a troubled kid, emotionally volatile and prone to outbursts, which worsened when his father died. The day Tyler was shot, he arrived home in a rage. He couldn't articulate to his mother what was wrong, but a few hours later he was seen in Northcote, Melbourne. CCTV vision showed Tyler stealing two large knives from a department store. Soon after, he phoned police and said there was a man near Northcote Plaza with a shotgun.

'Come and kill him, come and kill him,' Tyler urged police.

'We raced down there,' Richard Blundell told Silvester.

Blundell's eyes were green but red-rimmed. His head was shaved and his scalp was freckled.

Two female officers from a different station heard the call-out and followed in another car.

'Suddenly, in the middle of the roadway, staring us down was this young man, sort of leaning forward, staring at us with his hands behind his back,' Blundell said.

'It was not the run-of-the-mill job that you go to where a bloke's armed with two knives and he's having some sort of crisis. This was something different.'

In what other job was it 'run-of-the-mill' to face a person in mental crisis armed with two knives? I thought, curled on my couch.

Blundell unholstered his gun as he left the car.

Dods took over the story at this point. He commanded Tyler to show his hands, and Tyler revealed the two large knives. Dods demonstrated Tyler's stance; fists in line with cheekbones, holding imaginary knives pointed at the camera.

'And negotiations, such as they were, started from there. I told him exactly what we're trained to; I said, "Put down the knife, put down the knife".'

Dods and Blundell reminded me of the officers I had met in Narrabri, at the station. They looked young and strong, confident and friendly. Solid in a crisis. Dods's face was broad and honest, but he sat back deep behind his eyes somewhere. Jowls had grown around his chin too soon for such an athletic man.

Dods had a can of OC spray that night. When Tyler refused to drop the knives, Dods stepped towards him and released the spray. It hit the left side of Tyler's face.

'It's usually enough to debilitate even the biggest, angriest men,' said Blundell.

But Tyler didn't flinch. He turned and ran into the park. He was young and fit, disturbed, and armed near a busy shopping centre, close to Christmas. The police gave chase and put themselves between Tyler and the shopping mall, Dods said.

The camera lingered on Dods's face. He could hardly breathe. He rubbed his hand against his head. His body rocked back and forth.

Tyler walked towards him.

'He got closer,' Dods whispered. He wiped at his cheek and pressed his hands against his eyes. He wore a gold wedding ring.

Tyler yelled, 'Fucking shoot me, fucking shoot me.'

'And then the death threats came,' Dods said. '"I'm going to fucking kill you, you're going to have to shoot me".'

He shook his head in disbelief at the next memory.

'And then he took a phone call. I can't remember the exact words, but they were pretty much along the lines, "The cops are here and someone's going to die".'

Blundell saw Dods take a step towards Tyler and use the OC spray again.

'I can only describe it as a primary dose … it got him right in the face. At that point in my career, I had never seen anyone shake off OC foam as if it were water,' Blundell said.

Police fired ten shots within seventy-three seconds of locating Tyler, Silvester said in the introduction to Tyler's story. How many seconds of that had passed by now?

'They don't teach us to stand our ground and confront people, or to force that kind of confrontation. They teach us to withdraw, and that's what we did,' said Blundell.

The muscles in his jaw and throat worked double time to hold down the sobs rising in his chest.

Dods's gaze was steady.

'I'm still at a loss to know, if he'd come in arms' reach of me, how I was supposed to disarm him of both knives. Maybe I'd be lucky and get one. But whatever he's going to do with the other one wouldn't have been good for me.'

Dods's words had the upward inflection of a question. He asked himself this every day.

Dods drew his gun and repeated the order for Tyler to drop the knives. Tyler advanced towards him, still shouting: 'Fucking shoot me, fucking shoot me.'

'Eventually, I made it quite explicitly clear to him that if he kept advancing towards me he would be shot,' Dods said.

Tyler was now four metres away. Dods had only lethal options left, but he didn't want to take them.

'I thought a warning shot into the ground might bring him to his senses. I had nice soft grass rising up, there was no one I could see behind him at that stage, so I was pretty sure a ricochet wasn't going to go anywhere or into anyone … so I let the shot go at his feet, and really, he barely flinched … He was clearly focused on a terrible outcome.'

Dods walked backwards, but Tyler closed the gap.

'For all those who say if you've got time to shoot him in the legs, you shouldn't be shooting him — when they're two seconds away … you'll take that option rather than shooting them dead straight up. I fired two shots at his legs.'

It was a risk — not only of disciplinary action for acting outside his training, but a risk of Dods's own life if Tyler didn't stop.

'As soon as my leg shots had no effect, I heard three or four rounds come from my right,' said Dods.

Three were from Blundell, one from a female officer. None of them stopped Tyler. He was only a metre from Dods now, Blundell judged.

'It was at that point that I decided to fire the third shot, which was my last and …' Blundell exhaled like a frightened horse. He shook his head and closed his eyes.

'And ah … I probably shouldn't have, because at that stage in my line of sight there was no space between Tyler Cassidy and Dodsy. They were in my line of sight almost on top of each other.'

Blundell breathed in short, hard gasps. His composure broke completely.

'I actually thought I'd shot Dodsy,' he cried. It was the confession of a man who thought he'd killed his friend.

'I thought I'd shot him, because Dodsy put his hands up in the air and he yelled out, "Don't shoot me, don't shoot me!"'

Tyler backed Dods to the edge of the skate ramp, where Dods's back heel breached the edge of the concrete bowl. 'Cassidy was still coming, so it was at that point I realised, I'm just going to have to keep firing at this bloke's chest until he goes down.'

In the chaos of crossfire, Dods's mind was clear.

'It becomes a case of, well, now it's you or me, and I've got two little girls waiting for me at home. You have to draw a line through the sympathy and empathy at some stage, when the potential is that I'm not going to get home,' he told Silvester.

A barrister at Tyler's inquest suggested that police had the choice to retreat and lock themselves in their cars to prevent the necessity of shooting Tyler, and ameliorate the risk of the teenager hurting them.

'Our job is to protect the public whether we like it or not, and whether it sounds trite, that's what we signed up to do … It's a balancing act. If you don't respond, what are the potentials for disaster? You have to respond,' Dods said when that was put to him.

I thought of Dufty's remark at Elijah's inquest. 'When someone runs, you chase them.' *Was Dods articulating what Dufty and Rich had thought? That there was a potential for disaster if they let Elijah go? But Elijah wasn't armed when they chased him — what disaster did they imagine he might create?*

Tyler's death had lodged itself in Dods and Blundell's bodies. You could see the trauma coursing like blood underneath their skin.

'There is this concept out there in the broader community sometimes that shooting someone dead is just part of the job,' Victoria Police Chief Commissioner Ken Lay said to Silvester, 'and I guess that's what you see on TV on a regular basis.

'But I see some very, very damaged police members as a result of them being involved in police shootings. In forty years of policing, not once have I ever met a police member who has gone to work wanting to shoot someone dead ... It's the last thing we'd ever want to do, but the sad truth is, when it does occur, sometimes it's a very, very long way back for these members to being fully functional as they were before the incident.'

'Yeah. It does change you,' Blundell said. 'I think I said at the inquest, it takes over your life, becomes a pervasive force in your life that seeps into everything. You just become a bit darker and a bit more cynical and a little less happy and a little less relaxed, I s'pose.'

His grief was a mix of bitterness and wonder. The shooting had damaged his sense of who he was.

'It was eighteen months later I remember laughing at something, and I thought, "That's the first time I've really laughed, you know, *really* laughed — like I used to".'

The last word went to Dods.

'There is no closure the way I hoped there would be. Nobody has closure, because the fact remains that somebody is dead by our hand, or by my hand; so there's no, there's no changing that fact.'

Two weeks passed, then another two; still with no answer from Rich. The longer I waited, the more likely it seemed that Rich had closed the door.

I wrote to the NSW Coroner and asked for access to Rich's psychologist's report. The one that said he had PTSD and couldn't remember what happened in Cinders Lane. My plea for transparency to bring better understanding to a complex situation fell on deaf ears. The Coroner declined to release the report.

Rich was not communicating. Roger Best had stopped returning calls.

Greig Stier had retired from the NSW Police around the time of Elijah's final inquest hearing. When I reached him at home, he was heading to Queensland on holidays, but he agreed to speak to Rich and Dufty and ask if either of them would meet with me in Armidale.

'Don't get your hopes up,' he warned before he hung up.

43.

The only evidence it had snowed in Armidale was a bone-scraping wind and murky sky. The soft, white magic my daughter had hoped for had fallen in the night and melted when the sun rose. She threw herself on the hotel bed and sobbed with disappointment.

My husband fiddled with the tiny heater, and I wedged a towel beneath the door to stem the gale. The hotel I'd chosen had seen better days. The knobbly bedspreads were ten years old; electric-blanket dials poked out from beneath the mattress. Water glasses in paper bags and sachets of instant coffee sat near the mirror.

I'd made contact with Best again, finally, and heard back from Stier as well. Andrew had given permission for both men to answer questions about him. Neither man had an answer on whether Rich would speak himself.

Today was Sunday 20 July. Andrew had received my last letter asking to speak with him, through Best, two months ago. We were here until Tuesday. If Andrew didn't turn up by then, I would have to go on without him. He knew that.

Stella and Jonathon played Uno while I unpacked. They were my human armour on this trip: a fire at which to warm myself. I needed them to hold me here and to tug at me when it was time to go. I crawled into a cocoon of blankets to read through the questions I'd written for Rich. There were dozens of them, but they fell into three main camps. Was it possible for police to fulfil the public's expectations? What had the last five years done to him? What was missing from the story I knew about Elijah's death?

Cabin fever hit mid-afternoon, and we set off in search of food and greater warmth. The regional art gallery promised both, as well as the hope of easy distraction.

The gallery's restaurant was a glass box open to the view but protected from the weather. It was full of people soaking up the sun like plants in a terrarium. Children deserted adults for the lawn outside, where they rolled like rosy, squealing apples. Stella ran off to join them.

In one corner, multiple generations of a family were crowded around a long table. The women had artsy haircuts and laughed like butcherbirds. The men were tall and held babies against their woollen chests. Clusters of wine glasses spotted the table; they were celebrating something. One man caught my eye. He looked fragile beside his relatives. He responded whenever someone spoke to him, but he didn't initiate conversation. Something about the shape of his head plucked at me. Who in this town could look familiar? Was it Rich with a new hair colour and fuller beard?

I settled with the papers in a wedge of sunlight, but my eyes kept returning to the corner table. Then it dawned; the long, pointed nose, the gingery hair. Dufty.

Dufty had already told Greig Stier that he didn't want to speak to me.

What right did I have to step into his life when he'd given me his answer? I bargained with myself for twenty minutes. If he made eye contact, I would go over. My heart clenched at the thought. *If you don't ask, you'll never know if he might have changed his mind. What if Stier didn't really ask him, and just made up an answer?*

The bill was paid, children were herded, staff began to clear the long table. I hadn't made eye contact. Dufty walked out with the other men. I followed.

When I reached the footpath, they were gone. Relief flooded my chest.

A few early risers were drinking coffee or checking their postboxes in the mall on Monday morning. A pensioner on a scooter buzzed past, his breath puffing behind him like smoke from a tiny steam train.

Opposite the post office was the Armidale courthouse where Elijah's inquest had started. Its entrance was skirted in leaves and empty chip packets. Its black iron gates were padlocked. A sign on a notice board gave directions to a new courthouse.

Caffiends had moved a few doors down. The original site was an empty shell. Its windows were plastered with real estate posters, and junk mail covered the carpet inside. *What idiot was delivering mail to an empty shop?*

I sat on the steps of the post office and held down an urge to flee. The sun grew warmer and the mall began to fill. Junkies sashayed past with hoodies up, and farmers stepped out of utes into old brick banks. What was it about Armidale that unnerved me? It was the same feeling I got when I visited my hometown — as if my mouth and ears had been stuffed with cotton wool. I was returned to a silent past in which my voice did not exist. So few people in such a large space, and so little said between them. People in small towns liked to boast that they knew everyone, but they didn't really. Not in a real way. You could know someone for decades and never discuss more than the contents of their rain gauge. Proximity stood in for intimacy.

I checked my phone. No messages from Rich. I was meeting Roger Best in ten minutes.

In my memory, Armidale Police Station was a towering block of black glass and aluminium: a cold waiting room at the top of steep stairs, and a reception desk the length of an entire wall. When I turned the corner, I was reminded there were two stations.

A squat, redbrick one on the corner surrounded by a garden, and the new black glass and aluminium station. It was four levels high, not the tower I remembered. The steep flight of stairs behind the black glass door was only ten steps, and the desk in reception was a regular size.

A uniformed officer led me down a corridor into Roger Best's office, where lavender bushes peeked above the windowsill.

Best gestured for me to take a seat; he was on the phone.

His office was spotless. Folders on the bookshelf, a pot plant near the door, loose papers and a coffee mug on the desk.

Best had been Rich's immediate boss at the time of Elijah's shooting.

He was the one who broke to Rich the news that Elijah had died in Cinders Lane. It was Best who collected Rich from home and took him to his interview with homicide detectives, and who volunteered to run crowd control on Rich and Dufty's walk-through at 6am.

I listened to Best speak to whoever was on the phone. He asked if they were taking enough time off between jobs; he would make sure they got their overtime.

When the call was over, we laid the ground rules. Best was giving me his own views, not those of the police force. He had Rich's permission to speak to me, but he wasn't speaking *for* Andrew. Everything was on the record.

'I feel like I don't know anything about Andrew. Describe him for me,' I started.

'He's one of the best cops I've ever worked with,' Best said. Nice, smart, he'd do anything to help.

'If it wasn't for his family life and connection to this area, I would have forced him down to Sydney a long time ago, into the drug squads, where he would have shone in those roles targeting high-level criminals.'

Best had worked in the drug squad in Sydney before he came to Armidale, he explained. He'd only been in Armidale a short time when Elijah was shot. He was team leader of the Tactical Action Group (TAG) Rich was part of when the shooting happened. Two members of the TAG left the police shortly after.

'The team never really recovered to be honest,' Best said.

I mentioned seeing Dufty at the art gallery.

'Was his decision to leave the force connected to Elijah's shooting?' I asked.

'Whether this was *the* incident that caused Greg to leave the police or it was the final straw I'm not sure. More probably the final straw from my understanding,' Best said. He looked uncomfortable.

'What immediate impact did the shooting have on Andrew?' I asked.

Best cleared his throat and straightened his back.

'I would assess Andrew as being a very strong person and able to deal with adversity more than perhaps most people I know, but I wonder how accurate that is. I've thought back about how fair an assessment I made at the time, you know.'

'What do you mean?'

Best leaned against his desk towards me and clasped his hands into a triangle.

'Coming from a homicide background, you build up barriers, and deaths stop being overly traumatic. You just kick in and deal with it on a professional level. Those barriers you build up over a number of years, so seeing somebody killed, for me — it was just another instance of that.'

When Best broke the news that Elijah had died, Andrew broke down, Best said.

'That was the first indication to me of what a significant impact it had on him ... For me it was another traumatic event, and I dealt with it the way I've dealt with other traumatic events.'

It struck me as an enormous blind spot that Best would equate his own reaction to covering homicides with Rich's experience of taking a life. He had conditioned himself to survive the work he did, and assumed Rich had the same protective filters.

'It's been a learning time for me,' Best conceded. 'Of course, Andrew being Andrew, he kicked in I suppose the same way I do, back into that professional mode and just got on with doing his job, and it was only conversations with him over those years where I realised that me simply going, "Andrew's a very strong person and he will deal with this, no doubt, and come through it", has impacted significantly upon him.'

It was telling in a man whose compassion was so evident that he missed Rich's distress because he'd learned to suppress his own. The first time Best realised Andrew was not OK was when he spoke to Andrew's wife, he said. That's where Andrew was letting his feelings out. The strain only began to show at work when Elijah's inquest was referred to the DPP.

'He's quite relaxed and he likes to joke around and have fun in the office, and that wasn't there; and he's a practical joker and he's a good team person, and that wasn't there. I could just see he wasn't his normal self, and thinking about it — how could you be?'

Best shook his head.

'You think, in your own mind, you have done your duty — you have done what society asks of you as a police officer — and then to suddenly have that put up to the DPP to say, "Well, we think charges should be laid", it must have been extraordinarily stressful.'

'You weren't very pleased with the coronial, were you?' I said, offering Best an opening.

He looked me in the eye.

'No, I wasn't. I was surprised from the outset. To my mind, it seemed the counsel assisting had already made a determination in his mind and was proceeding towards an outcome … I think I mentioned in my email one of the examples …' and Best returned to Joan Whitburn's testimony. Best had a theory that counsel assisting didn't challenge Whitburn because her initial evidence aligned with the conclusion Hoy wanted to reach.

He counted off the evidence that the Police Commissioner's lawyer, Ray Hood, had extracted from Whitburn.

'It was a command system, it was on the table, she had to go over to the wall to use another phone because she thought that phone was broken. Then she found that in fact she'd been ringing the New Zealand emergency because she'd been over there for 6 months, and then rang Triple-0.'

I only remembered one phone, and it was on the desk not on the wall.

He had similar concerns about discussion of the crucifix position.

'Those little things, in my mind, were an indication that perhaps it wasn't really about working out exactly what happened and why it did happen,' he said.

'Why would counsel assisting want to reach a particular conclusion?' I asked.

Because there were people who believed the police should not investigate police in critical incidents like Elijah's death, Best said.

I'd heard the argument, but I couldn't see how an agenda to take critical incident investigations away from police related to proving Rich used fatal force without good reason.

Best believed Rich's account of Cinders Lane. Where the inquest findings suggested gaps in his evidence, Best was emphatic that the Coroner should have addressed any doubts more thoroughly. His greatest criticism of Elijah's inquest was that the process was not robust enough to reach the conclusions the Coroner came to.

'I don't think … well, I *know* the Coroner just didn't turn her mind to the possibility that what Andrew said took place,' he told me.

'I thought it was quite extraordinary that she was able to discount the evidence of that other fellow who said, "I heard Elijah say shoot me, shoot me".'

Best was talking about the only witness who'd corroborated Rich's claim: Andrew Schaefer.

Could he explain how only Schaefer heard Elijah's words when most of the other witnesses were much closer to Rich and Elijah than him? I asked.

Best's voice and face became animated.

'It's just that tunnel vision. There's lots of evidence of that in relation to witnesses faced with a fight-or-flight life-threatening situation; a gun and a knife, and they're just focused in and everything else washes over them. I think this is another example of where exactly that has happened.'

'But is there evidence of that number of people being subject to tunnel vision? I mean there were quite a lot of people in the laneway,' I ventured.

Best explained how a detective approached the question.

'So you flip it the other way: you go, OK, well if that's the case and no one else heard it, how did this other person hear it?'

Starting with the premise that Rich fabricated Elijah's comments to justify his actions, it followed that someone had to tell Schaefer 'what Elijah said' for Schaefer to repeat the lie. Who was in a position to do that? Best asked. Either the police officer who took Schaefer's statement, or someone else who Rich spoke to, he theorised.

'But that was never tested!' Counsel assisting didn't even attempt to establish how Schaefer came to give false evidence, if that's what the Coroner believed it was, Best crowed.

'Do you think, to be fair, that the Coroner expected she would be able to test Andrew on it — and that could never happen because he didn't give evidence?' I asked.

Possibly, Best said.

'Is it possible in the heat of the moment that Andrew could have imagined he heard those things, imagined that that was happening, but it didn't?'

'Yes, absolutely, but then how do you explain this other fellow?'

Best laughed.

'And then we go, "Hell, how on earth could he have heard it fifty metres away and why is he, who is fifty metres away, the one that hears it?" ... All those things should have been investigated by the Coroner. To just discount it like that was extraordinary and unfair. It didn't sit well with me at all.'

If you accepted that Elijah said, 'Shoot me, shoot me', took the crucifix position, and then moved towards Rich, it opened up another issue, Best continued.

'The whole avenue of what Mr Olen put in his statement, of why this ever happened in the first place — that notion of suicide by cop.'

I flinched. Suicide by cop was real, and it was what any officer would want to believe in Rich's situation. Stuart Thomas had examined the prevalence of 'suicide by cop' in his study of fatal police shootings in

Victoria. I remembered talking to him about it when we met.

Of the forty-five instances in a twenty-year period where Victorian police had shot and killed a mentally ill person, Thomas and his colleagues found a third of cases fitted the criteria of 'suicide by police'.

The criteria were an amalgam of elevated likelihoods. The person who was shot in a 'suicide by police' was more likely to have a serious mental illness; more likely to have a history of past suicide attempts and to be intoxicated at the time of the incident. They were more likely to have orchestrated a confrontation to provoke police attendance and to act aggressively once police arrived. 'Acting aggressively' meant they threatened police; they had a weapon and ignored police commands to put it down. It was also more likely that the person who was shot was already known to police as a criminal suspect or perpetrator.

This profile did not neatly fit Elijah.

He did have a diagnosed serious mental illness. He wasn't intoxicated when he was shot. Whether he was or had been suicidal was a matter of debate. Jeremy said Elijah's wrist-cutting episode the previous day wasn't a real suicide attempt; Elijah told nurses in Armidale he had been suicidal recently but wasn't now.

Elijah did approach police, but he asked them to take him to hospital; he didn't attempt to provoke them to violence, and later, when Rich approached him in Rusden Street, an unarmed Elijah ran away. Elijah may have had a change of heart between fleeing Rich and reaching Caffiends. It was possible he saw the knife in the kitchen and decided to die using Rich as his means. If I used Best's technique of stepping backwards from a conclusion through a justifying set of facts, that was the closest I could come.

'Throw in the fact that days before that, Elijah's talking about being killed by police …' Best added, and I interrupted him.

'That wasn't something Elijah started saying days before the shooting. The idea the police wanted to kill him was the whole basis of his paranoid delusions,' I explained.

'Well, where was that?' Best laughed in disbelief. 'That didn't come out!'

The Coroner and counsel assisting knew it, so did Rich's lawyers, I thought. But Best hadn't seen the brief.

We had talked for almost an hour already. I scanned the notebook on my lap.

'Talk to me like a police officer about the bread knife. How much damage could it have done?' I asked Best.

'How many times did you hear the counsel assisting say, "It was just a bread knife"? What it was, was a black-handled knife with a twenty-five-centimetre blade with a point on the end of it. A serrated blade — a twenty-five-centimetre silver blade with a point on the end of it,' Best repeated.

It was the second thing we remembered differently. The knife and Whitburn's phone.

'I thought it was a rounded end?'

'No, it had a point on it,' Best said without doubt. 'Trying to make an assessment of that knife in that scenario — all it is, is a knife. He picked up a knife with a serrated edge; in this case it had a point, but —'

'Because I think it is a very important point,' I interrupted. 'It's certainly played on my mind that it was a bread knife, and if Andrew knew that, how much damage could it do — did he really have to pull a gun on a man with a bread knife?'

'Well, we'll get the photos,' Best said politely. 'It's got a point on it, but even if it had the rounded end … it had the big silver blade, twenty-five to thirty centimetres long. If it had a round end, you couldn't stab, certainly, but you could slice. It's a weapon that was capable of inflicting death on somebody.'

Rich's words came back in a flash: 'I thought he was gonna stab me.' Then the image of Leanne Thomas sawing a bread knife across the arm of her pink fleece: 'I don't sort of think this knife would — you know — I'm cutting myself fairly hard there …' and the serrated blade dragging across the fabric.

'I suppose that's the point I'm looking to make,' I said. 'Because I don't know that it could. I pick up a bread knife and think you'd have to do a hell of a lot of sawing to even break skin with it, or you'd have to be using it with a lot of force.'

'It was a knife, it had a point, I saw it there on the ground. It could cut someone's throat, no problem at all. It was a scenario of Andrew being faced with a man with a knife and it was a potentially deadly scenario … and the fact that, like you said, it's in your mind as "just a bread knife", well, it was continually put forward in that way for a reason and it worked.'

It was the point Best returned to with multiple examples — the crucifix position, the nature of the knife, whether Elijah spoke or moved. Counsel assisting was pre-disposed to evidence that supported Elijah rather than Rich. Hoy and Gormly saw Elijah as unthreatening, but that wasn't Rich's view in Cinders Lane.

When I returned to the brief, I discovered that Best and I were both vulnerable to bias.

Police had photographed the knife lying in the gutter. Best was right. The pictures showed it had a squared-off tip, not round like I'd imagined. When I looked back through newspaper reporting on the inquest, *The Australian* had described it as a 'round-tipped bread knife' too. Looking at the photograph in front of me, you wouldn't call it pointed, but you couldn't call it blunt. I read Whitburn's statement again and my notes on her evidence from the inquest. There was no second phone in the room she called from.

But Best and I were united in our frustration over other things. No expert witnesses had been called during the inquest to discuss Elijah's mental state or explain how only Schaefer heard Elijah say, 'Shoot me, shoot me'. Then there were the legal machinations.

'The legal decision — the defence of silence …' I said.

The muscles in Best's face tremored with feeling. It was the NSW

Police Association who identified the risks involved if Andrew told his story to the Coroner, Best said. They were the ones who paid for Rich's lawyers.

'I know factually they drove that with Andrew and they told him the risk … Make no mistake, it is 100 per cent factual that the decision not to give his evidence was driven by his defence team.'

His barristers warned Rich he would 'leave himself open' if he gave evidence to the Coroner, and Andrew struggled with that advice, Best said.

'I know the conversations that were happening. It got to the point where Andrew said, "Look, I don't care about that aspect", and I said, "Mate, you know at some point you're just going to have to tell them no". They then moved onto the notion of, "Well, it's not just for you, you know this case will have far-reaching ramifications for others that come after you". So that was thrown into the mix in his mind that he's not just doing it for him; it's a risk for other police. That was put to him, I know that factually.'

Best gave one of his angry laughs.

'What was interesting, though, whether or not it was on Andrew's mind at the time, was the fact that he can't remember. The PTSD was an amazing thing.'

When did he become aware of Rich's memory loss? I asked.

'When we were driving down to Sydney. I still vividly remember the conversation; he said "You know I can't remember anything", and I said, "What the fuck are you talking about?", and he said, "From when I pulled my gun out, I can't remember anything". I thought about it and I said, "Well, that's not going to look good". He said, "I know".'

I imagined the two men in the car; Best driving, Rich looking out the window. Best glancing between Rich's face and the road, trying to take it in.

I studied Best's face for signs of doubt. He knew what I was thinking.

'I didn't for a moment contemplate that it was constructed, because there was only damage coming from it; it was only going to make things worse.'

'It did look pretty bad.'

I was wary, but Best's voice was calm.

'And he knew that, and that stressed him considerably. But I said, "Well, it is what it is mate, you've just got to deal with it again, another hurdle." But I found it just amazing that the mind could work in that fashion, that from when he pulled his gun out, there's just nothing there.'

Best raised his eyebrows and shook his head.

'Does that make sense to you?' I asked. My scepticism was audible enough to trigger Best's defences.

That was the notion of PTSD, he said.

'The brain just does things because it says, "I can't cope with this, I'm going to do this in order to cope".'

It summarised my own unscientific explanation — the brain shut down a set of conscious memories to protect it from things that were too awful to contemplate. Whatever the cause, Rich's body had done what it did to keep him sane.

'It was *far* worse for him to have to say in the witness box that he can't remember than it would have been to sit there and know his evidence, give his evidence, have those difficult questions in cross-examination, give his answers, and move on,' Best said.

One of the reasons people gave for doubting Rich's truthfulness, I told Best, was that he was working as a cop and carrying a gun when he was supposed to have PTSD.

'Oh, that's an interesting concept,' Best said, looking thoughtful.

Sometime after the incident in Cinders Lane, Rich was put through a re-enactment of a similar scenario, Best explained. Someone would have approached him with a knife, and the assessors would look for Rich's reaction — did he freeze or go to jelly?

'Now there's been no sort of indication of that type of a response from him in that,' Best said. The PTSD, in this instance, didn't affect Rich's ability to do his duties, so he was safe to carry a gun.

'I know it's different looking in than it is looking out,' he reassured me.

I'd been through my notes from the inquest hearing. Rich informed his barristers of his memory loss three days before he took the stand at the final hearing in 2014. His psychologist's report said Rich's memory of Cinders Lane had been compromised since 2010.

'When Andrew told you he couldn't remember anything, did you ask him why he didn't raise it when he first realised?' I asked Best.

'No, I didn't. I imagine if I were in the same position as him I'd be hoping it would get better. If you didn't understand what it was, and you're just having trouble recalling, you'd be thinking, "Is it going to come back? — I don't know." And I imagine he would have been deeply concerned about the fact of how bad it's going to look; now, whether that was kicking around in his mind, I don't know — but no, I didn't ask him that. I just found it extraordinary.'

The timing of Rich's memory loss was immaterial to Best, because he believed wholeheartedly that PTSD was the only thing that had stopped Andrew talking about Cinders Lane.

A terrible thought occurred to me for the first time.

What if Andrew's memory of Cinders Lane was intact when the legal tussle began over whether or not he would give evidence to the Coroner? What if Andrew could have told us at the beginning, before the Coroner referred the case? What if it was only in the years that followed that his mind buried the memories in order to survive?

'Do you feel like Andrew had a choice about the silence defence? Was it something that he ultimately made the decision to do or that he really didn't feel he had a choice about?' I asked Best.

'In all my conversations with him, we believed that he'd be giving evidence. That it would work out — this legal challenge was there to close a loophole in risks associated with giving evidence in that way. It would be closed, and he'd give evidence at some point. That was always his position.'

I nodded, my mind racing.

'So are you saying, in a way, Andrew was trying to keep a lot of people happy by following the legal process with the belief or the hope that he would be allowed to tell his story in the end?'

'Absolutely 100 per cent.'

I pressed him. 'Are you really quite confident of that?'

He was.

'That makes the findings a whole different story. How did Andrew take them?'

'In the standard Andrew way: "That's life, move on", but what's really happening inside you can only imagine. If Andrew's version is accurate, just imagine being in his position and being criticised in that way. It would be earth-shattering for you. Then throw in the fact that Elijah was suffering from a mental illness … and throw the fact in to Andrew's mind that Elijah was a lovely fellow — just horrible.'

We sat quietly for a moment.

'Will Andrew speak to the Holcombes, do you think? He was saying at the end of the last inquest that he wanted to …'

'To be honest with you, the findings have probably damaged that prospect. He's certainly strong enough to and understands the good that could come from it, but I think — you know, we were expecting from the tone of the inquest, we were expecting the findings to be, you know, problematic, but she took it to a fairly high level.'

I nodded.

'I was shocked by how absolute they were … I thought there was a great lack of compassion for Andrew.'

Best looked at me quizzically, as if I was laying a trap.

'Andrew's moving forward, as I am, going, this is just such a shit situation there's nothing we can do about it, move on … And I think the only way you can do that, like any tragedy, for the Holcombes or anyone involved in a terrible thing, you can just wait for time to do its healing, and there'll be those times that it comes back to your mind, but all you can hope is that the time in between is longer and longer. That's all you can do. And then at some point, it's not driving who you are.'

'I know they would like to meet with Andrew,' I said.

Best toyed with his keyboard and beetled his eyebrows.

'Well, that's certainly something we could turn our minds to.'

We both knew it wouldn't happen.

We shook hands. Best opened a door onto the verandah and showed me out through the garden of the old station.

I walked the single block to the top of Cinders Lane. Ambrose Hallman's office was on my left, one storey up. The blinds on his window were raised. The library where Ian Greenhalgh worked was in front of me. There was the back step where Anne Gilbert smoked, while she watched what she thought was a training exercise.

I walked to the spot where Rich had knelt over Elijah. To my right, close enough to throw a stone and crack the glass, was the window Joan Whitburn watched through. The building was leased by a law firm now. I pushed through the glass doors and stepped into reception. A man in a tweed coat greeted me.

'Can I help you?'

'Would it be possible, would you mind if — A young man was shot about five years ago just outside and a woman who worked in this building saw it.'

'Oh yes. The room she was in is just in here to your left,' he said, motioning with an open arm. 'Is that what you wanted to ask?'

'Do you mind? I won't be disturbing anyone?'

'Not at all.'

Like all of the spaces connected to Elijah's shooting, it was smaller than I expected. Venetian blinds covered the window. I poked at them tentatively, and the man in the tweed pulled them up with a clatter. The spot I had just walked from was right in front of me.

'A lot of people were very concerned when that young man was shot. It shocked — well, let's say it raised serious concerns for people in this town,' the man said.

I nodded. I could throw a tennis ball from here into the car park on the other side of Cinders Lane. You couldn't get any closer to what happened without standing next to Elijah and Rich. And she was safe, behind glass. Safe, like Schaefer, from the effects of tunnel vision?

I turned away from the window, back into the room.

'Did you know someone involved in the shooting?' the man in tweed asked.

I shook my head.

'Good luck,' he said kindly.

He held the front door open, and I walked into Cinders Lane.

There was nothing to do between my meetings with Best and Stier but wait. We spent hours in pubs playing cards and drinking soft drinks — anywhere there was an open fire. We warmed ourselves on huge plates of food, braved the park for the slippery dip, and raced through piles of fallen leaves. Jonathon and Stella filled the hours with activity. I wound the minutes tightly like thread around a reel. Each one was a chance for Rich to call.

'I know what he wants to say to them. He wants to say sorry.'

Greig Stier was making tea. It was Tuesday. The weather outside was still grey and frigid; piles of washing sat folded in baskets or draped over chairs to dry. Muddy riding boots toppled at the kitchen door. Stier carried fine, flowered mugs to the table. He could have been a farmer. His hands were thick and his jaw was set. He wore the woollen jumpers my father wore in the paddocks.

'I think Jeremy Holcombe is a really decent person,' Stier said. 'You deal with families in these situations and they aren't always decent, but he has been all the way through. Andrew has said to me he admires them. He thinks they're really decent people. He said to me, "I don't know how they can even look at me."'

Stier had been a cop since he was eighteen; he was forty-eight now, and recently retired. A detective inspector, a country boy, old friends with David Phelps. He was one of Armidale's most senior police at the time of Elijah's shooting. The job of telling Jeremy the details of how police killed his son was thrust on Stier.

Stier backed everything that Best had told me. Rich wanted to tell his story to the Coroner; he believed he would get the chance.

The Police Commissioner had threatened to deny vicarious liability for Rich if he gave evidence at Elijah's inquest, I said to Stier. Was that one reason he didn't speak — because he had to stay quiet if he wanted to stay a cop?

Stier sipped his tea and shook his head. The Commissioner would never have sacked Rich, he said. The threat to let him swing in the Holcombes' civil case was only a display of force: a bluff. The Police Commissioner spoke to Rich and told him he had the support of the police, Stier said. Andrew believed he'd get to tell his story when the legal challenge had run its course, he repeated.

I wanted to believe him. He cared about Andrew as much as Best did, and I trusted their sincerity. But it was hard to reconcile their assurances with Rich's choice at the final hearing.

After the revelations of the psychologist's report — Rich's PTSD and his memory loss — Jerram had offered Rich the chance to speak. Was there anything more he wanted to say? she asked.

Offered the opportunity, Rich didn't try to defend himself with an explanation or apology. 'I'm sorry I had no choice; I had to take Elijah's life to save my own.' 'I'm sorry I took Elijah's life, I made a terrible mistake.' He just said, 'No', and let the chance to end the story, by putting it into words, pass by.

Why? Why was I drinking Greig Stier's tea, not sitting in Andrew's kitchen now? His defenders' words and Andrew's actions didn't match.

'Do you think the decision to shoot Elijah was a terrible mistake or a terrible necessity?' I asked.

'It wasn't a mistake — he meant to pull the trigger. It was a deliberate act. A different person might have acted differently,' Stier said.

His careful answer made me wonder if his friendship with David Phelps had split his sympathies. I suggested to Stier that he had seemed to act as a bridge between the Holcombes and police during the inquest.

He set me straight immediately.

'My role was to defend our position — the cops' position, which in this instance wasn't hard with the evidence I'd seen and heard,' he said.

Stier could like the Holcombes and speak well of Elijah and still back Rich's decision to shoot. There was no malice in his belief that circumstances justified the shooting, and he scoffed when I asked if Rich might have made a different decision if he was better trained.

'It doesn't take special training, you just have to know how to communicate. They give us all this technology now — capsicum spray, Tasers, guns. I dunno if it makes any difference,' Stier said.

You had to be creative and use the resources around you, he said. Think; don't lean on technology and rules to fix a problem.

Stier was at ease defending Rich, but he commented more than once on how policing had changed since he joined at eighteen.

'Let it be said, police make mistakes. The fuck-ups that happened in this happened well before Andrew came on the scene. Putting Elijah in the back of the wagon, not getting hold of Jeremy when Elijah walked into the station. I could have found Jeremy in ten minutes,' Stier said in disgust.

Police weren't part of the community now in the way they were when he joined up. 'That's probably one of the reasons I left when I did.'

If modern police socialised outside work, if they played sport and got involved in the community, a cop in Narrabri would have known someone who could get in touch with Jeremy when Elijah turned up in Armidale, Stier said. Rich was the one left to carry the can for stuff-ups he hadn't made, Stier implied. With frustration in his voice, he told me Rich was one of the best cops in Armidale.

My phone vibrated with a text message. Jonathon and Stella were in the car outside; they'd come to pick me up.

Stier cleared the empty tea mugs from the table and took them to the sink.

'What did you make of the findings?' I asked him as I gathered my things together.

He crossed his arms and looked at me keenly.

'I said to Andrew, "You've read them, now put them in a drawer or a box and don't take them out again for three or four years."'

I pressed my forehead against the car window as we sped away from Armidale. A light, cold sleet was falling on the backs of sheep. Stella was asleep in the back, her head flopped forward like a blonde rag doll. Jonathon reached across and squeezed my leg.

'You OK?'

I nodded, my shoulders shuddering with sobs.

44.

Days after we left Armidale, I started my first full-time job in five years, as an investigative reporter at the ABC in Darwin. Work returned me to full health. First through its structure, then through the joy of finding myself in the middle of life again. I didn't forget Elijah or Andrew Rich, but my view of the world broadened beyond their sphere.

Then, two years after my last trip to Armidale, in August 2016, we broke the news to friends in Darwin that it was time to move back to New South Wales.

It happened on one of our last days in Darwin, on my way into the office. The traffic slowed, horns began to honk. *Someone's broken down.*

A young man in boxer shorts strutted through the traffic. He shook his bare chest, leaned across a bonnet and brought his fists down hard, then threw his head back and laughed maniacally. The cars in front of me had stopped at a set of traffic lights. Anytime a driver tried to inch forwards, the young man charged at it. Eventually, he lay down on the road, to block their path.

I swung out from behind the bus in front of me and turned in to a service station. Two men from the servo were watching the young man's antics from the footpath. They looked concerned. I parked and went to talk to them.

'Has someone called the police?'

They nodded.

'About fifteen minutes ago. They say they're on their way. Just worried he'll get hit, eh. Must be drugs,' said the older of the pair.

'Has anyone tried to get him off the road?' I asked.

'Yeah, he's got a friend who tried to talk him down a little while ago, but the idiot started throwing punches, so his mate left.'

'I might see if I can talk to him,' I said.

The two men stepped towards me.

'I wouldn't do that, Miss. He might be dangerous.' The younger man looked worried.

I walked to the traffic island in the middle of the road. I could hear the man's voice now. He was Irish.

He taunted the traffic then turned to someone invisible to berate them. His body was flushed and covered in sweat.

'Come on then, you cunts! Come and get some. Yeah, yeah, come on!'

'Hey, what's your name?' I called out.

He swung towards me and lifted his hands to shoulder height for emphasis.

'FUCK OFF! Yeah? Just fuck off.'

The Irishman giggled and turned in circles, veering into the path of the traffic. Horns blared.

'My name's Kate. Are you alright? Is there someone I can call for you?'

He ran towards me, grabbing his crotch.

'You want some of this? You want some?'

He pushed his face close to mine. I smelt alcohol.

'You stupid bitch. Leave me alone,' he groaned, then changed. 'You're lovely, you are. I like you.'

He rubbed his crotch and reached for my arm.

I backed away, and he cackled.

'That's right, FUCK OFF!'

I walked back to the men from the service station with a theatrical shrug of the shoulders.

'I think we should get him,' one of them said.

'Sure. How?' I asked.

'Ahmed and me will go and get him. I'm big enough, Ahmed's alright. The dickhead's going to get himself killed.'

The bus I had sat behind was still stationary at the lights. *Where are the cops?* I thought.

The two men strode into the traffic and grabbed the Irishman by the arms. He bent and twisted; he dropped to the ground and swore. Spit dribbled from his lips. They lifted him up and carried him to the kerb. He kicked out wildly at their legs, and they rolled him face down on the grass. Ahmed held his arms and the older man sat on his legs. A cheer went up from the crowd on the bus.

A police car turned the corner.

'Will you guys be OK? Do you want me to stay?' I asked.

'We're right, love,' said the older man, and Ahmed nodded.

'You're champions. Have a great day.'

I walked back to my car. It was already on the radio.

'Police have been called to a traffic disturbance on Dick Ward Drive. A bloke in his underwear running around in the traffic apparently,' the announcer chortled.

I parked my car and went to get coffee. A stranger approached me in the street.

'Excuse me?'

'Yes?'

'I saw you talk to that bloke in the traffic. I was on the bus. We thought he might swing a punch at you or something. You were brave.'

'I thought maybe I could talk him down. It didn't really work, did it? Thank God for the servo guys.'

We smiled at each other.

He wouldn't have told me I was brave if I was a cop, I thought as I walked away. He'd assume I knew exactly what I was doing and think it was just my job.

I had wanted to test my own theory and see if I could talk the Irishman out of his panic, like I wanted Rich to have tried with Elijah. It wasn't as easy as it sounded. It wasn't straightforward. It was frightening.

2017

45.

We sold our house and moved back to Sydney, to a suburb by the beach. Stella changed schools, my husband and I changed jobs, and we settled into a new but familiar life.

Early one morning, a year after the move, I rose in the dark and dressed. I kissed my sleeping husband and daughter and closed the front door quietly.

I drove over bridges and under tunnels, along highways that were never quiet, to a centre on Sydney's northern beaches.

A dozen people waited in reception. A woman with long blonde hair was checking names off at the front desk.

'Kate? Is Kate here yet?' she asked.

I raised my hand.

'I wasn't sure if I'd be on the list,' I apologised.

She smiled. 'I've put you down for morning and afternoon tea and lunch each day. OK everyone, come with me.'

We followed our guide across the car park and into a modern chapel. Thirty men and women, aged from their mid-twenties to fifties, filled two rows of tables that looked over bushland to the sea. Everyone was dressed in black or grey; there were a few dark suits, but mostly office civvies.

An athletic man strode to centre stage and rubbed his hands together.

'Good morning, everyone. Good to see you all here bright and early — I hope you slept well your first night? We've got a lot to get through.'

Chief Inspector Joel Murchie hadn't changed. The last time I'd seen him was at Elijah's inquest. He hummed with the energy of a whip.

'Now, why are we here?' he asked the room. 'To try and give

you practical expertise in dealing with people in mental health or suicidal crisis.'

It was eight years since Elijah's shooting. Every police officer in NSW had now had one day's training in mental health intervention from the Mental Health Intervention Team (MHIT) that Murchie ran: a vast improvement on the hour Andrew Rich had received. On top of the standard one-day course, the NSW Police put three hundred officers a year through an extra four-days' training. That's what I was here to observe.

In the twenty-odd years between Roni Levi's death on Bondi Beach in 1997 and the end of 2016, Murchie told the room, NSW Police had shot and killed a total of 38 people. On average, that was two a year. Evidence suggested well over half of those people had a serious mental illness. Since mental health training had been rolled out to every officer in NSW in 2014, police had fatally shot six people. None of those deaths had been examined by a coroner yet so their mental health was not confirmed, but three appeared to have been mentally disturbed.

'Ultimately, what we want to do here is change some attitudes about mental health. One of the things we want to do is get people in mental health crisis out of the back of police vans. Why? It's called mental health not mental policing — this is a health issue.

'The NSW Health Department admits their community mental health teams are under pressure.'

People scoffed in recognition. Murchie put up a hand of caution.

'They're complex jobs — the staff in those teams are overworked and not well paid. But guess who ends up dealing with the people who slip through the cracks? Good old Mr and Mrs Fix-it, NSW Police.'

Then Murchie came to a statistic I hadn't heard before. In April 2017, according to the World Health Organisation (WHO), depression had become the single largest contributor to global disability in the world, he claimed.

'We knew the numbers were on the rise but the WHO wasn't

expecting them to peak for a few years. Any ideas why mental health is getting worse?'

'Pressures of modern life,' someone piped up.

Murchie nodded.

'And it's cumulative. You think about being so depressed you can't get out of bed; if you can't get out of bed, what else can't you do? You can't go to work. What happens next? You're in financial stress. Pretty soon you're blueing with your other half, you might start drinking more than usual or taking drugs. It spirals.'

More and more people were struggling to deal with a daily load of pressure that was immense; any GP would give you anti-depressants, but often people didn't address the cause of the decline in their mental health.

He paced back and forth in front of huge windows, his hands clasped at his chest.

'Imagine you live in a quiet cul-de-sac. One afternoon, you hear a kerfuffle; the police turn up and bundle your neighbour into a police van. What are you going to think? That the neighbour is probably dangerous? You might avoid them, there's a stigma, right?'

A few heads nodded.

'Now, imagine it's an ambulance that takes your neighbour. What are you doing? Making a mental note to check on them when they get home, see if they're alright maybe? Different story, isn't it?'

Murchie explained that the aim of the four days was to teach the class skills to handle mental health crises. They'd learn ways to reduce the risk of injury to themselves and the people they were helping.

Joel Murchie and I had stayed in touch on and off since Elijah's inquest. I'd been keen since its rollout in 2012 to see the mental health training NSW Police now gave its officers. Now that I was back in NSW, Murchie had made it happen. I wanted to know if the skills police were taught would have helped Rich and Elijah in Armidale. Every police officer I'd asked directly maintained that Rich had done the only thing he could. But surely there were still lessons to be learned?

Early in the morning on the first day of the course, Joel Murchie revealed that he lived with a mental illness.

'The illness I manage is PTSD, and it affects me on a day-to-day basis.'

People's eyes slipped to the tabletop. He must have noticed, but Murchie didn't stop. He and his girlfriend went to Europe in 2002; on the way home they stopped in Bali, he told the class.

'Friends from Australia were flying in to meet us. No one had mobile phones back then, so we agreed on a place to meet when they got in.'

9.30pm at the Sari Club in Kuta, a favourite nightspot with Western tourists.

'My girlfriend and I got there on time. The Sari Club was packed. We scored a table near the front door next to the security guard; we were pretty happy with that. The plan was we'd spot our friends as soon as they came in, we'd have a drink and decide where to go next,' Murchie said.

An hour later, their friends had not appeared. By 11pm the club was heaving, and Murchie and his girlfriend decided to bail. She went to find the toilet; he got on the dance floor while he waited. A few minutes later, Murchie heard what sounded like a gas bottle exploding. He went to the door to look outside. The security guard was gone, and a motley-green minivan was parked across the footpath. He knew straight away there was something wrong.

'I was about twenty metres from the van when it went up. I was blown off my feet; my nose and face came off. When I came to, there were body parts and dead people all around me. It's amazing to think now that I actually walked out and climbed over a wall. When I couldn't find my girlfriend, I went back in to look for her.'

The bombs had been set by Islamic extremists targeting Western 'infidels'. Two hundred and two people were killed and hundreds injured in three different locations. The Sari Club was by far the worst hit in what became known as the first Bali bombings.

Murchie clicked a remote control and a photo of his face appeared on a screen behind him.

'See my black eye in that picture? That's where my nose came off and hit my face.'

He clicked the remote again.

'When I got out of the club I pulled my T-shirt over my head, and you can see here where the skin on my back came off with the T-shirt.'

A picture of his arm and torso flashed on screen.

'I was 109kgs then — I played rugby league on weekends. When you get badly burned, everything swells up. My arm there is the same thickness as my torso. Have you heard of Fiona Woods, the burns doctor who won Australian of the Year? She pioneered a special spray-on skin. Well, I was her guinea pig.'

The room was silent. No one moved or made a sound.

'I had to do a lot of rehabilitation. I was lucky I had very skilled, capable people to help me. I wanted to get back to work as soon as I could.'

Murchie wore a compression suit under his uniform when he went back to work, but his passion for the job was gone.

'I loved being a cop, but I couldn't raise the enthusiasm I used to have before.'

He told the class he found himself getting angry at small things; feeling depressed, afraid, hyper-alert to threat. He took seven months off to get the help he needed.

'I still get nightmares. I can get angry or anxious very easily, but I've learned how to manage it. I do a lot of physical exercise. I don't drink alcohol, I eat well. I'm not ashamed to live with a mental illness. It's all about removing the stigma. No one is immune.'

His tone was bright, but the words were short and sharp. He clapped his hands.

'Time for morning tea. Enjoy the sunshine out there, see you at twenty past for the next session.'

It was the first time Murchie had told a training group his story.

'I like to keep the course fresh. There was no reason not to tell it in the past, I just decided to try it out this time,' he told me.

He bared his teeth to approximate a smile.

'I manage a mental illness, too,' I said.

'What sort?'

My stomach lurched.

'Depression, and anxiety.'

Would he doubt my intentions? Would I lose his respect? It had taken so long to get this far.

Murchie nodded and looked away.

'No one is immune.'

There were two other permanent teaching staff on the MHIT with Joel Murchie. Martin Collis was a psychiatric nurse, with silver hair that stood straight up. He'd worked in institutional asylums, community homes, emergency response units, and hospital emergency wards in a career that spanned forty years. With his bright-blue eyes behind large glasses, he looked like a friendly owl.

Martin taught mainly psychiatric subjects: how to identify different mental illnesses; how to avoid and de-escalate a crisis; and the side effects of medication.

'Mental health is about functioning,' he told the class. 'You all have a job, so you have money. You have somewhere to live … yes? What about relationships — a partner, friends? A pet? Something or someone that loves you?'

Heads nodded in confirmation. Martin walked along the rows.

'These are all things that support you and help you function. When you start to take things away from a person's life, it can fall apart very quickly. Like you would if I took things away from you.'

Later, he asked for a show of hands of police who'd dealt with someone who was psychotic. A forest of arms reached for the ceiling.

'Psychosis will change the way a person thinks, feels, and behaves, such that they lose touch with reality. Delusions and hallucinations are common, and they can appear through any of the senses. The hallucination you need to be aware of is the command auditory hallucination. It's when people hear the voice that tells them to, "Go kill the neighbour. Kill the cop."'

If they were dealing with a person having this kind of experience, they should neither confirm nor challenge the reality of the voices, Martin instructed.

'If you challenge the delusion, you may become part of their conspiracy. If they tell you a story about what they believe is happening — that someone is watching them, for instance — think how you might feel if you were them. Try to connect with their emotions. "That sounds really scary, you must be very frightened".'

'Have you ever seen people with the tin hats?' he asked, and half a dozen people nodded.

'We have a regular lady who comes into one hospital wearing only the best quality cookware on her head.'

The room burst into laughter. I had never seen a person in a tin hat. I'd thought the stories were apocryphal.

'She drives a Mercedes. Her headwear stops messages being put into her brain. To the person who is psychotic, the hallucination or delusion is 100 per cent real,' Martin emphasised.

'Some delusions are delusions of reference — things that talk to you or send you messages, like the TV or radio, or you think there are special messages in the newspaper for you.'

I thought of Elijah's certainty that Facebook posts from Allison and their friends held special orders and instructions for him.

Martin pressed the remote control and two x-rays popped up on the screen. One showed a skull covered in straight white lines. Some lines were entirely buried in the bone, others poked above the skin. At the crown of the skull, like Excalibur in stone, a bright white rod plunged deep into the x-ray's shadow.

'This patient, a 44-year-old man with a history of depression and deliberate self-harm, presented at a hospital emergency department. He told staff he had hammered nails into his head over a period of three months.'

I felt myself recoil from the screen.

'He kept the wounds clean with antiseptic and hid them under his hat. A psychiatric service sent him to emergency after he inserted a masonry nail, almost thirteen centimetres long, into the top of his skull and started to experience weakness on his left side,' and Martin pointed to the bright white rod.

The room inhaled. The second x-ray showed a different skull, with lines like looping doodles inside the forehead. This patient used a drill, said Martin.

'You can see here where he's drilled a hole in the skull and pushed wire into the hole. The wire was the binding from a sketch pad. Now this man, he was thirty-two years old, made an excellent recovery.'

'You can't un-see the next image I'm going to show you. It's gory. If you'd rather not see it, please look away.'

Up came an image of a young man on his back. There was grass beneath him, and, somewhere nearby, a footpath. He wore jeans or dark trousers, maybe a beanie, and he cradled a tangle of blooms — red, pink, and pearl — across his belly.

'This shows you how real the delusion is for people. I can't say why this particular man disembowelled himself, but it's common in cases like this for people to believe they have a chip in their body somewhere that is transmitting messages, or that part of their body is evil and they want to remove it.'

I stared, fascinated. My mind could not accept the image was real. Was this how police processed the trauma they witnessed, by accepting their brain's message that the horror was 'not reality'?

Martin gave classes on identifying and handling people with different mental illnesses. Speak slowly, give people time to respond; count to ten before you asked the next question. People who were depressed had difficulty communicating. People with psychosis were over-stimulated already.

'There's no cutting corners with these jobs; you have to take your time.'

Build trust and rapport, he told the class. Assess the risk, check the person's history of violence; establish communication, monitor your speed and tone of voice.

'Don't act overly officious. The person is sick, they are not necessarily criminal.'

Empathise, he said repeatedly. Try to imagine how frightened they must be.

'So you're writing a book? That must be a really interesting thing to do.'

A man with glasses and a boyish face bent down to make eye contact. I was standing by myself, like I had at every break.

My saviour smiled encouragingly.

'It is. But this is interesting, too, for me, I mean,' I stumbled. 'Are you finding it useful?'

'Oh yeah, absolutely. We're desperate for this stuff.'

'Do you get many call-outs for mental health jobs?' I asked.

He nodded vigorously. 'Lots.'

A second cop joined us with a cup of coffee.

'Do people get violent very often, in mental health call-outs?' I asked.

'Sometimes things get physical. I've had to pile on on a few occasions,' said the second cop.

I hesitated.

'Have you ever had to use your gun?'

'I've had to take it out a few times.'

'I've never had to unholster my gun in eighteen years as a police officer,' said the first cop. 'If I ever, God forbid, had to shoot someone, it would be my last shift on the job. I'd give it up.'

A significant proportion of non-bizarre paranoid delusions involved police, Martin Collis told the training group. It wasn't clear why, but it might have to do with being figures of authority, he said. There was no getting away from it; they would be starting on the back foot with most seriously mentally ill people they came across.

It was why the course included a session taught by two people with a mental illness, as well as a carer. The session was Murchie's favourite.

'It's the part of the course where you really see the lights go on for people,' he told me. 'You watch; you'll see attitudes change in front of you.'

The presentation was in the middle of the week. Two middle-aged men and an older woman sat at a table out the front of the class, like an interview panel for an unnamed job. The men, James and Kieran, had schizophrenia. The woman, Lyn, cared for her schizophrenic son.

James wore a polo shirt with the MHIT logo. I guessed he was in his forties. He stayed seated to address the group, reading from notes through round, rimless glasses.

James took the room to the years before his illness surfaced. He was popular at school; a passionate musician and a good sportsman, dux of his year twice in high school, he said. His first experience of mental illness was depression and insomnia at the age of fifteen. In year twelve, he made school captain. By that time, he was playing saxophone with professional musicians twice a week and studying for the HSC. His illness was real, but it hadn't slowed him down. That was when the delusions started, James said in a gentle voice.

'I started having ideas in my head as though my friends were talking about me in another room.'

His delusions became stronger and more frightening as he got older.

'I would hear voices telling me to go the airport to meet with spiritual leaders. One day, in the emergency department of a hospital, I told the doctor I was going to die in five minutes,' he said.

Neither James or his parents could work out what was wrong, and James was finally scheduled. He spent months in hospital, but he didn't like being there.

'I was picked up twice by the police, having escaped my ward. I presented at five different hospitals before I received my diagnosis.'

The diagnosis of schizophrenia came three years after he started hearing voices. James was twenty-one. Against advice, his parents took James out of hospital and brought him home to take care of him.

'I never took my continuing mental health for granted. I've been back to hospital at times for psychosis and depression. Medication is not always enough, and past experience does not deliver immunity,' he told the class.

James spoke with almost no expression. It was as if someone had edited out the highs and lows of his natural voice. It was a side effect of the medication he was on. There were days even catching a bus was difficult, James said.

'The prognosis for my recovery is better than the community perceives. Stigma is still part of our society. As a community, we need not be afraid because we all have needs and barriers. Thank you.'

James didn't smile, just nodded his head at the applause.

Kieran stepped out from the behind the table and hitched his pants with a grin. He had a pale Irish face and long earlobes. He ambled over to the front row of students and touched a bearded man on the shoulder.

'Sorry to pick on you, mate, you alright if I do this?'

The bearded cop blushed.

'Yeah, sure mate. No problem.'

'See how your friend feels when I do this? Embarrassed, self-conscious? That is how I feel when I have tactile hallucinations,' Kieran explained. 'It is a raw, emotional experience being sick — it's very painful.'

His hallucinations were really intrusive thoughts, but he felt them on his body as if he was being touched, he explained. It was 'really distressing'. Sometimes he saw bars of light moving between people in a conversation.

Kieran told the class he'd received a diagnosis of acute psychosis at twenty-eight. He tried to describe how psychosis felt.

'When I first had delusions, a leaf falling at a particular moment of thought would make me think that Jesus or Mary were talking to me. I also had delusions of place, so if I sat in a certain seat in a café, a certain person would speak to me.

'Once, I imagined I was listening to a conversation between Kylie Minogue and Nick Cave about a song they were recording together, and Nick said his next song after that would be a hymn. And it was! So maybe I got that one right,' he joked.

He caught a bus from Sydney to Darwin during one psychotic episode and stumbled off the bus onto Darwin's main street in the middle of the night.

'I didn't know anyone and I had nowhere to stay. I walked a lot.'

He spent a few nights at the Salvation Army and a backpackers' hostel on his Darwin trip. He remembered waking up one night on the side of a highway, wrapped in a tent with a dingo circling him. He still didn't know how he got there or who found him.

'I woke up the next day in a psych ward. It was my birthday. It hurt.'

Kieran rolled onto the insides of his feet until the heels of his sneakers touched. He still had persecutory delusions and tactile sensations every day, he said.

'The delusions and psychosis don't care how hard a person tries to get it right.'

His psychosis would come on with very little warning. It could last between one and four hours and happen once or twice a week when he was really ill, he said. There was no self-pity in Kieran's words. He was matter-of-fact and funny.

Kieran and James both had a watchfulness about them. An edge of nerves, eyes that darted when anyone came near. They couldn't control when their psychosis would visit, and it filled them with apprehension.

They came to these classes because they needed to know that in the midst of a crisis, the people in this room would understand that their illness was not the sum of them.

I thought of how my jaw had clenched when I told Joel Murchie that I managed a mental illness. Exposure felt like a risk every time. How painful must this be for James and Kieran — to tell a roomful of people they didn't know the intimate details of their condition?

The carer in the trio, Lyn, said she didn't know how she could have coped over the years if she hadn't been able to turn to the police. She couldn't talk to family or friends about her son's illness, because of the stigma. But when she was scared or at her wits' end, the police would always come, she said. They had escorted her son to hospital twenty or thirty times in twenty-seven years. Lyn was proud of her son and grateful to the police for helping them both survive his illness. 'Thank you,' she said, 'and take care of yourselves.'

Dozens of people approached the trio to shake hands when the session finished. The gratitude from police was palpable. A layer of assumptions had been dismantled. Kieran and James were humorous and intelligent. Lyn, who had no one else to turn to, needed the police and was grateful for their help.

Joel Murchie caught my eye and smiled.

On my drive home across the city each afternoon, I replayed the classes in my head and filtered my judgements of Rich's failings through the knowledge I had gained. Recognising and engaging with people who were psychotic; mental health and young people, and older people, and cognitive disability. Mental health and substance abuse; the side effects of psychotropic medication. I had as much theoretical understanding now of how to de-escalate a psychiatric crisis as any police officer in NSW, at least as far as police-provided training went. How confident was I that I could use it to dissuade someone from hammering nails into their head? I had freely judged police in the past for failing to achieve these things *without* any training.

The crucial ingredient in a psychiatric crisis, it seemed to me, was fear, and the triage treatment for a deeply frightened person was genuine human contact. But making that connection was not straightforward. Police still had to keep in mind that identifying someone as mentally disturbed didn't bestow unlimited power for police to direct or contain that person. Dawn Pointon's class on Section 22 of the NSW *Mental Health Act 2007*, was designed to teach officers the extent of their powers over people who were mentally ill, and how to use it effectively.

Dawn was a sergeant with a background in trauma counselling. She was fit and brisk; a warm, swift-moving bird with a ponytail.

'If we are using Section 22 of the *Act*, we are taking away a person's liberty,' Dawn told the class of officers. 'We try to get people to realise it is a very, very important use of power.' She rattled off the checklist police must fulfil before they could detain someone for the purpose of taking them to a mental health facility.

'Is the person committing or have they recently committed an offence?'

'Have they recently attempted to kill themselves or someone else? Is it probable they will kill or attempt to cause serious injury to themselves or someone else if you do not detain them?'

'And is it better to deal with this person under the *Mental Health Act* rather than according to another law?' Dawn finished.

I answered her questions with Rich in mind. Elijah had not committed an offence, other than driving without a licence, which no one had raised in five years of court cases; the car was not stolen, although Rich believed it was. No one told Rich that Elijah had self-harmed recently, so as far as Rich knew, that was not a risk factor. There was no evidence to support the idea Elijah would hurt someone if the police did not detain him. Rich had no power to detain Elijah under the *Act*, or any other law.

'What if they need help, but there's not enough there for a 22?' a man with a sharp nose asked Dawn Pointon.

'You can try the ambulance service,' Dawn said, and the whole room groaned.

'Paramedics have a much lower threshold to meet in their use of Section 20 of the *Act*,' Dawn continued. 'For [the police force] it's got to be that a person is homicidal, suicidal or both.'

The law required a crisis before it gave police the power to step in, but even I knew that, in reality, that wasn't what happened on the ground. If the health system used the *Act* in the way it had been written, staff at Armidale Hospital would never have asked Rich to find Elijah. If police used Section 22 to rule, Rich would have told the nurses he didn't have the power to return Elijah unless he'd become a danger to himself or someone since leaving the Emergency Department.

Police, paramedics, and hospital staff all appeared to accept blurry boundaries when it came to the delivery, release, and retrieval of mentally ill people under the *Act*.

When I asked Martin Collis, away from the class, why a nurse or doctor might ask the police to bring a voluntary patient back, he said the answer would always depend on the circumstances.

'I know why you're asking the question,' he said.

But why did it need to be police, I asked? Why didn't someone from the hospital go?

'Well, police are mobile,' Martin pointed out, 'and they've taken a sworn oath to protect the community; public safety is their role first and foremost.'

But they weren't the only people with the authority to act under the *Mental Health Act*, he stressed. There was also a memorandum of understanding (MOU) between the police force and the department of health that gave directions on what to do before health workers called the police, he explained.

The original MOU had been in place since 1998, 'but people didn't know it was there,' Martin said.

A new, updated MOU had just been signed, but old or new, there were things medical staff were supposed to do before they called police.

'Like what?' I asked.

'Search the grounds. Notify their security to do a broader search. Look around the ward; maybe they're in the toilets. So you need to do those obvious things.'

Martin's words jogged a memory from the brief. Acting Sergeant Aiken had called the hospital while Carla Rutherford, Robyn O'Brien, and the doctor were discussing Elijah's departure. The nurse who took the call told investigators that Aiken requested that hospital security be asked to look for Elijah in the grounds. Aiken, who had taken Elijah's confession and arranged his transport to the hospital, appeared to have given directions to hospital staff that followed the MOU to the letter.

'Then, what was agreed in the old MOU, and it's in the new one too,' Martin continued, 'is that they call the community team — depending on the level of risk involved.'

'What else is in the MOU?' I asked.

'Call the family,' Martin said.

Next of kin was a standard detail collected during triage, when staff took Medicare and health-fund details, he explained.

It had never occurred to me that Armidale Hospital could have tried to contact Elijah's family — that responsibility had always been laid at the feet of the police.

There would always be cases where it was absolutely the right thing to do for medical staff to call the police, Martin stressed, and he told me stories of violent outbursts by mentally ill people that he had tried to assess in hospital emergency wards.

But did the MOU's guidelines on 'leaving without permission' apply to a voluntary patient like Elijah? I asked.

Martin sighed. The subject seemed perturbing to him.

In the MOU that was active when Elijah presented at Armidale Hospital, the answer wasn't clear. It depended on how you read the document, but all of the language about people leaving without permission referred to involuntary patients, he said.

Martin was far more comfortable interpreting the new MOU that had just been signed. There were no fuzzy lines in the latest agreement between police, paramedics, and the Department of Health when it came to someone in Elijah's situation, and to who was responsible for retrieving him — or not.

The hospital remained 'the lead agency in locating and returning' a person who left a facility in mental distress or disarray, and that applied whether the person in question was a voluntary or scheduled patient.

The first thing staff at the hospital were asked to do was make a risk assessment, including the likelihood that the person would harm themselves or someone else. The hospital or health facility was expected to try and find the person before they called police, unless their assessment of the risk the person posed was serious and immediate.

If the hospital thought the person was a risk, they were to call police at the nearest station (no tasking a plainclothes cop who'd just walked in). 'A request for police assistance is based on the risk the person poses and not solely on their legal status,' the MOU spelt out.

'You know, I feel sorry for that mental health nurse, too,' Martin said, returning to the situation I'd described with Elijah at Armidale Hospital.

'Why?'

'Well, was she accredited to schedule Elijah?' he asked.

'No.'

'From what I understand, he left very quickly, didn't he? Really, the person who is doing the assessment should have the power to make decisions about scheduling, too.'

Of course.

If Carla Rutherford had had the power to schedule Elijah, she could have told him he was an involuntary patient and kept him in hospital instead of letting him walk out.

But he didn't qualify; he wasn't a threat to anyone. That's what Rutherford told the inquest.

But it wasn't what she said to other staff that day.

The way I read the MOU that had been current when Elijah arrived at Armidale Hospital, he didn't fall within its boundaries. He was a voluntary patient in the Emergency Department, and the MOU appeared to apply only to involuntary patients. Regardless of the now-defunct MOU's ambiguity, neither Carla Rutherford nor Andrew Rich had followed its suggestions, or the legislative power of the *2007 Mental Health Act* (NSW), in acting to have Elijah brought back.

Andrew Rich had made the final fatal mistake, but there were failings that did not belong to him in the can he was left holding in Armidale.

It was 5pm when I turned in to my driveway.

At 7pm, the NSW police shot a man at Sydney's Central Station.

Early reports online were sketchy. A young man had walked into a florist shop at the entrance to the station and attacked the elderly owner with a broken bottle. The police had appeared, and the man with the bottle had run at four officers, allegedly holding scissors.

By morning, mobile phone footage of the shooting was on YouTube, and Manuel Theoharas, the florist, had spoken to reporters.

'The way he was holding the broken bottle he could cut my neck … or anything … He could have run out there while he was holding the scissors to hurt other people. I feel sorry for him but … I could be dead.'

The police didn't have a choice, Theoharas said.

'He was cutting his face and neck and all over his body … then he started breaking all this stuff in the florist, so I called police,' a witness told *The Daily Telegraph*.

'They came and tried to grab him but they couldn't so they shot him, maybe three or four times, and he went straight down.'

When I arrived for class at 8am the next day, Joel Murchie was in the car park taking calls. He must have been up for hours. The class filed into the chapel quietly.

The man who was shot at Central Station appeared to have a history of mental illness, Murchie said. Investigators were looking at indications it was a suicide by cop, but it was early days; a thorough investigation would bring out the details. Murchie was checking the mental health training status of the officers involved.

The mood in the room was glum.

The morning's presenters were waiting in the wings: Scott Weber, president of the NSW Police Association, and Allan Sparkes, a decorated former detective senior constable.

Murchie introduced Scott Weber first, and ducked outside to take another call.

Weber looked like a politician, with his thrust-out chin and high hairline. He jumped straight into the shooting at Central Station the minute he took the floor.

Police were criticised no matter what they did, he told the room. If they shot an offender, they were trigger-happy; if they didn't, they were leaving the community unprotected. The Police Association would defend the industrial and legal rights of every member, he thundered.

His tone brought to mind the emails police had written to *Four Corners* when Elijah's story aired — a mixture of hurt and outrage.

I rolled my eyes internally at Weber's theatricality, but he wasn't entirely wrong. If I was a police officer who had shot someone, I might believe, as Weber was encouraging me to, that the public was against me. I might be grateful for the Police Association's pugnacious defence of my actions under pressure. I might believe that only other cops could ever understand what it was like.

Allan Sparkes was a different man to Weber. His warmth lit up the room. Sparkes had saved a drowning boy and won Australia's highest bravery award for it. He was tall and solid, balding on top, with a misshapen nose and rubbery ears.

'I'm not here today to talk about being brave,' Sparkes said, then relayed the terrible things he'd experienced as a police officer. The bombing of Sydney's Hilton Hotel in 1978. Three people died, including a police officer. As a probationary constable, Sparkes had climbed onto the awning of a building across the road to gather body parts in plastic bags. Two decades later, he headed a police operation to end a siege at a house in Crescent Head on the NSW north coast. Two police officers had been shot dead. One was a close friend of Allan's. He worked for hours in sight of his dead friend's body, in uniform on the lawn.

Ten months later, Sparkes crawled into a flooded drain to save a drowning boy. It was this heroic act that released years of trauma stored by his mind and body.

He stopped sleeping, he couldn't concentrate, his body screamed in 'indescribable physical agony'. He began to have nightmares about murdering his family.

'Twenty years ago, if you disclosed that you were struggling, your career was over,' Sparkes told the hushed room.

So he didn't ask for help. He settled on a different way to end his fears and pain.

'I kissed my wife and daughter goodbye one morning. I went to work, I took my service revolver out of my locker, and I went to the bathroom to shoot myself. A colleague saw me and said, "Are you OK?" I said, "No, I'm fucked", and he said, "Well how about we take you home?"'

Sparkes saw a counsellor with his wife the next day. The counsellor wanted to schedule Allan, but his wife, Deb, refused.

'So the counsellor told her to take every knife out of the house when we got home.'

Sparkes was sedated for two weeks to rest his mind and body before he started appointments with a psychologist. The stigma of mental illness at the time was far greater than it was now, he said. At the time, he lived in a large town on the coast; there was no escape from judgement.

'I was the local president of the rugby club. I was a senior cop sitting in a waiting room that was also the waiting room for the methadone clinic, with all the heroin addicts. All I wanted was to get back to work.'

He discussed his shame when the Police Force discharged him instead of giving him the support he needed.

'My sense of self and worth was completely shattered.'

How much had the culture changed in the twenty years since Sparkes's experience, I wondered. Was Rich's choice to stay silent about his memory loss a calculated judgement to protect his job?

Sparkes told the class that he lived with overwhelming fear for years before he recovered. His presentation ended with a video full of snapshots from his life. The last one was a photograph of a rising sun taken from a boat.

'My wife and children were asleep below, so I saw the sun rise on my own. This was the final leg of our trip; we sailed around the world together, and this very moment I realised I wasn't afraid anymore,' he said. 'So I took a picture to remind myself of how it felt.'

What chance did the four police officers involved in the shooting at Central Station have of escaping mental illness? What other traumas would they accumulate in the years ahead of them? If anxiety, depression, or PTSD took hold of them, which of today's presentations would they lean on to survive? Could Weber's anger save police from paying the price of the things they were asked to do? How many people had the strength to endure the hell Allan Sparkes had lived through to regain his wholeness?

When it was time for him to leave, Sparkes shook my hand and looked into my eyes.

'Feel free to call me any time. I'm happy to help if there's any way I can.'

I approached Scott Weber at the end of the session and explained I was writing about Elijah Holcombe. I wanted to know more about the Police Association's views and choices in defending Andrew Rich, I said.

'I don't know,' Weber hedged. 'You'd better put some questions in an email.'

When I sent him questions the following week, he thanked me for the message.

'PANSW can't make any comment.'

The closing session on the final day was a series of role-play scenarios. There was nothing to gain by watching them, I thought; I decided to say my farewells and disappear.

'But you can't go yet! This is the best part,' Dawn protested. 'You have to stay.'

Joel Murchie had already chosen six participants; each pair would face a different scenario with a person in mental crisis.

The class was held in a lecture theatre. Murchie herded everyone on stage and called up the first two officers.

'A call's come in from a well-known suicide spot. No one has approached the subject, but she's standing close to a cliff edge. Take a minute to chat, remember what you've learned this week. Good luck.'

Half way up the rake of seats, Dawn stood cradling a bottle of booze. Her long blonde hair was pulled around her face; she was whimpering and talking to herself.

Mark and Joe conferred in whispers then separated into position. They moved towards Dawn from different directions, keeping their actions slow and steady.

'Hello, Ma'am, can you hear me?' Mark said.

Dawn kept muttering.

'Ma'am, my name's Mark, I'm a police officer. We're here to see if you need any help. Can you let me know if you can hear me?'

Dawn stopped muttering and froze.

'So I think you can hear me … like I said, my name is Mark. Would you like to come back on this side of the barrier Ma'am?'

'Don't come near me!' Dawn shouted, and took a step towards the edge.

Mark's arms went forward instinctively.

'OK, OK, we're staying where we are. What's your name? Will you tell me your name? Can you turn around so I don't have to talk to your back?'

Joe hung back, and Mark kept talking. Things were moving slowly. As his questions to Dawn piled up unanswered, a red flush began to creep up Mark's neck.

When Dawn was coaxed to reveal her name — Barbara — Joe jumped into the conversation.

'Barbara, my name is Joe, I'm a police officer like Mark. Can you tell us what's been happening?'

The ball was now in Barbara's court, and the exchange began to shift.

'Has something happened, Barbara?' Joe prodded.

'You don't care what's happened to me. No one cares.'

The words spewed out of the curtain of blonde hair.

'We do care, Barbara. I care. We want to help you,' Mark said awkwardly. He had a sharp-featured face and a no-nonsense voice, but I could tell he was doing his best to drop his cop act.

'Would you come back over this side of the barrier? It's dangerous being so close to the edge.'

'I'm not scared,' snapped Barbara.

'Well, you're scaring me, I'd like you to step back,' Mark replied. 'Just one or two steps for me.' He was a husband or boyfriend in that moment, concerned and gentle.

The back and forth went on for minutes, the two men taking turns. Joe was the voice of calm and reason soothing Barbara out of her chaos. Mark was the one who gave directions.

Barbara revealed that her partner was abusive. She had two small daughters she couldn't protect. She was a useless mother, there was nothing to live for, it would be better for everyone if she killed herself, she said.

'I'm sure your little girls don't want you to do that. I bet they love their mum; they need you,' Joe said gently.

'It's hopeless, I'm shit. I'm going to jump.'

'Don't do that, Barbara,' Mark's face creased with effort. 'I'm reaching out my hand for you to grab. I'm reaching out to you, Barbara, can you hear me?'

Barbara muttered and swayed and finally turned around. She stretched out her hand to Mark, and the class whooped loudly.

The second scenario was a mother and daughter conflict. Mum was drunk, and the teenage daughter had locked herself in the bathroom. Their fighting was so loud the neighbours had called police. The daughter told officers through the bathroom door she was cutting herself with a razor.

The two young officers, one male, one female, looked a little overwhelmed. The physical barrier of the bathroom door forced them to take things slowly; the only way they could get the girl out was persuasion. She told them she loved her Dad, 'but Mum's a bitch'. After fifteen minutes of negotiation, the male officer reached an agreement with the girl. If she stopped cutting herself and opened the door, they would call her dad to see if she could stay with him for a while.

The 'bathroom door' cracked open an inch, and the auditorium filled with applause. The two young officers blushed with relief and pride.

For the last six years, I had invested police with magical powers they didn't have. The trite realisation that they were just people in uniforms dawned in every scenario I watched. I had presumed police were equipped for whatever we asked of them — that's why they had the job, because they knew what to do when no one else did. But watching them game-plan different mental health crises where success did not rely on the use of force, they were as self-conscious and tentative about exposing themselves to another human being as I was.

I had come to the course with one main question: *What was the MHIT teaching police that might lead to fewer shootings of mentally ill people in crisis?*

The answer was compassion — for the person in crisis and for themselves. Pragmatic cops would squirm at the idea, but to make a connection with someone who was frightened, you had to be able to reach your own feelings. Mark's vulnerability with 'Barbara' on the cliff edge, admitting he was scared for her — 'I'm reaching out to you' — was what brought her across the line. The teenage girl locked in the bathroom responded to the offer she could speak to her father, not commands to open the door.

The course asked officers to connect as humans first. When crisis threatened, if they could find a way to connect with a person's emotional need for comfort and reassurance, they could bring the temperature of the situation down. Making that connection without forfeiting control was a fine line to walk, but it was the key to de-escalation.

The lesson as it applied to Elijah was *not* to reach Cinders Lane.

Stuart Thomas had picked the dynamic in his research with the Victoria Police.

'It's about escalation and what triggers crisis,' Thomas had said in Melbourne, five years ago.

The standard police approach to a crisis was to establish authority quickly; securing obedience relied in part on fear or respect for the person in authority. Rich approached Elijah the way the force had taught him to, but the training failed them both; it didn't serve the circumstances.

If Rich had been taught to relinquish the need for immediate control and to connect with Elijah, the fatal thread of fear between them might have broken before they reached Cinders Lane.

I had made the same mistakes Rich made in Rusden Street with the man on the road in Darwin. I knew how long it took for people's words to reach me when I was sick — I should have known; I should have done it better. But I wanted the Irishman 'tidied up'; I wanted to 'fix' him without his chaos touching me. So when I failed to connect within a couple of minutes, I walked away. I gave up on both of us. I denied my own vulnerability when I could have used it as a bridge.

Rich had made the same choice as me, after Elijah's shooting. He had pushed his vulnerability down beneath layers of legal warnings. He chose Weber's path. Shut down, shut up, don't feel or talk about it. *Hide the pain in silence and it will disappear.*

Martin Collis taught police the opposite.

Take time to connect. Imagine the other person's fear and pain.

I had to try to reach Andrew Rich one more time.

46.

The man shot at Central Station was identified as 30-year-old Danukul Mokmool.

The media had tracked his family down by the time I was driving home from the role-plays.

Mokmool's brother criticised police for shooting the young man they all called 'Dan', but admitted in the same breath that Dan may have encouraged the officers to fire on him.

'I guess he was trying to make a big scene. He told the cops to obviously shoot him. He just wanted to die, I guess,' he said.

According to his family, Dan was on daily medication and had struggled with mental health problems since he was twenty.

'I'm guessing he got really paranoid at stuff. Thinks someone was trying to kill him or what not,' Dan's brother told reporters.

Two weeks after the shooting at Central Station, police officers capsicum-sprayed, tasered, and then fatally shot a man at his flat in Grafton, on the mid-north coast of NSW.

'It's an unfortunate situation and from what I've been briefed on, police have undertaken their tactical option textbook,' Assistant Commissioner Max Mitchell told journalists.

'No police officer wants to shoot an individual,' he said. 'It is traumatic.'

But the trauma wasn't over yet. Four weeks after the Grafton incident, NSW police shot a mentally ill man, near Bathurst in Central NSW.

Media reports said Ian Fackender had threatened police with a samurai sword. Police had arrived at the 47-year-old's house 'following a call from staff at a local health agency who expressed concern about the man's behaviour'.

'It's one of those situations that police sadly sometimes find themselves in. From what I've seen thus far, I believe their actions in many ways are commendable as well as what I would say justified,' Assistant Commissioner Geoff McKechnie told the media.

McKechnie had spoken to reporters in Armidale after Elijah's shooting, eight years ago. Now, here he was again.

The police were shaken and receiving counselling, McKechnie told the crowd, but: 'We mustn't forget the family of the deceased man as well. There's family out there this morning that are grieving the loss of a son, a brother perhaps, a relative. Our thoughts are certainly with those people as well,' he said this time.

'No one knows what happened at the moment, so you can't pass judgement,' the dead man's neighbour said.

47.

1 Nov 2017

Dear Andrew,

... The book I have been working on and which I hoped you would contribute to will be published next year in 2018. As a courtesy, I wanted to write and let you know ... I wanted to ask one final time if there is anything you would like to say or have included in the book, before it goes to print. Anything at all.

Kate

48.

It is mid-March 2018, and I have not heard from Andrew Rich. I understand he's left the police force, but his life and thoughts remain a mystery to me.

A couple of months ago, I drove north to see the Holcombes. Jeremy has built a house on the coast and Tarney is putting up a shack with timber logged from the block of land they bought. They have solar panels and a generator for power; no running water, but the vegie patch is rich. Laura and Jordan live nearby. Fiona moved back to Wee Waa before Christmas.

I take my medication most days. It is a small rebellion to skip a few tablets, but more than that and I can feel the pain that lurks beneath my skin, waiting to pounce.

Stella is eight and growing like a weed. My husband and I just celebrated our tenth wedding anniversary. I am loved with all my flaws and strangeness, and happier than I ever hoped to be. I know now that my parents' silence was a symptom of helplessness, not a lack of love or care. They never learned how to help me with my illness because they had never received that help themselves. If their needs had been met by the adults in their lives when they were too small to be self-sufficient, it may have equipped them to help when it was my turn.

Elijah's image rarely visits me these days; more often, the picture I see is Rich.

He stares into the dark above the bed until a fearful roaring fills his ears and a single shot rings out. He has no choice; he cannot hold the memories down and he cannot drag them up at will. The silence the Holcombes hoped he would fill is now the place where Andrew lives. A mind left in pain must do something to survive.

When he finds a way to ask, the Holcombes will be waiting. When he finds his words, Andrew's waiting will be over, too.

Mine is. Telling Elijah's story broke my silence.

We hide what we think is unspeakable in silence, believing if we starve a thing of words it will disappear.

But the thing we hide will wait forever for the night the door is left ajar. It will wait with bated breath for the one who can bear to witness all the pain we hold.

We all wait for Elijah in our own way, putting off our challenges until someone wise can tell us what to do. But no one is coming. We have to work it out ourselves.

Elijah Holcombe

ACKNOWLEDGEMENTS

First, I would like to thank my mother for listening to the teacher who asked her for $50 to buy my sister and me a box full of 'good kids' books' in primary school. The change those books delivered to my worldview is still alive inside me. It is thanks to my sister's precocious mind that our teacher suggested the box that changed my life.

Thank you also to:

Kay Masman, Tracey Durrant, Ruth Rudge, and Alison Manning (*A Mind of One's Own*), for unlocking doors.

Life-filled friends Ivan O'Mahoney and Tash Clark, who more than anyone else in the world are responsible for this book coming into existence.

All of the ABC colleagues who encouraged and supported me, including Sue Spencer, Quentin McDermott, Sarah Ferguson, Rachael Brown, Alison McClymont, and Ruth Fogarty.

My port in a storm, Jenny Brockie.

Darwin writers Miranda Tetlow, Kylie Stevenson, Jen Pinkerton, and Clare Atkins — the best and brightest of fellow travellers.

To the lawyers, academics, police officers, and psychiatrists, many of whom are named in this book, who contributed to my understanding of the complex issues in it — a heartfelt thank you for your patience and trust, particularly those who asked not to be named but were still willing to share their expertise and knowledge.

My respect for police and the nature of their work has only grown greater through the openness and honesty of Inspector Roger Best, former Detective Inspector Greig Stier, former Inspector Joel Murchie, and the students and staff I met at an MHIT training session.

To Grace Heifetz, my agent, whose judgement, instinct, and wisdom is unparalleled — you are awesome.

To the Scribe posse — Henry Rosenbloom, Marika Webb-Pullman, Sarina Gale, Cora Roberts, and Allison Colpoys, thank you for welcoming Elijah into your fold and for treating his story with such respect.

I am forever indebted to the Holcombes for letting me into their lives: for their trust and endless patience, and their love.

To the people who have held me together over the decades; who have sat on roundabouts in the rain (Mel and Pip) and let me live on their couches for longer than was polite or convenient (Mel, Alo, Pip, the unnamed lady from Queensland); thank you all for getting me here (you too, Noah).

To our daughter, Stella, whose entire life so far has been lived alongside Elijah's story — one day I hope you will understand how much Elijah helped me through this book, to give you and the world all that is inside me.

But most of all and always, to the funniest, most buoyant man in the world — my husband, Jonathon Hunyor, who has gifted me the hover-shoes of happiness and loves me even when I cannot put them on. Thank you for our life.